INSIGHT
GUIDES

Sweden

Edited by Doreen Taylor
Editorial Director: Brian Bell

APA
PUBLICATIONS

SWEDEN

ABOUT THIS BOOK

This book had its beginnings—though nobody recognised them as such—in the late 1970s when its project editor, **Doreen Taylor**, met a member of the Swedish Embassy in London. Friendships developed with many of the Swedes who come to London and a long-distance love affair began with Sweden itself, sometimes conducted on extended visits to make radio programmes or write articles.

As a Scottish journalist, broadcaster and travel writer, Taylor feels an affinity with Sweden. On those early visits, however, she found she had to disabuse herself of many generally held misconceptions about the country. Sweden was not a dark, cold place where people scuttled between their warm houses. In spring and autumn the country was full of flowers or berries and in summer, it could be very hot, and Stockholm seemed full of tall, bronzed Scandinavians. Swedes laughed too—a lot. As well as being project editor, Taylor wrote several chapters, including the one on Stockholm—"my favourite European capital".

Passionate feelings

One frequent comment about Swedes is certainly true. Despite their grumbles at home, they have a proud love of country, something that shows in two articles by one of Sweden's most eminent journalists, **Inga Wallerius**. She wrote about the Lapps, a people she knows well, and about conservation, a subject she feels passionately about as a member of Greenpeace.

The other native-born Swede in this book, **Anita Oxburgh**, left Sweden in the 1970s with her English husband to settle in Scotland. "Sweden is often described as boring and conformist—most often by Swedes themselves," she says. "Seeing it from the outside, I think it offers an amazing amount of variety for a country with such a small population." As an independent television producer with her own production company in Edinburgh, she worked in many parts of the world but still missed Sweden... "the warm light summer nights, the cold, crisp winters and the celebrations! Swedes are great celebrators." She and her husband have now gone back to live in Sweden.

Several other contributors are American or British, who live and work in Sweden. **Terry Greenwood** has been there one of the longest, married to a Swede with whom he runs a successful press agency. His Swedish is near-perfect—though he has never quite lost his London accent—and he sometimes feels himself more Swedish than the Swedes.

Other writers work from Sweden for foreign publications, often in the financial world—which is not surprising in view of Sweden's financial and industrial successes. The doyen of the American journalists must be **Bob Skole**, who has lived in Stockholm for many years and is also married to a Swede. He is fascinated by fishing and by the paradoxes of Sweden's attitude to nuclear power, particularly since the success of the Green Party in the 1988 General Election.

Jack Burton has spent four years in Stockholm and claims "I had the good fortune to move to Sweden on the eve of what has been probably the most interesing period in its modern history." Born in New York, he travelled widely in Scandinavia as a university student, including a semester at the University of Oslo. Although primarily a

Taylor

Wallerius

Oxburgh

business journalist, he has also taken part in several British and Dutch TV documentaries about Sweden. He is now a correspondent for the *Financial Times* in Sweden.

Louis Borgia is one of those widely travelled American journalists you meet all over the world. A native of Chicago, he has been the Sweden correspondent for *Travel Trade Gazette (TTG) Europa* "for longer than I care to remember." Both his own lengthy spell in Sweden and the fact that he has a Finnish wife helped him write The Immigrants' Dilemma, and Finn-Finns, Finn-Swedes and Swede-Finns—an attempt to unravel a distinction that often foxes foreigners.

H.J. Hardy remembers the first McDonald's opening in Sweden in the early 1970s when he was still a poor student. Today, there are McDonald's all over Sweden but Hardy no longer believes that Sweden is the European version of America despite its ubiquitous bars. "Just scratch the surface and you'll find a deep rooted Europeanism that strongly pervades every aspect of Swedish life." As a pure Anglo-Saxon (with an American voice) he is concerned about the Swedish lack of an equivalent of the word "please", an omission that worries visitors.

Three British writers wrote the bulk of the Places section. **Philip Ray** is a business journalist involved in the travel and airline industries who in recent years has specialised in Scandinavia. He has travelled extensively in Sweden, from Riksgränsen in the north to Ystad in the south, but finds it depressing that in such a vast country he still has so much to explore. He has an affinity with the wide open spaces of Sweden but not with the long dark winters. In business terms, he is critical of Sweden's approach to tourism, which he believes tends to be a bit parochial.

A brief 1950s visit to the three Scandinavian capitals as a young industrial reporter began what has become **Robert Spark**'s enduring fascination with the Nordic countries. But his real chance to get to grips with the country as a whole came in 1985 while he researched and wrote a motoring guide to Sweden, *Drive Around Sweden*. "It was then I realised how little Sweden is known outside its own borders," he says. He claims people either have preconceived ideas, which are often wrong, or only the haziest notion of the country, and Spark is an eager proselytiser of his own view of Sweden's major attractions—"space and solitude, with the knowledge that at the same time you can enjoy very civilised amenities and everything works when you need it."

John Lloyd specialises in writing and photographing travel and outdoor activities. He first went to Sweden in the depths of the winter of 1978. "I remember being thoroughly impressed with the way road and rail were kept open even when there was constantly falling snow." It gave him a taste for Swedish winters, confirmed in 1987-88 when he travelled from Gothenburg to Lappland by train, a 24-hour journey with deep snow all the way... "yet the train still arrived at Kiruna bang on time."

In Britain, particular thanks are due to **Barbro Hunter** and the Swedish National Tourist Office in London and to **Brian Bell**, Apa Publications' London-based editorial director, who guided the book through all its stages of production. In Stockholm, the Swedish Tourist Board and the Swedish Institute both gave valuable assistance.

The maps were drawn by **Kaj Berndtson Associates** and proof-reading and indexing was handled by **Rosemary Jackson Hunter**.

Borgia

Ray

Greenwood

Lloyd

CONTENTS

HISTORY AND FEATURES

TRAVEL TIPS

Five identical wooden huts stand in the centre of a quiet town square in Central Sweden. Under the trees they look like the country cottages that are the pride and joy of many Swedish families. But these have a serious purpose, as the offices of the various political parties during a General Election.

Deep in the 20th-century Swede and in the fabric of modern Swedish society is the aim of equality, so no party is allowed even the advantage of a superior campaign headquarters. Yet not much more than 100 years ago, backward Sweden had one of the most polarised societies anywhere, with great riches and power living alongside harsh privation.

A knowledge of the rapid change that transformed the Swedes from country to city dwellers and turned poverty into comfort helps the bemused foreigner to understand something of Sweden and its people.

Village mentality: Although they may seem sophisticated city dwellers with an astonishingly high standard of living, at heart Swedes have not moved far from the village. They have all the seriousness of the peasant farmer, well aware that it needs only a metaphorical bad harvest for everything to fail.

Although Swedes are generally serious talkers, they have their own private humour, the humour of the small community which is difficult for outsiders to understand, and the most deflating jokes about Sweden are told by Swedes themselves, among themselves.

To the world outside, Swedes maintain a smooth self-satisfaction with everything Swedish which infuriates their Scandinavian neighbours. The reason is obvious. Deep down the Swedes know that their present affluence comes from a willingness not to rock the boat, to conform to common beliefs, and have faith in their own society. They do grumble and argue, but consensus thinking has a strong patriotic streak and a deep love for the land itself.

Particularly on high days and holidays it

Preceding pages: Royal Marines Music Corps at Nynäshamn Annual Tattoo; telephone time at Smögen, Bohuslän; Swedes learn to swim early; Stadshuset, and modern Stockholm. <u>Left</u>, sailing boat skipper. <u>Right</u>, Saturday auction.

can seem as though the country holds more Swedish flags than Swedish people. Not for Swedes the cynical British habit of turning their national flag into carrier bags and holiday shorts. Everywhere, the gold cross on the blue background stands out against the sky. On a windy day in Gamla Stan, the old city of Stockholm, the cords crack against the flagstaffs, and flags fly back from the shoals of pleasure boats on lake and archipelago.

At the least excuse, Swedes don their national costumes, which vary from region to

region, to sing and dance to the old tunes. When German-born Queen Silvia began to wear national dress on Swedish National Day and during the Midsummer festivities, her subjects were delighted.

But nowhere do you see the national flag more often than fluttering like streamers on the long flagpoles outside the Swedish *stugor*, the small wooden country houses that many have inherited from parent or grandparent. The fact that 90 percent of the population still lived on the land at the start of this century has left a strong inheritance of cottages dotted over the countryside, sometimes in small groups, sometimes isolated.

Many are now beautifully restored in a blend of traditional shape and decoration and modern comfort. Nothing makes a Swedish family happier—unless it be messing about in its small sailing boat—than packing up for a weekend or a month in the *stuga*, out in "the nature". Note that nature gets a definite article. *The* nature somehow stresses its importance, and helps to explain why the Green Party did well in the 1988 election, when it gained its first seats in Parliament.

One-issue country: When Swedes do argue, they argue forcibly and are intensely irritated by British circumlocution and unwillingness to say clearly what they mean. But though the Swedes argue hard, they tend to argue in

women—in fact, all Scandinavian women—enjoying a great deal more equality than most. During their run, all these issues are argued about in homes, workplaces and discussion groups; eventually a consensus view is absorbed into Swedish life.

Communal life: All this harks back to the small community, where people were dependent on one another. However long it took, it was necessary to find an agreed solution if the village was to survive and neighbours live in reasonable harmony. In the same way, a Swede has the preoccupation of the country person with his neighbours' doings and will not spare criticisms. But this does not mean that when the need

teams, putting points for and against whatever is the current coffee-room issue.

Sweden is a one-issue country, however. One year, all the posters on Tunnelbanen (Stockholm's underground) exhorted everyone to eat low-fat margarine instead of butter. The next year, newspapers were full of articles on the powers of social workers to take children into care; before the 1984 election, the only issue was the Wage Earner Funds (a plan to give trade unions a stake in private companies). A big debate on the need for men to express their emotions followed hard on the heels of women's equality. The women's debate resulted in Swedish

arises those same neighbours do not cooperate together. In small communities that was necessary and the habit has persisted. How significant that the best-known word Scandinavia has given to the rest of the world is *Ombudsman*, the arbitrator who tries to mediate between interested parties. It is a very old Scandinavian word.

Another Swedish word, *Lagom*—which does not have an English equivalent but means something like "just right" or "sufficiency"—goes a long way to describe the Swedes' consensus way of life. *Lagom* is neither all good nor all bad but sums up the Swedish Middle Way,

The emphasis on absolute equality can seem stuffily bureaucratic, as irritating to the Swedes themselves as to a foreigner. But the Swedish attitude is always positive. Swedes actually want to know about faults in their system or way of life and a familiar question to a departing visitor is: "Well, what do you think we've got wrong?" If the guest is open enough to list a few less than ideal facets, the answer could well be: "Ah, yes, but you must come back again and see what we are doing to put them right!"

As the biggest and most prosperous of the Scandinavian nations, Sweden is in much the same position vis-à-vis Scandinavia as England is in relation to the rest of the United Kingdom, and the United States to Canada. Like the English, Swedes quite unconsciously believe that they are better than their fellow Scandinavians. They tell jokes about the Norwegians (looked on as "blue-eyed" or naive) and are amazed when told that Norwegians relate precisely the same jokes about Swedes. Swedes and Danes simply cannot understand each other's thought processes or even accents (though neither finds difficulty with Norwegian). Both Danes and Norwegians resent Swedish "superiority", in much the same way as the Scots, Irish and Welsh are irritated by English assumptions of knowing best.

A Swede abroad: When they travel, Swedes, like Americans, become intensely patriotic. All the pride of country normally held below the surface becomes vocal, particularly in males—with a certain justification. Swedes can truthfully boast: "In Sweden, nobody is poor or homeless. We may pay among the highest taxes in the world but then we have a cradle-to-grave welfare system, and we're one of the most generous donors of overseas aid." Or he could just say: "*Sverige är fantastisk!*" (Sweden is fantastic!)

The second stereotype—that of the long-legged, blonde nymphomaniac—is equally untrue. The Swedish attitude to sex is matter-of-fact, and stems from a countryside tradition that regarded unmarried partnerships as acceptable and common, as they are at present. None of this implied promiscuity; nor does it today. In all northern European nations, you see a similar inheritance, however

overlaid it may have become by religious strictures. After all, in these cold climes the warmest place in winter was in bed!

Swedish taboos are based much more on alcohol, and there is a strong streak of morality in laws that make spirits prohibitively expensive in restaurants, time-consuming to buy in the state liquor stores, and drinking and driving a crime serious enough to preclude dropping in for a drink.

Top stays off: This means that Swedes, like all Scandinavians (except perhaps the Danes), have little idea of social drinking. Once the top is off a bottle, it rarely goes back. Nothing shows this more clearly than Stockholm's Tunnelbanen. From Sunday to

Thursday, people sit quietly, minding their own business. On Friday and Saturday, traditional drinking nights, everything changes to raucous singing, loud voices, and ribald remarks. Even then, Tunnelbanen has few of the terrors of the New York subway or the latent dangers of London's underground, but many women prefer an expensive taxi home.

As with other aberrations, this one does not last in a land of consensus. By Sunday everything is peace. In the Swedish national village of today, as in the past, people know each other and have to get along together. In that situation, Swedes are well aware that "*Lagom är bäst*"—*Lagom* is best.

Left, a summer folk festival. **Right**, time off on Stockholm's Concert Hall steps.

Sweden's history is a patchwork, with periods of economic and political greatness contrasting with longer periods of decline in international importance. One factor has remained constant: the significance of the sea and of the country's inland waterways.

From prehistoric times, the distant ancestors of today's Scandinavians were seafarers and fishermen who used the sea, lakes and rivers as the easiest means of transport through their densely forested lands. Later, as Vikings, their long voyages ranged over every part of the then known world.

Not for Sweden the glories of the early Christian church, when earnest monks chronicled the doings of kings and prelates. Sweden did not become Christian until the 11th and 12th centuries, so the country's written history began late. If there were triumphs, they were remembered only in legend and saga.

The Vikings were Sweden's first conquerors and traders, followed by the monarchs of the Vasa dynasty who extended this small country's boundaries far into Europe. At that time its leaders constantly looked over their shoulders to Russia in the east, the traditional source of threat. Not until the 19th century did Swedish preoccupations shift towards the west. Abruptly, the government renounced all pretensions to conquest and has since lived within its own boundaries. In the 20th century, its hardest fought campaigns have been for peace between nations, and it has become a strong supporter of the United Nations.

But long years of war had left a legacy of poverty and hardship and Sweden entered the 20th century as a poor, backward nation dependent largely on subsistence farming. In less than 100 years, however, the country has transformed itself into a model of peace, prosperity, neutrality and good living. Today's Vikings travel across the seas by air and their conquests are confined to the commercial.

In the beginning: Sweden's known history began 10,000 years ago. As the melting ice

Left, rock carving at Tanum. **Right**, Viking runestone at Täby , north of Stockholm.

crept north, a peninsula of land grew on the northern edge of the European Continent. This was land in the raw, a turmoil of melting glaciers and seas that burst out of earth that could no longer restrain them and great areas tilted, rose and fell, pressed by gigantic subterranean forces. A thousand years later, a single great cataclysm severed what became Sweden from the land that is now Denmark.

As life became possible, Stone Age hunters followed the melting glaciers north.

Modern archaeological finds of implements and camp sites witnessed the slow establishment of settlements and agriculture, as these primitive people began the long evolution from hunters and gatherers to farmers.

Already, these unknown people had established a rapport with the sea and, by 1500 B.C., their trade routes extended to the Danube. Bronze began to appear in Scandinavia, thanks to these early traders who almost certainly brought back the raw materials and the knowledge. Sweden's own rich deposits of copper and tin were not discovered for many centuries, and it was some 500 years later that the Swedes began to make iron for themselves. One of the earliest chroniclers to mention these northern tribes was the Roman historian Tacitus, who visited northern Europe in the first century A.D. He wrote of a people who appear to be from Scandinavia called *fenni*, but his successor Procopius gave the more evocative description of the people of Thule (Scandinavia) as skiing hunters.

Tales and tombs: The pace of history began to pick up about A.D. 500 when the fertile valley surrounding Lake Mälaren grew into a centre of power. This was the start of unending minor wars and feuds, a tradition inherited by the later Swedish nobility, as the Svea tribe began the struggle to supremacy

The *Ynglingatal*, a 10th-century Norse poem about sixth-century Uppsala, claimed that these grave mounds belonged to three members of the ruling family, Aun, Egils and Adils. Another member of the same ruling family, Ottar, was killed at Vendel, north of Uppsala, which has a mound known as Ottar's Mound.

More came to light about the society of these times when excavation of the mounds began in the 19th century. Archaeologists unearthed not only the burned remains of humans and animals but also precious objects and utensils, which indicate an ordered way of life in Uppsala in the sixth century. What is certain is that, by the beginning of

over its neighbours. The Svea tribe gave its name to Sweden or *Sverige* (the Realm of the Sveas) and its base was Uppland (then called *Svitiod*), centred on Old Uppsala.

The contemporary Anglo-Saxon Beowulf saga, more historical fiction than history, describes with awe the exploits of several Swedish "kings", or tribal chieftains. According to Beowulf, they fought in massive horned or winged helmets, slashing at one another with jewelled longswords and wicked spears. The impressive burial mounds of three of these kings are major tourist attractions at Old Uppsala, near the site of Sweden's last heathen temple.

the early Viking era , the militant Svears had already expanded into territory to the west and south, covered by the present-day counties of Västmanland and Södermanland. They were the power in the land.

The marauders: During the next 500 or 600 years, the Scandinavians entered the European theatre in the role of marauders. Their first recorded appearance was in the late-eighth century at the succulently rich abbey of Lindisfarne on the northeast coast of England. It was attacked, plundered and burned by "vicious barbarians from Outer Tule. So primitive they are, they spared not the library from the torch nor the timid monks from the sword." By the year 1000 the Norsemen had learned the value of books in barter and destroyed no more libraries.

Such lamenting reports of the destruction of one of European civilisation's major centres of book illumination and learning were not taken seriously by the court of Charlemagne. The idea of unexpected, pillaging savages was preposterous—at first. They soon learned their error for, within a few years, Charlemagne was defending the long coastline of civilisation against the Norse. The standard Christian prayer of the English soon included the plea, "Protect us, Oh Lord, from the wrath of the Norsemen."

Overpopulation at home seems to have

been the primary reason for the sudden appearance of the Vikings, a name derived from the Nordic word for bay or shallow inlet. At first they were simply summer raiders but, as this became more organised and part of the way of life, superior ship-building technology, superb seamanship, and a lack of respect for the European Continent's established moral code were the reasons for their virulent success in ravaging Europe.

Their methods of construction allowed

Left, ruined fort at Björkö, Sweden's first "city". **Above**, 11th-century bronze fertility god from Södermanland.

their longships to withstand heavy seas by twisting through surging waves, and the ship's shallow draught made it possible to beach the craft in extremely shallow waters for surprise attacks on unsuspecting setlements. The Viking strategy depended heavily on hit-and-run tactics, but later many Vikings came to trade and settle in the lands they had terrorised.

Sailing east: Swedish Vikings directed their longboats eastwards across the Baltic, first to the Baltic coasts, then deep into present day Russia along the rivers Volga and Dnieper. The rivers, and short portages across flat lands, in slow stages at last brought the Swedes to Constantinople, or as they called it, Miklegård—the big city. The attraction of the east was tremendous. The Swedes developed trade with the Byzantine empire and the Arab domains, and set up short-lived principalities in Russia such as Rurik at Novgorod. Many Norsemen remained in Byzantium as an elite imperial guard, described by an Arab chronicler as "huge mustachioed angels, of evil disposition and smell."

Throughout Sweden, but especially in Skåne, Gotland, Öland, and Uppland, these proud travellers raised large flat stones inscribed with twisting serpents and legends and inscriptions which give insights into Viking society. "Commemorating Wulf and Alderik who died fighting out east in the big City. This stone was raised by their mother, Bodil." She had probably not seen her sons since they first turned their longboat east years before.

The profitable trade in furs, honey and amber in the east led to the founding of Kiev by Swedes around A.D. 900. The Swedes brought back from the Black Sea and Constantinople gold, silver, luxury cloths, and trinkets such as the small gilt bronze Buddha found at the excavations of the early town of Birka, on Björkö.

This island on Lake Mälaren (the lake where Stockholm now lies) was the site of Sweden's first "city", a crowded, dirty but rich trading centre, with an interest in luxury items and precious metals. At Birka coins from as far away as Arabia and Ireland have been found, a tribute to the skilled seamanship, ruthlessness and endurance of these Norse trading-warriors that has never been equalled.

Once the Vikings had drawn Europe's attention to Scandinavia, the continent could not leave its northern neighbour alone. The first purpose was to spread the Gospel, in the pious hope that Christianity might change the Viking temperament.

In the ninth century, the first notable Christian missionary arrived. He was Ansgar, who landed on Björkö in Mälaren. Here he founded a church and converted some islanders; but, after two brief visits, Ansgar returned to Germany as Bishop of Hamburg. Sweden's conversion was only skin-deep and, in A.D. 936, a successor missionary, Bishop Unni of Hamburg, was murdered in Birka. Sweden had to wait until the second half of the 11th century for true conversion, and paganism died only slowly during the next two centuries.

Pagan rituals: The clerical scholar Adam of Bremen left a picture of Norse paganism when he included Scandinavia in his history of his own bishopric. Although Adam relied on existing records and contemporary accounts to describe the temple at Uppsala, the last bastion of the "olde ways", there is no reason to believe his accounts are more or less than the truth.

Here was the heart of paganism, Adam wrote, a structure covered in scales and wreathed with serpents and dragon heads. A heavy golden chain girt the heathen temple to contain the evil of the idols Thor, Odin and Frej. Even more fearsome was the sacred grove alongside the temple, its branches hung with the sacrificial remains, "seven males of every species from man to the lowly cat."

By the middle of the 12th century, paganism was officially out of fashion. King Erik Jedvarsson, later Saint Erik, the patron saint of Sweden, had been converted and with "sword and word" saw to it that his subjects bowed to the word of the Lord.

While the Christian church struggled for souls, the kingly families of Erik and Sverker struggled for temporal power. From this time, Sweden began to emerge as a country

separate from Norway and Denmark and to turn its attention to conquest. Swedes living along the Baltic had long had trading and raiding links with the east Baltic coasts, but now they began a serious colonisation of Finland. This led to the eventual absorption of that country almost as part of Sweden itself, a state that lasted for some 800 years.

The German centuries: German traders had become a familiar part of life on the small island that became Stockholm at the mouth of Lake Mälaren. But the 13th century

brought the turn of the German Hanseatic trading cities, grouped under Lübeck, eager to get a foot into the Swedish door. The Hansa ship was the "cog", designed for cargo, not for men and weapons like the swift Viking longboats. But the effect was the same.

The German merchants conquered through commerce and eventually gained almost total control of Swedish foreign trade and its domestic economy and politics. Many new towns grew up to accommodate the lively commercial activity instigated by the Hansa and the German traders lived alongside but not with their Swedish neigh-

Left, the God Thor as early Scandinavians saw him. **Right**, a 10th-century silver crucifix.

bours. They were particularly strong on the Swedish island of Gotland where they left medieval walls and part of their trading city.

During the next few centuries Germany dominated the Swedish world. German manners were *comme il faut*, German architecture was fashionable. Even the Swedish language assimilated many of its present grammatical and other linguistic forms from the Platdeutsch of the Hanseatic traders.

The concentration of interests on Stockholm, which was becoming important as the country's political centre, led to the advent of a noble class in Sweden. As early as 1280, King Magnus Ladulås had introduced a modified form of European feudalism. To the country were known familiarly as "big farmers", and were descendants of the early chiefs. Now, true nobles began to make their appearance. Many of these families still exist, such as the once royal Bondes (meaning farmer), Svinhuvuds (Pigheads), Natt och Dag (Night and Day), Bjelke (Beam). Feuds were endemic and ballads and chronicles record the bravery and the treachery of these struggling families.

Major revelations: By the 14th century, the shadows of the Dark Ages had lifted. Monasteries and convents flourished in Sweden and brought medical knowledge where had previously been only home remedies. Saint Birgitta founded her order of Catholic nuns

some extent, this countered the old Viking democracy, where the chief was but first among equals, but the ordinary farmers held tightly to their ancient rights and privileges and forestalled the implantation of full European feudalism.

These verbal rights were written down during this period, to form Europe's oldest body of written law. This system of rights for the ordinary man was brought to England by the Vikings centuries earlier. It survived there and by adoption in the United States in the form of bylaws—a word derived from the Norse for "village ordinances."

Up to this point, the important families of

and the convent of Vadstena. Her mystical *Revelations*, often on political and religious themes, were Sweden's first major contribution to European thought. Guided by one revelation, she eventually went to Rome, where she worked to establish her order. She was canonised in 1391.

By this time, Sweden and the rest of Scandinavia had acquired enough sophistication to object to the heavy political and economic control of the Hansas and, in 1397, the three countries formed the Union of Kalmar. It involved an undertaking that all Scandinavia should have one and the same monarch, at the start another influential woman of the

14th century, Queen Margareta of Denmark.

Margareta's new, loose-knit domain was enormous and not easily ruled. But she maintained the union, especially at times when external threats were serious. Her greatest success was in using the danger of such incursions to strip the Hansa of some of their power, though the League continued to exert political and commercial influence for several centuries.

Miners' revolt: As the most advanced of the three Scandinavian states, Denmark dominated the Kalmar alliance, but the whole period of the union was marked by conflict between the monarch on the one hand and the high nobility and intermittently rebel-

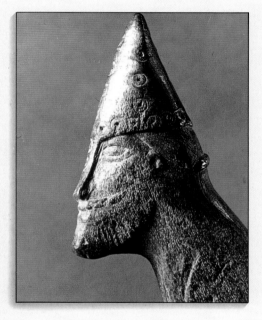

lious burghers and peasants on the other.

In 1434, intolerable Danish tax demands coupled with general social anxieties and differences led to a revolt against Margareta's successor, Erik of Pomerania, by Sweden's first great national hero, Engelbrekt Engelbrektsson. A minor noble, he raised the peasants and miners from his native Dalarna, and stormed towards Stockholm. There, it is said, Engelbrekt forced the council to support him by taking one mem-

ber, a bishop, by his collar and threatening to throw him out of the castle window.

Despite his successes, Engelbrekt was murdered by Bengtsson Natt och Dag, the son of one of his enemies, but his legend lived on. The political might of ordinary people had become evident.

King Erik was deposed but nationalism spread. The struggle continued between powerful families who were for or against the union. The Hanseatic League conspired, more often than not now with the complicity of the Swedes, and the Danes threatened.

Against this background, another national hero emerged. Sten Sture changed Sweden's history and yet he was not of royal birth. Through his leadership in 1471 at the Battle of Brunkenburg just outside Stockholm, Sture gained a decisive victory over the Danes. Although the Kalmar Union still had nearly 50 years to run, this fierce victory— and later Sten Sture's actions as statesman rather than soldier—saved Sweden from being reabsorbed completely into the northern union.

First Parliament: By this time Sweden had a national assembly (the Riksdag) of four estates—nobles, clergy, burghers and peasants—the first step towards parliamentary government. Swedish nationalism and a renewed alliance with the Hansa, as well as a struggle emerging between church and state power, led to more Danish attacks. In the early 16th century, the Riksdag voted to burn the fortress of the Archibishop of Sweden, a pro-Dane named Gustav Trolle. In the event, Trolle was merely forced to resign and was imprisoned.

In 1520 the Papal Court excommunicated Sten Sture the Younger (successor to the Elder) for this act and Kristian II had his justification for invading again. To save their city, the burghers of Stockholm opened the gates, and Kristian (known as Good King Christian in Denmark) retaliated with an enormous feast in the palace where he assembled all of Sweden's leading nobles. On the pretext that the Papal excommunication released him from any promises of safe conduct, Kristian (called the Terrible in Sweden) then chopped off the heads of 82 of Sweden's finest and of many innocent bystanders unlucky enough to be there at the time. This "Stockholm Bloodbath" was the catalyst that raised the nation.

Young Gustav Eriksson Vasa escaped the Stockholm Bloodbath in which his father, two uncles and a bother-in-law were killed. He was in Denmark at the time, held hostage by King Kristian, who was trying to force talks between Sweden and Denmark.

By the time Kristian was killing his kin, however, this resourceful young man had already escaped from Denmark, slipped into Sweden to rouse the countryside, spurred on by news of what had happened in Stockholm. After hard fighting, Gustav Vasa

manager or an enlightened landowner.

Gustav Vasa's reign merely coincided with the Swedish Reformation, and did not bring it about, but he was quick to make use of it. His struggle against the Danes was also a struggle against the Roman Catholic Archbishop Gustav Trolle, whose accusations of heresy had led to the Bloodbath.

Trolle had fled into exile at Gustav Vasa's victory and the Pope refused to consecrate a successor, but the bishops were still unruly and it suited Gustav's policies to support the

subdued Kristian and the Danes, who retreated south, killing and burning as they went. In 1523, a grateful nation invited Gustav to take the Swedish throne.

Though Gustav still had many further struggles against dissident factions in his own country, centred around the Sture family, he set about enhancing the power of the king and reorganising the government, the monetary system, the administration and the army. Nothing escaped his attention. He ran Sweden as though it were his family estates and his vision set the country on the road from the Middle Ages to a national state. Today he could have been an innovative

Reformation. Though he was not particularly religious, like Henry VIII of England, Gustav needed money and less interference from Rome.

His success against the Danes cost money, however, as did his internal struggle against rival factions, which continued throughout his reign, and later foreign campaigns. He was also in debt to the Lübeckers, who had continued to involve themselves in Swedish affairs by providing funds to fight Kristian. In his great need, the wily young king was not slow to see the rich pickings in the churches and monasteries. He confiscated Roman Catholic property and prepared the ground for a state Lutheran religion.

One of Gustav Vasa's closest advisers was Olaus Petri. A man of humble birth, he was known as the Father of the Reformation in Sweden, and the country's first "modern" writer. Early in Gustav's reign, he translated the New Testament into Swedish and later went on to produce many volumes of Lutheran thought.

Petri was a fearless preacher of the Lutheran doctrines, and was for two years chancellor to Gustav, backing the young

and long-reaching. He not only succeeded in bringing about the supremacy of state over church in order to curb the power of the nobles, he also strengthened the monarchy by making it hereditary. When he recalled the Riksdag in 1544, it was to reform it, and to plan what became a form of national military service, to make Sweden the first European country to have a standing peacetime army.

Though he curbed some traditional Swedish liberties and ruled firmly, Gustav Vasa

king's reforms. It was perhaps inevitable that two such strong characters should quarrel and in 1540 Olaus Petri was sentenced to death for alleged complicity in a plot against Gustav Vasa—in fact, his only "crime" was in refusing to divulge a secret of the confessional. Gustav reprieved his old counsellor who then produced his most famous work, a history of Sweden up to 1520, titled *A Swedish Chronicle*.

Gustav's achievements were remarkable

Far left, early portrait of Gustav Vasa. **Left**, Gustav's statue at Mora. **Above**, Vadstena Castle, one of the many built by the King.

was more than a straightforward autocrat. He was a great orator, he had charm, he was not uncultured, and he both loved and played music. He was also a successful trader, who became the country's richest man, with treasure hoards in Gripsholm and Stockholm castles. But his greatest strengths were his skills as organiser and manager, his ability to give Sweden a sense of nationhood.

When he died in 1560, Gustav Vasa had welded his country together, made it strong and had not neglected his duty to the dynasty. In three marriages, he produced 11 children, thus securing the Vasa rule for more than a century ahead.

After the death of Gustav Vasa, the succession was confused. His three sons—who became Erik XIV, Johan II, and Karl IX—struggled against one another, and there was a seven-year period when Johan's son Sigismund, who had become King of Poland, occupied the Swedish throne.

The eldest son, Erik, was at first a competent and popular king, supported by his brother Johan. Under the Vasa prosperity, Sweden grew in ways other than conquest. The University of Uppsala, which had been founded in 1477, flourished, and the Vasas encouraged immigration by Belgian Walloons, Scots, and Germans, who were knowledgeable in the working of iron into swords and cannons. Sweden was abundantly endowed with deposits of pure iron and copper and in the flickering torch-lit caverns of Bergsland, the Dalarna miners prized out the precious ore with primitive implements and little care for human life.

With weapons and a standing army, Sweden had become a military power. The Vasa sons now looked for expansion in trade and territory in what became the Seven Years War of the North, after which Denmark accepted the *status quo* and renounced claims to the independent state of Sweden.

Family infighting: But jealousy between the brothers was incessant and Erik began to fear his brother Johan, safe in his base as Duke of Finland. Backed by the youngest brother Karl, Johan led a revolt; the Riksdag agreed to depose Erik, who died insane.

Johan's mistake was to allow his son Sigismund to become King of Poland while he was successor to the Swedish throne. After Johan's death, a few troubled years under Sigismund led to the reign of the youngest Vasa son, Karl. The tests of strength continued but Karl asserted his authority with cruel force and curbed the nobles' power by executions and banishments. In 1611, he handed on the succession of an established and confident monarchy.

With the accession to the throne in 1611 of

Left, Swedish monarchs from Gustav Vasa to Oskar I. Right, Gustav II Adolf's statue in Gothenburg.

Karl's son, Gustav II Adolf, Sweden acquired a miliary genius. Gustav Adolf was intelligent, his education was thorough and, having a German mother, he spoke both German and Swedish. He had all the strength, determination and enthusiasm of his celebrated grandfather, Gustav Vasa. One difference was Gustav Adolf's belief in the Lutheran faith. His piety induced him to hold regular prayers for his army in the field.

He was backed by an equally robust chancellor, the aristocratic Axel Oxenstierna.

The two believed that Sweden was surrounded by enemies who thought themselves stronger and that its friends had no understanding of Sweden's difficulties. It was a good basis for conquest.

The War of Kalmar, which Gustav Adolf fought at the beginning of his reign, regained parts of southern Sweden from the Danes and in 1617 the Peace of Stolbova left Sweden in sole control of the Gulf of Finland. But in Poland, Johan's son, Sigismund, still laid claim to the Swedish throne. Gustav Adolf moved fast, with a surge of Swedish troops across the Baltic to take Riga after a six-week siege. The Baltic began to be known as the "Swedish lake."

The start of the Thirty Years' War in 1618 involved Sweden in the wider conflict. Over the next years, Gustav Adolf's army drove far into Europe and pressed south to the rich trading area of the Vistula. After the defeat of Sigismund at Mewe, it marched into Poland, where Gustav Adolf defeated the Polish cavalry at Dirschau, to give Sweden a strong presence in Europe.

After these successes, Gustav Adolf spent several less satisfying years of intense diplomacy with Denmark. He also tried to bring together the Scandinavian countries and the participants in the Thirty Years' War.

Strange premonition: In 1630, the king

he had perfected with his well-trained army.

Gustav Adolf's aim was to unite all the Protestant countries and his diplomacy-on-the-march continued until just before the final battle, at Lützen, near Leipzig. The November day was misty as Gustav Adolf's Swedish and Finnish troops fought the Catholic Imperialist army. Few saw Gustav Adolf's death because the mist had again swirled low. He was shot three times and died immediately. As rumours of his death whispered along the lines, the Småland companies almost wavered until Gustav Adolf's chaplain, Fabricus, began to sing the hymn "Sustain Us By Thy Mighty Word." Inspired to vengeance, the Swedes won a

sailed again to Pomerania on what was to be his last campaign. Gustav Adolf had the satisfaction of knowing that he had brought low the power and prestige of his Danish rival, Christian IV, and had the support of his Riksdag and people. Yet the sense of foreboding was strong in his last speech to the Riksdag, almost as though he knew his fate.

The Swedes marched firmly across Europe and crossed the Elbe. The decisive battle of this year was Breitenfeld which lasted five hours, with the Imperial cavalry charging and charging again. By sunset, it was a clear victory for Gustav Adolf and his veterans, thanks to the new military tactics

battle so fierce that one-third of the army fell alongside its king.

Gustav II Adolf was Sweden's most successful military leader. He made Sweden a great power, captured huge territories in the Baltic, the east, and south as far as Poland. He also made his country for the first time more powerful than Denmark. He was the Lion of the North who sent back treasures from Europe that are now to be found generously spread over the Swedish palaces.

His military innovations, advanced techniques and trained army won battle after battle but they did not stop the fatal bullet at Lützen in 1632.

Infant heiress: When Gustav Adolf fell, his daughter Kristina, whose name figures in many Swedish towns and institutions, was only six years old. But she had the advantage of her father's chancellor, Axel Oxenstierna, who became Regent during her minority.

Oxenstierna continued the king's policies at home and overseas. The formidable army in Europe subdued more German and Slavic domains and, by 1645, Denmark had ceded to Sweden some of the provinces in south Sweden which had traditionally been part of Denmark. Oxenstierna and the foremost nobility soared high in the see-saw of power between throne and council by introducing a new constitution which placed effective

she decided to abdicate, probably because she was drawn to the Roman Catholic faith. After she stepped down in 1654, she travelled through Europe and shocked her former subjects when in Rome she announced her conversion. And so the daughter of one the great champions of the Protestant faith renounced it. As a final irony, with her to Rome she took many of the same treasures her father had plundered from the Catholic rulers of Europe.

Continued greatness: Although Kristina had gone, Sweden's power continued to grow. In 1658, Sweden astounded Denmark by a surprise attack, partly due to Karl X Gustav's luck. The winter of 1657-58 was

power in the hands of the nobles.

When she came of age, Queen Kristina presided over a shining Baroque court filled with massive silver furnishings and dark intrigues. She had been well educated for queenship and gathered around her the brilliant young minds of the age. But, by now, the relationship between Kristina and her elderly chancellor was not sympathetic and the country stagnated.

In one of history's unexplained decisions,

Left, Kronan Skansen, one of two forts dating back to Gustav II Adolf's Gothenburg. **Above**, the Battle of Lützen, where Gustav II Adolf died.

one of the coldest in a century and froze the sea between Sweden and Denmark, and between Denmark's first and second main islands. Though two squadrons of horses and riders fell through the ice, an army of 1,500 cavalry and 3,500 foot soldiers came safely across and overran the island of Fyn almost before the Danes knew what was happening. The Treaty of Roskilde gave Sweden all the provinces in the south Swedish mainland which Denmark had traditionally ruled.

The last decades of the 17th century saw the tentative start of an Age of Enlightenment. This came to maturity in the 18th century, as it did in many parts of Europe, as a time of scientific discovery, a flowering of artistic talent, and of freedom of thought and expression. One of its first exponents was Olof Rudbeck. From Uppsala, he became Sweden's first internationally recognised genius, contributing significantly to medical and scientific advancement, with discoveries such as the human lymphatic system.

But, as the 17th century ended, with the country still at the height of its political rather than intellectual powers, Sweden produced its greatest romantic warrior king, Karl XII. Every European country has its royal figure of romance and how much Karl's reputation derived from the fact that, of his 21 years as monarch, he spent 18 away

at the wars is not clear. To many, he is Sweden's greatest king—certainly to those of a romantic and nationalist temperament.

All Karl XII's successes and failures were inextricably mixed with European issues, the struggle between Protestant and Catholic, and the race for trade and sea routes. His strong personality brooked little opposition and, three years after he came to the throne as a minor, he first showed his military skills by landing on the nearest main Danish island of Sjaelland. This led to an early peace treaty and left Karl free to turn to the east.

Meanwhile, Tsar Peter of Russia had declared war on Sweden and Karl hurried through Estonia to relieve Narva. Soon Poland was involved in the war, and Karl's victorious army swept through Poland, taking Warsaw and Krakow, as well as Danzig. By 1705 Poland had signed an alliance with Sweden against the Russians.

In his mission to save Europe from the Russian bear, over the next years Karl rampaged over Germany and Russia. But, in 1709, at one of the most important battles of the 18th century, the Swedes met their match. Everything conspired against the Swedish army. Karl had already been wounded in the foot and had to command from a litter. At the end of a day of victory and defeat, the Swedes retreated to Perevolotjna, where the king was at last persuaded to cross into Turkey.

From his distant "court" in Turkey, the frustrated Karl attempted to guide his realm and, at times, almost persuaded the Turks to go to war against Russia. By 1714, Karl realised he must return to Sweden and he made a journey of more than 1,300 miles by horseback across Europe to Straslund in Germany. That he did the journey in 15 days with two companions says much for the King's determination and endurance.

Only Straslund and Wismar remained of the vast Swedish European Empire. At Straslund, Karl was still not safe from the alliance which had formed against him, and eventually he fled secretly to Sweden. Fifteen years after his first triumphs, Karl devised plan after plan to defeat his traditional enemies, the Danes. In 1718, he invaded southern Norway to besiege the border fortress of Frederiksten. On 30 November, he went out to inspect his troops when a bullet struck his skull and he died instantly.

Swedes still argue whether it was a Norwegian bullet or one from the gun of a disaffected Swedish soldier, tired of the long wars, which killed Karl. There have been many theories but no proof.

Next to Gustav II Adolf, Karl was undoubtedly Sweden's greatest military genius. But while the former left Sweden powerful, Karl left the country divested of all its conquests except Finland. From the moment the fatal bullet found its target, Sweden ceased to be a great fighting power.

Left, Queen Kristina, by David Beck in 1650. **Right**, Sweden's most romantic king, Karl XII.

CARL XII.

The death of Karl XII and the end of long exhausting wars left Sweden shrunk in size, weak, and forced to negotiate from an inferior position. Above all, the council and Riksdag were tired of absolute monarchs and warfare. The lack of an obvious heir provided their opportunity. In 1719 the Riksdag introduced a constitution which again curbed the royal prerogative and stated that the monarch was obliged to endorse all laws passed by the Riksdag. So began the era called the Age of Freedom.

At first the crown went to Ulrika Eleonora, the dead king's sister, whose husband Fredrik of Hesse was close enough to the army to make a successful bid for the throne on behalf of his wife. Under the new constitution her powers were curbed and the Riksdag refused to recognise her husband as king. Her short reign was marked by a Parliament determined to assert itself and, after a tense year, she stepped aside in 1720, enabling her husband to take over as Fredrik I.

He, too, was threatened by rival claimants to the throne and, over the years, Sweden's cautious path was plotted by the Finnish politician Arvid Horn, who trod a delicate diplomatic road to compensate for Sweden's weakness and, when Fredrik died in 1751, the Swedes had the satisfaction of knowing that the successful claimant, Adolf Fredrik, had at least a few drops of Vasa blood.

As democracy began to gain a foothold, the estates of the Riksdag also took on the job of nominating the members of the council and, though its own proceedings were still a well-guarded secret, the Riksdag passed a Freedom of the Press Act in 1766, the world's first attempt at press freedom which is still in force today.

In political terms, this era was dominated by two factions, the Hats (mercantile nobles or Whigs) and the Caps (liberal commoners and urban traders similar to Tories). In diplomatic terms, Sweden was lucky in having a leader whose cautious temperament suited the age. During the 1720s and 1730s, Arvid

Left, the botanist Carl von Linné (Linneaus) in Lapp dress after his Lappland expedition. **Right**, Gustav III.

Horn continued to steer Sweden through dangerous foreign shoals. Despite minor alarums and Russian inroads and the swings in the allegiances of the Caps and Hats to foreign powers, he contrived to keep an insecure peace with the old enemy, Denmark, as well as Russia and Prussia.

In 1718, the wars of Charles XII had killed not only the king but also many of the strongest young men in Sweden and Finland. Bad harvests added to the economic problems. Although Sweden remained primarily an

agricultural country until late in the 19th century, the Age of Freedom saw the start of a transformation into a trading nation.

The government encouraged mining of iron in the many small works, and copper from the great mine of Falun. Hand manufacturing of many kinds also began. Swedish ships carried Swedish goods all over Europe and further, through companies such as the new Swedish East India Company, which lasted into the next century. The ships carried iron and returned with luxury items such as silk and provided young Swedes with an adventurous challenge.

Scientific pioneers: Away from these affairs of politics, diplomacy and trade, the Age of Freedom was also an Age of Science which produced a royal flush of original thinkers. High among them was Swedenborg, a scientist who edited the first Swedish scientific journal but is also known for his studies on the human brain and his religious writing. Nils Rosén was one of the earliest to study and practise pediatrics. He was also an anatomist and a pioneer of innoculation against diseases.

Carl von Linné (Linnaeus), a student of the first great scientist, Olof Rudbeck, developed his theories that plants, like animals, reproduced sexually. It became the basis for his great work *Species Plantarium*, which

This outpouring of science and scientists, many of whom worked closely together, led to formal co-operation in 1739 when the Swedish Academy of Science was opened in Stockholm, with Linnaeus as one of its founders. Sweden began to gain prestige on the wider stage, and many botanical pilgrims came to Linnaeus's garden in Uppsala.

At home, scientists used their talents to advise the new industrialists and the farmers—practical scientific work that laid a foundation for prosperity and future study. Although it continued into the reign of Gustav III, it was inevitable that such a flood could not continue at the same volume indefinitely. In any case, Gustav III did not en-

classified 8,000 plants. Linneaus travelled widely in Sweden and pronounced on many subjects. His disciples travelled further, to China, Africa, North America, and two Swedes joined in Captain Cook's Antipodean expeditions.

In the field of astronomy, Anders Celsius invented and gave his name to the 100-degree thermometer and established Sweden's first astronomical observatory at Uppsala. Sweden also produced good chemists: Bergman, the founder of chemical analysis, Wallerius and Cronstedt and, most famous of all, C.W. Scheele, the first man to analyse air as oxygen and nitrogen.

courage freedom but another form of enlightenment. His sphere of interest was the arts and the encouragement of a national Swedish culture.

Autocracy returns: During Gustav III's reign, the Age of Freedom gradually faded, though study of science and economics continued. He was influenced by his mother, Louisa Ulrika, sister of Fredrik the Great of Russia, a strong-minded woman who had spent her life in political schemes and in grooming her son for the monarchy. At the age of 23, Gustav III started out as a golden figure. He was proud of being the first Swedish born king since Karl XII, and was well educated for his role. He loved France and the theatre, where he both wrote and acted, and his sense of drama loomed large throughout his 23-year reign.

In the Riksdag, the Caps were supreme, moved by common cause against the Hats, who represented the nobility. Gustav III was beset by threats from Russia and Prussia; in the countryside, two bad harvests had raised political discontent. In 1772, the king organised a bloodless *coup d'état* that condemned the aristocracy and demanded a return to the ancient constitution but, essentially, gave him absolute power.

War declared: Like his predecessors, Gustav did not escape conflict with Russia. In to Sweden and a surprising naval victory at Svendsund, when the Swedish fleet sank 50 Russian ships, which led to peace and, against all the odds, left Sweden with its reduced territory intact.

This unlikely victory did not make Gustav III a notable warrior, and his fame lies not in his political or military skill. He is remembered for the upsurge he encouraged in all the fine arts. Though the king loved France, he was a patriot who founded Swedish drama when he built Stockholm's Dramatic Theatre, replaced the French actors in his mother's theatre at Drottningholm, and hired Swedish actors and writers to develop a native theatre. The most important of the arts

1788, he declared war, partly in the hope that external strife would allay the unrest caused by his growing despotism, partly to make the most of Russia's preoccupation with a Turkish war. At first, Gustav succeeded in pushing far into Finland but the support of his Finnish officers could not be guaranteed and a group of more than 100, the Anjala Confederation, made contact with the Empress Catherine in an attempt to restore the Finnish boundaries of 1721. When the Norwegians invaded near Gothenburg, Gustav returned

Left, Gustav III's court at Drottningholm. **Above**, a performance at Drottningholm Theatre.

in the Golden Age was opera and, in 1782, Gustav opened the magnificent Royal Opera House alongside Strömmen, where Lake Mälaren pours into the beginnings of the sea. Gustav commissioned the first opera in Swedish at the Dramatic Theatre, followed three years later by *Thetis and Peleus*, which he planned, staged six major tragedies and other plays, in four of which the king himself took part.

Gustav's old tutor Olof Dalin was one of the earliest of this age of writers with his popular critical essays in *Then Swenska Argus*, (The Swedish Argus). Most unusual of the early writers was Carl Bellman, a natural troubadour who wrote poetry about the ordinary people of Stockholm's taverns and markets. Another in the same mould was Jakob Wallenberg, whose robust words were Bellman's prose equivalent, Carl Cristoffer Gjörwell described nature, and another distinguished poet, Johan Kellgren, helped Gustav translate his plays into Swedish—the king knew French so well that he always wrote that language better than Swedish.

Many more poets and prose writers clustered round Gustav when, in 1786, he established the Swedish Academy of Literature. Modelled on the French Academy, its main task was to ensure the purity of the Swedish language; now it is better known for its

award of the Nobel Prize for Literature. Gustav also founded the Musical Academy in 1771, the Literary, Historical and Antiquities Academy, and the Academy of Art.

Gustavian life was rich in culture and the court went to the theatre and opera in silks and brocades. The middle classes also prospered in the atmosphere of expanding commercial contacts abroad. Only the old noble families felt neglected. Gustav III had manoeuvred them out of their traditional roles and political power and replaced them with more pliable commoners and the newly-great, dubbed *parvenues*.

So much of Gustav's energies had been centred on his artistic protégés that he may have been lulled into a false sense of political security. He was not a true tyrant, more a despot who sincerely believed in individual liberties. As with so many Swedish monarchs, he had become more and more autocratic as his reign passed, and this was the era of the French Revolution.

The curtain on Gustav's drama came thundering down at an opera masquerade in 1792. A group of conspirators from many parties formed the plot and a disgruntled minor nobleman, Jakob Anckarström, shot Gustav III. The king died from an infection a few days later in the cold of the Royal Palace. Anckarström was broken on the wheel and the Golden Age was at an end.

Afterthoughts: The Gustavian era trailed on for another 17 years under the young king, Gustav IV Adolf, but the spark was gone. Gustav Adolf's one real achievement was land reformation, which gave the 18th-century peasants the independence of the long-gone Viking times.

There was also one last gasp of territorialism. The Swedes had already fought an unsuccessful war over Pomerania, but this was the time of the Reign of Terror in France. Gustav Adolf felt the fear that gripped all European monarchs. He embarked on a campaign against France which eventually found him in opposition to Russia. Russia immediately abrogated the treaty of Armed Neutrality between the two which had left Finland as part of Sweden. In 1808, Tsar Alexander invaded Finland. For the Swedes, the campaign was disastrous. The Finns were disillusioned, and the Swedes forced to retreat back to the Gulf of Bothnia.

Under the Treaty of Fredrikshamn signed in September 1809, Sweden lost Finland for the last time. Gustav IV Adolf had already abdicated in April and, by 1810, Sweden had made peace with all its enemies. Old Duke Karl (who had once been regent to his nephew Gustav IV Adolf) resumed the role under a new constitution as Karl XIII. This allowed power to move gradually from king to Riksdag, the end of autocracy and the start of Sweden's democratic monarchy.

Left, "First Drink of the Morning", the troubadour Carl Michael Bellman by Tobias Sergel. **Right**, the Royal Dramatic Theatre, Stockholm.

Once the last faint link to the great Vasa dynasty was gone, Sweden elected the French Marshall Jean Charles Bernadotte as Crown Prince. By 1810, the new prince had converted to Lutheranism on his way north to Sweden, taking the name Karl Johan.

The election of a Frenchman as heir to the throne and the loss of Finland to Russia the year before turned Swedish eyes away from the east. As Sweden's interests and identity became more and more involved in Western Europe, foreign policy lost much of its preoccupation with its great eastern neighbour, though that did not preclude treaties with Russia.

At the time, many believed that a French marshall was bound to be no more than an emissary of Napoleon, but Karl Johan soon proved them wrong. A few weeks after his arrival, he took over state affairs when the elderly Karl XIII had a stroke, and later became the legal regent. The Swedish aristocracy remained hostile but Karl Johan steered a quiet course through the tangle of European diplomacy. By 1812, Sweden had broken its long-held treaty of alliance with France and in 1813, after campaigning in Europe, Karl Johan allied Sweden with Russia and Prussia against his former leader, Napoleon. In return, Karl Johan gave up Swedish Pomerania, Sweden's last toehold on continental Europe.

He was even more determined to prise Norway from Denmark and unite it with Sweden. Although Denmark agreed, the Norwegians were less than delighted at being handed over like a parcel and wrung many concessions from the Swedes before agreeing to a loose-knit union under the Swedish king. The new union struggled on for almost a century but had the effect of arousing Norwegian nationalism still further until, in 1905, Norway's separation into a sovereign state became inevitable.

Curbs on the throne: In 1818, the former French marshall became King Karl XIV

Johan under the 1809 constitution drawn up during the *coup d'état*, which separated and rebalanced the powers of government and monarch. Though Karl XIV Johan was himself a conservative, a liberal opposition began to form during this period and expanded during the reigns of his son, Oskar I, and his grandson, Karl XV. By 1862, Sweden had local self-government and four years later the reform of Parliament abolished the four estates which had formed the Riksdag for over 400 years and reduced

it to two chambers. From this time until 1974, the monarch's power has been only marginally greater than it is today and history has become a chronicle of Riksdag and people. In 1971, the Riksdag became a single chamber and a new constitution in 1974 gave the present king, Carl XVI Gustav, purely ceremonial functions.

The Napoleonic wars and the loss of Finland left Sweden low in morale and poorer than it had been for a century. The earlier growth in trade stagnated and agriculture meant poverty and even starvation for the large numbers who earned a living from the land. The greatest potential

Left, King Carl XVI Gustaf and Queen Silvia in the Bernadotte Apartments in Stockholm's Royal Palace. **Right**, King Karl XIV Johan, the former French Marshall Jean Charles Bernadotte.

EXODUS TO THE NEW WORLD

In the last decades of the 19th century and the early years of the 20th, more than a million Swedes, around one quarter of the population, left Sweden. So many came from the poor agricultural areas of Småland, Bohuslän and Värmland that some exchanged a Swedish village at home for small American communities in Minnesota and Wisconsin that also spoke only Swedish.

Their story is best summed up in the emigration trilogy of the 20th-century writer Vilhelm Moberg, *The Emigrants*, *Unto a New Land*, and *The Last Letter Home*. Moburg was a Smålander and he wrote about his own people who left the county's stony ground for a better future. This was turned into two films by Swedish film-maker Jan Troell, with Liv Ullmann and Max von Sydow in the title roles.

The motives of the Swedish emigrants were not simple. Unlike the Highland Scots, forced out in the Clearances by their own chiefs, who found sheep more profitable than people, the Swedes were not obliged to leave. But changes in agriculture from communal crofting villages to individual farms had split the old communities. Even in their new farms, families were separated from neighbours and neighbourhoods they had known for centuries. Some moved first to the city, and then to America; others went direct to build a new life for themselves, encouraged particularly by the United States Homestead Act of 1862 which promised land almost free to settlers who dared to travel west.

To the United States, the Swedes took their traditional virtues of hard work, thrift and honesty and, given the wide open opportunities of the New World, many made their fortunes. The new settlers sent back glowing accounts of their lives in America, and a great deal of money to support those left behind. They came home to visit their relatives with undreamed of wealth in their pockets and gifts for their families. These signs of prosperity, in turn, encouraged others.

The whole movement became highly business-like. Shipping companies used agents to recruit new settlers and so provide passengers for their ships, and introduced a system of pre-paid tickets for emigrants to send home for a younger brother or sister, or even a widowed mother. Some agents were rogues who preyed on the would-be settlers and disappeared with their money. Other newcomers were robbed and cheated when they arrived in New York. But by far the greatest bulk of the emigrants prospered and added to the success of their adopted country.

In Sweden, this mass movement of people coincided with the start of the country's Industrial Revolution, just when the new mills were beginning to attract workers to towns and cities. Gradually, the administration realised that Sweden was in danger of losing too many of its youngest and most able citizens. In the early years of the 20th century, the Riksdag began to encourage people both to stay and to return, and compiled a survey of what had brought about the exodus. It revealed a sorry tale of oppression, poverty and discontent with life in Sweden.

In all, around one-fifth of all those who had emigrated came back to Sweden, many of them bringing their new riches to put money into the poorer areas. Swedes have always had a great love of country and the possibilities of bettering themselves was the real lure of America. When they had done that, they could sometimes afford to come home. Others waited for three or four generations before the pull of the past drew them back to Europe. In 1968, a group which included Vilhelm Moberg founded the Emigrant Institute —the House of the Emigrants — in Växjö in the centre of Småland, the largest European archive on emigration. It has 2,000 Swedish-American church and club record books and a library of more than 25,000 volumes.

More than anything, the emigrants helped those who remained behind through the realities revealed in the 1908 survey. These alerted the powerful to the ills and indignities of a system that was still far from egalitarian. Though the connection is not fully proven, many of the sweeping democratic reforms of the 20th century which changed Sweden for ever owed much to the insights provided by those 19th century Swedes who left for a better life.

for disaster was the population explosion, which took numbers in Sweden from less than two-and-a-half million in 1800 to more than five million by 1900, due in part to a much reduced death rate which had earlier balanced births.

In the first decade of the new century Gustav IV Adolf had begun agricultural reform, but the real father of the Swedish agricultural revolution was one of his contemporaries, an estate owner in the southern province of Skåne with the Scottish sounding name of Rutger Maclean. Some 20 years before Gustav Adolf introduced his land enclosure laws of 1803 and 1807, which prevented the sub-division of land into ever

persisted and, when he died in 1816, most of his tenants were able to buy their farms. Maclean's example took a long time to filter through and was, in any case, not suitable for every area of Sweden but the greater productivity it brought did something to put food in the growing number of stomachs.

By the second half of the century, Swedish transport, which had changed little since the days of Gustav Vasa, began to improve. Water had always provided trading and travelling routes and the wide expanses of Lakes Vänern and Vättern in the centre of the country were natural waterways. Baltzar von Platen's Göta Kanal, which opened in 1832, made full use of the lakes to link east to west.

smaller, uneconomic portions, Maclean had already reformed his own estate into manageable lots and abolished some of the near-feudal duties of his peasants.

At first, this reform was less than a success and met with bitter hostility (in Dalarna for example, some peasant tradition lingered well into the 20th century). There were also casualties and, if an independent farmer failed, he was usually reduced to the status of crofter or landless labourer. But Maclean

Left, the Emigrants' Statue at Karlshamn, Blekinge. **Above**, Hagdahl's painting of emigrants leaving Gothenburg.

In 1853, the engineer Nils Ericsson took charge of railway building and began the construction of a part-state, part-private network to link not just existing cities but to open up new areas for the future.

Lively inventions: Rail transport encouraged the new forest industries to make use of Sweden's endless wooded acres for saw-milling and later wood-pulping, and by the last decades of the century, the first glow of the Swedish inventive genius had begun to show in men like Gustav Pasch, who invented the safety match; Lars Magnus Ericsson, whose invention of the table telephone led to the start of the international company which bears his name today; and, of course, Alfred Nobel, the inventor of dynamite. These and many more set the economic stage for the country's swift industrial development in the next century.

The Riksdag introduced compulsory education and elementary schools in 1842 and better education led to many popular movements. Frederika Bremer was one of the founders of the women's movement, and wrote many books, from her early *Sketches of Everyday Life*, to her polemical novel *Hertha*, which put the women's cause. Late in the century another writer, Ellen Key, shocked Swedish polite society with her support for free love. In the country, where

sex was considered natural and marriage after the conception or birth of a child was almost a custom, these ideas were less startling. In 1921, Sweden was among the first to give women full suffrage—though women who owned property had long held local voting rights.

Growing industrialisation created a new social class of workers and the abolition of the medieval guilds of craftsmen in 1846 led to new associations which were the beginning of trade unions. In the light of the success and power of Swedish unions today, there's irony in the fact that the first union, started in 1874 for tobacco workers in Mal-

mö, was founded by Danes, afraid that the unorganised Swedes might move into Denmark and lead to lower wages there.

Heavy-handed: The start of unions led to many inconclusive strikes. The first notable confrontation happened in 1879 in Sundsvall where the sawmill owners proposed a 15 to 20 percent reduction on already minimal wages. Oskar II sent his troops to face several thousand strikers and, though no violence occurred that day, many were alarmed at the official high-handedness. Workers began to realise that they must organise to win and more militant socialist trade unionists were soon taking over these "liberal" unions. What became the largest of the trade union federations, Landsorganisation (LO) had also formed.

Other popular movements included the formation of free churches and a crusading temperance league. The co-operative movement was very strong in 19th-century Sweden and most far-reaching of all were the beginnings of what later became the Social Democratic Party. Its progenitor, August Palm, converted to socialism in Denmark; a radical and eccentric trouble-maker, he was expelled from Germany and imprisoned when he returned home. He started a radical newspaper and, from prison launched the congress that founded the party.

But Palm was a wayward founder and a steadier guiding hand for the new party came from Hjalmar Branting. He had been an early associate of Palm but realised that the latter's disruptive influence would kill the infant party before it could walk. In 1892, Branting succeeded in having Palm declared unfit to lead the party and took over himself. For a long time, he was the only party-affiliated Social Democrat in the Riksdag, but between 1895 and 1905 party membership multiplied by more than a factor of six to 67,000 and returned 13 to the Riksdag.

This new Social Democratic Party expressed the hopes and aspirations of an industrial population that exploded in size before and during the Industrial Revolution. With the workers behind it, the party could scarcely fail and, more than anywhere else in Europe, the 20th century was to belong to the Swedish Social Democrats.

Left, founder of the Social Democrats August Palm. **Right**, early feminist Frederika Bremer.

In the long term, Sweden's late Industrial Revolution has contributed much to the country's remarkably swift rise from poverty to prosperity. By the time Sweden was ready to move on a large scale from agriculture to industry, the country already had universal education and a network of railways, planned with foresight to open up new areas and serve new communities. After almost 100 years of peace, the country had stability with an expanding population settled in existing communities, small rather than large, and spread over wide areas.

Nor did the potential workforce lack skills. In the traditional communities a small farmer had to be his own blacksmith, carpenter, mason and more, and these diverse talents were useful not only to those who emigrated to America but also to their relatives who migrated from farm to factory. The new industrial workers could turn their hands to most tasks.

The cities drew in thousands and many more moved into the smaller towns as new mills opened up. Although sickness and poverty lived in the cramped houses and noisy factories even more than in the villages, Sweden was fortunate in avoiding the overwhelming size of the dark satanic mill towns of other parts of Europe.

Thinking ahead: There was also money to pay for expansion and new industry because industrialised Europe needed timber and iron, the raw materials which Sweden had in plenty. If the government and the new industrial class had been short-sighted, Sweden could have lived for many years on money from the export of raw materials. Instead, those exports were the means of paying for the new industries built on Swedish inventions and the ability to exploit them. A tradition of careful husbandry encouraged early industrialists to use their profits to start more companies rather than for personal pleasure.

From the start, the government took an active part in providing the rail and road infrastructure, in paying for the opening up of the northern mines, and for other purposes

Left, making stainless steel at Nyby Bruk. **Right**, inside Börsen, Stockholm's Stock Exchange.

beyond the means of a private company. Even then, Sweden had discovered that the best combination for industry was a partnership between private and public interests. The pioneers also realised quickly that it was as important to market their products as to make them. (See "Sweden's Humane Capitalism," page 67, and "Industry's Astonishing Success," page 127).

Despite the swift and relatively harmonious success of its Industrial Revolution, Sweden did not escape the Depression of the

late 1920s and early 1930s. The price of iron and grain fell, unemployment rose sharply and discontent matched its curve. Strife broke out between communist workers and industrialists, mine owners and the government. It culminated in a strike-breaking episode at Ådalen in Ångermanland when soldiers who were called in fired on the crowd, killing four strikers and a woman bystander.

Fight for neutrality: By the 20th century, Sweden had already started along the road to neutrality and non-alignment. In 1912, the three Scandinavian countries declared their agreement on a policy of neutrality. As a result Sweden took no part in World War I.

During World War II, Sweden's neutrality was strained when all three of its closest neighbours, Finland, Denmark and Norway, were involved. Ties were strong and popular support ran high when the Soviet Union invaded Finland. Informally, Sweden sent supplies and arms, and individual Swedes fought alongside the Finns. Despite German pressure over Norway and Denmark, Sweden's neutrality held; but World War II put an end to any latent pro-German feeling.

In the early days of the century, Sweden began to take the rough road from government by aristocracy to democracy and, between World Wars I and II, from democracy in general to Social Democracy in particular.

prime minister in 1921.

In 1932, Per Albin Hansson took over the premiership and, from then until 1976, the Social Democrats held office, sometimes in coalition with the Agrarian Party (now the Centre Party) with a short break in 1936. During World War II, Per Albin Hansson headed a coalition government. It is the longest reign of any single party in government in the democracies of the West. The bourgeois parties ruled between 1976 and 1982, when the Social Democrats returned to office to continue as the ruling party through the 1980s.

Although in its early days Swedish Social Democracy was influenced by Marxism and

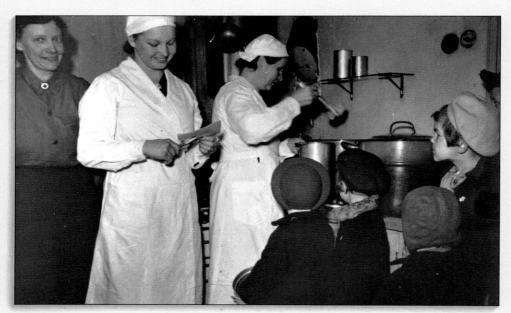

Although for centuries monarch and aristocracy had disputed, the transformation went surprisingly smoothly; few were killed, few executed and none transported. Even more amazing is the *volte face* to consensus and equality in a land which as late as the 19th century was still a sharp divide of powerless peasants and privileged aristocrats.

Despite the Russian Revolution and Finland's fierce struggle in a Civil War right on Sweden's doorstep, the Social Democrats avoided revolutionary tactics and, under the veteran Hjalmar Branting, moved carefully, often in coalition with the Liberals. Branting became Sweden's first Social Democratic

international socialism, it is essentially a Scandinavian brand with no connection to the Eastern Bloc. It is highly adapted to Swedish needs and lives alongside and co-operates with capitalism. There is a small but tenacious Communist Party which normally supports the Social Democrats.

Cradle-to-grave security: When Per Albin Hansson came to power in 1932, the Social Democrats began to plan a welfare state, aided by Socialist thinkers and writers such as Gunnar and Alva Myrdal. World War II shelved the proposals but their introduction began immediately after.

After the war, first Hansson and then his

successor Tage Erlander began the long process to make Sweden the world's most comprehensive welfare state. His policies concentrated on social reforms aimed at "levelling out social advantage and disadvantage" and, on the face of it, first Erlander and then his successors, Olof Palme and Ingvar Carlsson, have largely succeeded. Sweden has almost no poor people, Swedes appear classless and equal. But in fact there are still large differences in the distribution of wealth and, although almost as many women work in paid employment as men, few have yet reached the higher echelons. The high taxes which pay for the welfare state are a constant point of debate.

Olof Palme's time as prime minister from 1969 was broken between 1976 and 1982 by a coalition government of the three bourgeois parties—Liberal, Moderate, and Centre—in various combinations. But these years did little to shake Sweden's consensus way of life.

More and more, Palme was assuming a greater role as intermediary and arbitrator on the international scene and his assassination in February 1986 shocked the world as much as it stunned his native land.

This tragic event severely shook Swedish confidence and seems to have provoked or led to a new and somewhat uncharacteristic influx of power politics, political scandals

Peace at work has been greatly helped by the closeness between the Social Democrats and the unions, and through an economic policy based on tripartite discussions between these two and the employers' federations. This straightforward relationship continued as long as the unions held to the policy of solidarity but is wearing thinner now that many individual unions are eager to negotiate better deals for their own members.

Left, Finnish children find refuge in Sweden during World War II. **Above**, the Globe, Stockholm's new sports arena, exhibition and conference centre.

and a straying away from the normal courtesies of Swedish politics. Before the 1988 election (which gave the Riksdag its first new party for decades when the Green Party won seats) the Social Democrats were besmirched by political indiscretions and the bourgeois opposition was splintered by ideological detail.

It is as though Sweden has turned away from a second period on the international stage, for purposes of peace rather than war, to preoccupy itself with domestic problems of high taxes, the labour market, concern for energy sources, and Sweden's own environment, both physical and social.

It may be Sweden's long-held traditions of neutrality and its position as a buffer between the power blocks, but from a population of only eight million it has produced a remarkable number of dedicated peacemakers of international repute.

World War II, in which Sweden was relatively untouched, saw the start of this trend, when in 1939-40 (during the bleak Finnish Winter War against the Soviet Union), many Swedes opened their homes to Finnish children. After the German attack on Denmark and Norway, a stream of refugees crossed the long border between Sweden and Norway and many Danish Jews also found asylum in the neutral country.

From this period, the names of two humanitarians stand out: Count Folke Bernadotte and Raoul Wallenberg.

Count Folke Bernadotte had high connections and a Royal name. He was the nephew of King Gustav V, and an army officer as well as chairman of the Red Cross. His talent was for negotiation and he was one of the first to recognise that, whatever a country might think of the Nazi regime, it was better to treat with it than to allow its victims to die. His first success was to secure the release of thousands of Scandinavian prisoners, and later prisoners of other nationalities, from the concentration camps.

In 1947, Bernadotte's already proven skills recommended him to the United Nations Security Council, which was seeking someone to mediate in the delicate situation between the Jews and Arabs in Palestine.

Bernadotte moved to Palestine but, though he successfully negotiated a ceasefire, both sides rejected his terms of settlement of the war. He was also faced with many who had a vested interest in making sure that he didn't succeed and were prepared to go to any lengths to continue the struggle. After a number of threats against his life, his car was ambushed in September 1948 and he was shot down by Jewish extremists.

Raoul Wallenberg's aim was also to help the Jews. When in 1944 the United States established the War Refugee Board to save Jews from Nazi persecution, the Board's Stockholm representative called together a group of Swedish Jews to suggest candidates suitable, brave enough, and willing to go on a rescue operation to Budapest.

At this point, the lives of Folke Bernadotte and Raoul Wallenberg came together because Bernadotte was the first choice. When the Hungarian Government would not accept him, Wallenberg was appointed. The 32-year-old member of the great industrial and banking family became First Secretary of the Swedish Legation in Budapest and began his dangerous mission. His best pro-

tection was his authority to deal with anyone he chose and to use diplomatic couriers outside the normal channels.

By the time Wallenberg arrived in Budapest, he was too late to save two-thirds of the Jewish population. Already, 400,000 Jews had been transported to the camps, but there were around 200,000 left in the capital.

Wallenberg's first step was to start to issue protective passports and to open "Swedish Houses" all over the city, where Budapest Jews could take refuge. He used everything from bribery to threats and blackmail, and it is said that as many as 100,000 Jews owe their survival to Raoul Wallenberg.

But the saviour could not save himself and his own fate is veiled in mystery. At the end of the war, Wallenberg fell into the hands of the Russians, who seem to have believed that he was a spy. They later declared that Wallenberg had died in captivity and have since refused to re-open the question, though eye witnesses claim that he was alive and still imprisoned as late as the 1970s.

Many in Sweden are reluctant to believe that this brave man died as early as 1947, and his family and voluntary associations are

Apart from the establishment of the Peacekeeping Force, Hammarskjöld's main achievements were to arrange the release of captured American pilots from China. He was also the champion of the small states of the United Nations, and the guardian particularly of the interests of the Third World against the major powers.

His stewardship ended when he decided to send UN troops to the Congo after Civil War broke out in the area in 1969. As the political repercussions of Hammarskjöld's actions

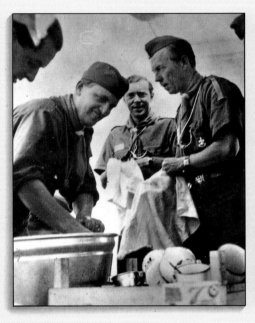

still tireless in their efforts to find out what happened to Raoul Wallenberg.

When the United Nations was established after the war, its first General Secretary was a Norwegian, Trygve Lie. He was succeeded in 1953 by another Swedish peacemaker, Dag Hammarskjöld, who became the founder of the UN Peacekeeping Force. Hammarskjöld was an economist and had been a civil servant and son of a former Swedish Prime Minister of Sweden.

Left, Raoul Wallenberg. Above left, Count Folke Bernadotte (on right) at a pre-war international Scout camp. Above right, Dag Hammarskjöld.

spread, Russia demanded his resignation, but Hammarskjöld remained.

It was in the Congo that this independently-minded man met his death in mysterious circumstances, as so often has been the fate of the peacemaker. In 1971, when Hammarskjöld was on a peace mission to that war-torn country, his plane crashed, killing all on board. The reasons have never been explained and even today many speculate that this too was an assassination.

Sweden's principal woman peacemaker, Alva Myrdal, was also closely connected with the UN and was the first woman to achieve a position as a top ranking director within that organisation, when she became head of the Department of Social Affairs.

But her main contribution to the cause of peace was her tireless effort to promote disarmament and peace during the 1960s when she was involved in the Geneva Disarmament Talks. Through what must have been a series of dispiriting meetings over a number of years, she held on to her belief that in the end commonsense would prevail. In 1964, she was one of the founders of Stockholm's International Peace Research Institute (SIPRI) and its first chair. She published a number of books and articles. In 1980 she was the first to be awarded the Albert Einstein Peace Prize, and in 1982 the Nobel

were to combat unemployment and to promote social reforms, building on the work of his predecessors. In foreign policy, however, he broke new ground. He argued constantly against colonialism and the arms race and, during the 1970s and 1980s, he became one of the world's foremost champions of oppressed peoples.

As a member of the Brandt Commission, he helped to formulate proposals for narrowing the gap between North and South, and his own "Palme Commission" presented a concrete plan for reducing armaments and increasing global security. He too was involved in the work of the United Nations when he acted as mediator in the Iran-Iraq

Peace Prize. She died in 1986 at the age of 84.

That same year, the most recent of Sweden's peacemakers, Olof Palme, was gunned down in a Stockholm street as he strolled home from a visit to the cinema with his wife.

Even before Palme became Prime Minister in 1969 at the age of 42, he had already begun to acquire an international reputation, mainly in connection with the Vietnam War. For several years, his robust condemnation of American policy in Vietnam led to acrimonious exchanges with the United States administration in Washington and also occasionally with the US Embassy in Stockholm.

In domestic politics Palme's priorities

war at the request of the Secretary General.

As Prime Minister, Swedes had naturally concentrated more on Palme's domestic policies than on his international achievements, but his death and world reaction to it opened their eyes to his international reputation as a peacemaker and statesman. For more than a year, the spot on the pavement where he died was indicated by its tributes of flowers. His grave is marked by a simple stone in a churchyard nearby.

Above, Alva Myrdal and Olof Palme at the United Nations. **Right**, a Swedish destroyer off the coast of Gästrikland.

THE NON-ALIGNED NATION

Sweden's King Karl XIV Johan was the first to lay down his country's long-lasting belief in neutrality. In the 1830s he assured both the Russian and British governments that Sweden had abandoned all thoughts of regaining the provinces on the eastern and southern shores of the Baltic lost as a result of the Napoleonic wars. Sweden would not want to do anything to endanger the calm it enjoyed or its existence as a state.

That was the official position—but there were forces within the country which challenged it. The loss of Finland in 1809 to Russia was a blow to Swedish national pride. The aristocracy in both countries had close connections, and Swedish was the official language of Finland.

The union with Norway entered into in 1814 could in no way make up for the loss of Finland. The Norwegian Parliament attempted several times to obtain some control over foreign policy for fear that they would be drawn into conflicts by Swedish activism. Only a policy of greatest constraint could keep Norway and Sweden united; but, despite all efforts, the union was a source of conflict and it was dissolved in 1905.

During the years before World War I Sweden, feeling under threat of attack from Russia, moved closer to Germany. It became clear though that the Germans were only interested in using a friendship with Sweden as a threat to Russia and the implications of getting drawn into a war were obvious. A few days after war was declared, Sweden issued an official declaration of neutrality.

Towards the end of that war, neutrality was under strain as civil war broke out in Finland between the Russian-backed Reds and the Whites. Victory for the Reds was a threat to Swedish security but it was felt that military intervention would entail an even higher risk.

By 1920 Sweden was more favourably placed than ever before. Germany and Russia had lost the war, an independent Finland emerged, German influence over Denmark had disappeared, and none of the other Nordic states was under obligation to a great power. Even Estonia, Latvia, and Lithuania had become independent. Sweden now concentrated its efforts on limiting the growth of power in other countries through the League of Nations, including efforts to promote limitations of armament. Sweden, in fact, adopted unilateral disarmament as early as 1925.

Sweden stayed out of World War II officially but a number of volunteers from the Swedish forces remembered their close links with Finland, now subjugated, and joined the White Army to fight with the Finns against Russia.

At the same time, Sweden recognised the urgent need to rearm. Denmark and Norway were both occupied by the Germans after surprise actions in 1940 and press and public opinion in Sweden put pressure on the government to take sides. The Germans applied even greater pressures and Sweden was under threat of invasion.

The coalition government decided to keep Sweden out of the war at almost any cost and reluctantly conceded to German demands to transport troops through Sweden. This was then—and still is—seen by many as undignified and immoral. Others feel that because Sweden stayed out of the war, it was able to make a humanitarian contribution which outweighed any military contribution.

After the war, recognising the need for protection, Norway and Denmark joined NATO, Finland signed a treaty of friendship and mutual assistance with the Soviet Union in 1948, but Sweden resolved to maintain its non-alliance in peacetime, leading to neutrality in war time. It has also been very active in the United Nations, promoting peace and disarmament.

But armed neutrality puts Sweden in something of a cleft stick. In order to maintain an up-to-date defence, Sweden has to have an armament industry. An armament industry supplying only its indigenous needs would be an intolerable drain on the nation's resources and Swedish manufacturers have had to look for customers elsewhere. This has led to the hypocritical situation where the peace-loving and peace-promoting Swedes are among the world's biggest exporters of armaments. As in 1925, unilateral disarmament does not seem to be on the agenda.

Any summer Saturday you will see the typical Swedish family setting out for the day, a boat on top of the Volvo or Saab, picnic and swimsuits in the back; or they might have packed up the evening before for a weekend at the family cottage or the grandparents' home.

Almost certainly, there will be no more than two children in the car, for native Swedes are scarcely even reproducing themselves, with an average of 1.7 births for every two adults. This figure is complicated by the higher birthrate among the immigrant communities and the likelihood of more than one marriage. The Swedish divorce rate, at something over 50 percent of all marriages, is one of the highest in Europe or America. But, whatever the method of calculation, the birthrate is low.

In cities, a flat is still the most likely home, most often rented from the local authority or one of the housing associations, which must conform to laid-down standards and rents. But flat-dwelling does not imply poor housing. Many have large rooms in gracious buildings and all are comfortable, with light, heat and other services included. More often than not, they are surrounded by gardens and play areas. Go down to the basement, and you'll be amazed at the lines of bicycles and the immaculate laundry room with big washing machines and dryers for the tenants' use.

The dream of home ownership has also taken root in modern Sweden and, in addition to the suburban flats built to meet the post-war housing shortage, many suburbs of private houses now stretch out from the bigger cities. From the road, these often show a dull uniformity; but move closer and everything is different. Many are grafted on to older communities and inside they are individual and luxurious and all have Sweden's greatest asset, space. On the outskirts of towns, only 50 metres from the garden you come to the tall conifers of the forest, with tracks to walk in summer and ski in winter. The sides of the roads are like meadows, full of flowers, and a lake will rarely be far away.

Left, Swedes eat outside whenever they can. **Right**, making the most of winter.

No wonder Swedes like their bicycles.

The couples who live in these flats and houses are as likely to be unmarried as married. Some never marry but wedding pictures that show a couple of children along with the bride and groom are commonplace. Around four out of every seven partnerships are unwed. Under Swedish law, couples have much the same rights to property and inheritance whether they are married or not and, on divorce, joint custody of children is very common. This can call for so much

contact and co-operation between the former marriage partners that you sometimes wonder why they didn't simply stay married. Around one family in five is headed by a single parent.

A familiar sight on a Swedish street is a happy gaggle of pushchairs, toddlers, and young women. They are children from the *dagis*, the day-care centres provided by all local authorities in Sweden to look after children when their parents are at work.

Some 85 percent of all Swedish women of working age have a job outside their homes, over 90 percent when you narrow it to women with children over school-age, which is seven in Sweden.

Yet the first aim of the *dagshem*, (day home) to give it its full title, was not to help working parents. The movement for day care in the 1930s was part of the wider plans of the early Social Democrats. Along with good housing and schools and health education, they wanted to give everyone the opportunities that had been available only to the small minority of those with comfortable means.

A *dagis* place costs 60,000 Skr (approx £6,000) a year but parents pay only around 10 to 15 percent, and the rest comes from local taxes. The main benefit of the system today is that it enables parents to work without worry. Some cities still have a scarcity of

which Swedes expect. Just as strong was the push from the women's movement in the late 1960s and 1970s when many Swedish laws changed to meet their aspirations.

In 1974, the Swedish Government abolished maternity leave and substituted up to a year's parental leave with very little loss of pay, open equally to both parents to indicate that children were the concern of fathers as well as mothers. Either parent of a child under eight can elect to work only 75 percent of normal hours and accept a proportionately lower salary. Parents can also take time off to look after a sick child.

Since then, almost as frequent a sight as the group from the *dagis* is the young father

places and the government is committed to ensuring that one is available for every family which wants it. As an alternative, some parents have combined to found their own *dagis* and, in every case, standards are high, equipment good, and the children spend a lot of time out of doors. As well as the *dagis*, *fritids* (free times) are open to school children, to fill the gap between the end of the school day and the time the parent collects them after work.

Nowadays, high taxation and high prices usually compel both partners in a family to go out to work. A single income is rarely sufficient to keep up the high standard of living

sitting on a park bench with his newspaper, shopping bag and push chair, or making his way round the supermarket with child and trolley. Men's attitudes have changed a lot faster than they have in other parts of the world, but not as fast as many Swedes hoped. Only some 20 percent of men share parental leave after a birth, and few of those remain at home for longer than a month. Apart from single fathers, men do not often opt for the shorter working day, partly because average salaries for women are still below men's and a family usually loses more when the father works part-time. Other couples elect to share the shorter working day and both work part-time, but this is more common in the professions than on the shopfloor.

This peculiarly Scandinavian form of family life is so universal that women who elect not to work are a rarity and sometimes looked on askance. But it is a busy life, the working day starts early and, in winter, the morning departure for the *dagis* and the evening return is always in the dark, and the family assembles tired after a day at its separate pursuits.

A lot of entertaining is centred on the home, but during the week families have little time for family and social pursuits, or even to enjoy their beautiful Swedish homes. Swedish children learn early to stand on their

whether early independence disrupts family life. But, though Swedish teenagers have most of the good things of life, their problems seem neither greater nor smaller than those in all Western societies and vandalism and overt signs of disaffection are few.

Weekends are the time when families and friends get together, but there is a growing feeling among Swedes that they have too little time for themselves and their families. People are tackling the issue in the usual way, talking and arguing, trying to come up with an agreed solution.

Even success itself is being redefined to mean self-development, the need for good personal relationships and family life, in-

own feet and are among the most independent in the world. Like the children of an Israeli *kibbutz*, they take their values as much from their friends as they do from their parents. Children's interests are looked after by their own Ombudsman and a law forbids parents to hit a naughty child. Swedish parents live with these constraints and have much the same hopes and fears for their children as do parents everywhere. They worry about the effects of materialism and

Left, a bicycle made for three. **Above**, a familiar sight, an expedition from the *dagis*, the day care centre.

stead of merely amassing more and more goods. "They want to fish, to sail, take part in family life, to read and indulge in different hobbies, and to find another direction for their lives," is how a rising young economist puts it.

Although it is still mainly what the Swedes call "the intellectuals" who hanker after this "doing their own thing," the possibilities are widening. Whatever the outcome, Swedish society would never send one partner, the woman, back to the kitchen. Much more likely is an increase in job-sharing inside and outside the family and an even greater involvement by both men and women.

SWEDEN'S "HUMANE CAPITALISM"

The expression "the Swedish Model" conjures up two distinctly different images. One is renowned worldwide for being leggy, blonde and blue-eyed. The other is more likely to cause the greatest excitement among economists, although it too enjoys its share of global fame.

Sweden's reputation as a model of economic planning rests on three essentials: the close collaboration between business, Government and labour. This is the partnership that this century has helped to transform one of Europe's poorest countries into one of its richest. The Swedish system of economic checks and balances has also created a society largely free of the inequalities of unbridled capitalism and the inefficiencies of authoritarian central planning.

It has been dubbed *The Middle Way*, from the title of a best-selling book. Published in 1936, this first brought international attention to a country that had solved the problem of mass unemployment which then haunted the Western world. Fifty years on, the Swedish model continues to attract foreign admiration, not least from the super powers.

Example to America: Today, when Americans are preoccupied with declining industrial competitiveness, a recent US Senate report proclaimed: "Sweden's success in securing both competitiveness abroad and a high living standard at home makes the Swedish experience well worth studying."

Meanwhile, Soviet officials frequently cite Sweden as the example they would like to emulate in achieving *perestroika*, and study teams from Moscow are becoming a familiar sight in Stockholm.

For all but six years, since 1932 Sweden has been ruled by the Social Democratic Party, tempting one to say that the country represents "Socialism with a Prosperous Face." But that would be misleading. Sweden does not conform to standard definitions of socialism. More than 90 percent of industry, for example, remains in private hands. Perhaps "Humane Capitalism" would more

aptly describe an economy able to provide full employment, generous welfare services, and a narrowing gap between rich and poor.

Although it is often said that the Social Democrats have moulded Sweden during the past half century, this is not the result of some master plan. While the Social Democrats' goal may be ideological—in simple terms, full employment in an egalitarian society—the means they have employed to achieve this are strictly pragmatic. They determine their tactics by circumstances not

dogma, which reflects the national preference for consensus and compromise rather than conflict.

The Swedish Model was born in response to the major crisis of the 1930s: the Great Depression. When the Social Democrats assumed office in 1932, one out of four workers did not have a job, but the party started with several advantages in combating unemployment.

For one, it naturally enjoyed the confidence of the large trade union movement for which it served as the political voice. Moreover, the long-time acrimony between business and labour was beginning to dissipate.

Left, wood pulp mill—timber and forest products are important in a tree-covered country. **Right**, Swedish fathers take their turn at child care.

The year before, the country had been shocked when soldiers fired into a crowd of striking workers at the small sawmill town of Ådalen, killing several. This unprecedented event, which warned Sweden of the dangers of class conflict, coincided with the suicide of Sweden's greatest financier, Ivar Kreuger, and the collapse of his global match empire.

Events like these undermined the self-confidence of the business community in standing up to labour demands, and the ground appeared ready for compromise on both sides to meet the new challenge facing Sweden.

In any case, the Social Democrats themselves were quickly shedding their Marxist beliefs and, to achieve power, they had to co-operate with the conservative Agrarian Party (now the Centre Party) which guaranteed that no radical ideas would be imposed.

The Social Democrats were fortunate too that their Finance Minister, Ernst Wigforss, was at that time one of the few senior government officials in the world who was familiar with the writings of the British economist John Maynard Keynes.

Sweden adopted an expansionary Keynesian programme of spending its way out of the 1930s Depression, by curing unemployment through public works projects and other measures to stimulate the economy. The Government realised then that a profitable private sector would lead to the creation of more jobs, and a key ingredient in this policy was to keep corporate taxes as low as possible while avoiding the nationalisation of industry, a step that won the confidence of the business community.

Hard-pressed regions: To ensure that industry re-invested its profits instead of hoarding them, in 1938 the Government set up an investment reserve fund. Under the system, still in existence, companies can place up to half of their pre-tax profits with the Central Bank in exchange for tax write-offs. The Government then determines when these funds can be used to stabilise fluctuations in business cycles, keep control over excessive profits and create employment in periods of depression. The fund is also used to direct investment to hard-pressed regions and to encourage the even distribution of industry throughout the country.

But the generous treatment of companies

as the source of the nation's prosperity does not stop there. Untaxed reserves for inventory and wages, liberal depreciation rules, and interest rates and dividend reductions are offered as further tax relief to persuade firms to expand their factories, increase their technological development and hire more workers.

For example, Swedish companies spend a high percentage of their profits by international standards on research and development which enables them to maintain a competitive technological edge in world markets. Although the nominal corporate tax rate is a steep 52 percent, the average firm pays only 14 percent of its profits in tax. As

one corporate president put it: "The Social Democrats like rich companies, but not rich individuals".

The biggest step towards the construction of the Swedish Model came on a dark December day in 1938 at a seaside resort hotel in Saltsjöbaden, just outside Stockholm. Here, at a historic meeting, business and labour reached agreement on rules to regulate collective bargaining and industrial disputes.

Through the early part of the century, the trade unions, centred around the Swedish Trade Union Confederation (LO), and management, represented by the Swedish Employers' Confederation (SAF), had been bitter enemies. Strikes and lockouts multiplied during the 1920s and early 1930s, and disrupted economic performance. When the Government threatened to intervene and impose order in the labour market, both the LO and SAF, worried about losing their power to the State, agreed to try the resolve the issue between themselves. After two years of negotiation, aided by an improved economic climate, they signed the Saltsjöbaden Agreement.

Under the peace pact, unions were required to give advance notice of any planned industrial action, thus providing a cooling-off period for talks and arbitration. The

otherwise acerbic account of Sweden, *The New Totalitarians.* "It ensured the proper distribution of the benefits of technology, and the efficient use of a small country's resources. It mobilised the industrial power of Sweden in a way normally open in peacetime to a dictatorship alone."

By the eve of World War II, the basic elements of the Swedish Model were in place. The Social Democratic Government enjoyed the trust of the labour movement and had won the support of industry, while capitalists and workers had established a mutually beneficial relationship through the Saltsjöbaden Agreement.

But the reason why this triumvirate of

Swedish labour market soon became one of the calmest in the world. Equally important, the Saltsjöbaden Agreement laid the foundation for centralised wage negotiations, which contributed to stability in economic planning and restrained wage demands and inflation.

"The Saltsjöbaden Agreement guaranteed employers peace to build up their factories and expand their business," commented British journalist Roland Huntford in his

Left, making Skania trucks at Södertälje. **Above**, the Saltsjöbaden Agreement in 1938 brought peace to Swedish industry.

Government, industry and labour has endured primarily reflects the national character. Swedes tend to be highly disciplined and harbour respect for authority. Until recently, Sweden had a thoroughly homogeneous population, which helped promote the quest for compromise.

Moreover, social values favour the group over the individual, the legacy of an agrarian society, and the security-minded Swedes find safety in numbers. Sweden is perhaps the most organised nation in the West today, with a multitude of interest groups and organisations serving as the building blocks of society.

This has made it easy to implement the agreements reached between SAF and LO, the biggest organisations in the country. SAF's word is regarded as law within the private sector. The blue-collar LO speaks for half of the nation's highly-unionised labour force of 4.4 million and its activities influence the behaviour of Sweden's second largest trade union group, the white-collar Salaried Employees' Confederation (TCO), which accounts for another quarter of the workers. For its part, the Government has at its disposal a strongly centralised and sophisticated administrative structure that dates as far back as the mid-16th century.

The various strands of official Sweden are further woven together in a consultation process known as *remiss*. Whenever a major change in law or policy is contemplated, a Commission of Inquiry is set up. The resulting recommendation is often a consensus decision that enjoys the backing of all the participants in the process. It is a system in which "everyone wins something", according to one observer.

Despite its success, the Swedish Model has been criticised for creating a corporatist state, albeit a democratic one, ruled by interlocking elites of business executives, civil servants and top union officials. This collusion of interests is symbolised by occasional meetings of the powerful at the Prime Minister's summer retreat at Harpsund where current problems are informally discussed.

While Sweden may strive for an egalitarian society, there is little doubt that its corporate world remains an oligarchy, dominated by a few family dynasties. The Wallenberg banking family alone is estimated indirectly to control one-third of Sweden's gross national product through holdings in many of the country's biggest multinationals.

Policies such as wage solidarity promote the concentration of business ownership by weeding out inefficient firms, and the Government lends its support to big business through its control of national pension funds, used to buy corporate shares and thus give the State a powerful say in which companies should grow.

It is argued that a small, export-dependent nation such as Sweden needs to concentrate its resources on big companies in order to compete and survive against bigger industrial countries, and a recent Parliamentary Commission that examined corporate ownership defended the present structure by explaining that strong ownership makes companies more efficient.

One often-cited example of successful collaboration between industry and the State concerns the dismantling of the shipbuilding sector, which in the early 1970s was the second largest in the world. Faced with cheaper competition from the Far East and a surplus in world demand, the Government encouraged the shutdown of the shipyards.

Thanks to the country's re-training programme, the displaced workers had a chance to find new jobs at car manufacturing plants that were built with Government support near their old workplaces. It is close co-operation such as this, say supporters of the system, that has allowed Sweden to enjoy almost full employment since World War II.

But prosperity has brought rising expectations and growing disenchantment in its wake, to subject the Swedish Model to internal strains. No longer satisfied with comfortable wages, the unions started to push for economic democracy in the mid-1970s, and they succeeded in placing employee representatives on the board of directors of any company with a staff of more than 25.

This worker participation in corporate decision-making was actually welcomed by most businessmen, who believed it would give labour a more realistic assessment of the problems that Swedish industry faced and thus improve co-operation between the executive suite and the shopfloor.

But the corporate community violently opposed another proposal to increase union power. This was to establish union-controlled funds, financed by a corporate profit tax, that would be used gradually to take over Swedish corporations, through the purchase of their stocks. These so-called "wage earner funds" marked a radical departure since it was the first time that the labour movement had vigorously campaigned for worker ownership of the means of production.

To business, it was the first major step in the march towards socialism and the resulting debate over the issue threatened to tear asunder the spirit of co-operation that supported the Swedish Model. But, in a typical Swedish compromise, parliament passed a watered-down version which has done little to transfer corporate ownership to the workers, and it is estimated that the wage earner funds control only one percent of the total value of Stockholm's Stock Exchange.

Another threat to the Swedish Model appeared in the 1980s with a growing split within the labour movement, which was once bound together by its devotion to wage solidarity. Friction exists between white and blue-collar unions because of the former's interest in seeking higher salaries. Another division has appeared between workers in private industry and the large army of public sector workers, who run the country's extensive welfare system and now constitute almost 40 percent of the national workforce.

Private industry workers favour industrial

compete to get the best possible pay deal. Although companies approve of the development because it takes into account differences in profitability among various industries, it also makes economic planning uncertain and pushes up inflation. The latter has in recent years in any case been relatively high because full employment has given the unions a strong hand in wage talks.

Now that it has achieved its main goal of a rich society with work for all, there is a growing belief that the Swedish Model is past its prime. Economists say the Swedish economic structure has become too rigid.

The Government has signalled its readiness to support a more competitive, market-

peace and have a sense of loyalty to their employers because they believe their well-being depends on their companies doing well. But critics claim that the public workers have little incentive to keep labour relations calm. In the 1980s, they staged several large, crippling strikes and have emerged as the most militant sector of the labour market.

This declining cohesion of the labour movement has, in turn, led to decentralised wage negotiations, as individual unions

Above, insurance office at Bergshamra— Swedish working conditions are of a high standard.

orientated economy through, for example, an extensive tax reform that will encourage a more efficient use of capital investment. The creation of the European Community internal market has hastened this process. Although Sweden has so far refused to join the European Community, it has pledged to harmonise its laws and policies, which will open up what has previously been a tightly-controlled economy.

By the turn of the 21st century, the Swedish Model could no longer exist except in faint outline. In its place Sweden may see something that could perhaps be called the European Model.

Some of the most fascinating contradictions of the human character came together inside Alfred Nobel. How, for instance, could one man both found the renowned Nobel Peace Prize, awarded each year to those who have made the greatest contributions to world peace, and at the same time be the father of Sweden's vigorous armaments industry, which today provides a substantial amount of the weapons held by one half of that same world against the other?

Alfred Nobel was born in 1833 in Sweden, one of three brothers. He clearly inherited his talents as a chemist and inventor from his father who went bankrupt in Alfred's early childhood. Despite the bankruptcy, Nobel Senior moved the family to Russia where he became a very successful industrialist.

Well-travelled: Life in St Petersburg gave Alfred the chance of an international education. He was particularly well tutored in chemistry and, in addition to Swedish, spoke French, Russian, English and German. Nor was he confined to Russia. As a young man he took educational trips all over Europe and even as far as the United States, before joining his father in St Petersburg as a chemist. In 1853, the Nobel family moved back to Sweden, leaving Alfred's two brothers, Robert and Ludwig, to look after their father's business interests.

An early interest in explosives was also stimulated by Alfred Nobel's father, who in Russia had invented new and efficient land and sea mines which the Russian armed forces used in the Crimean War. Alfred went further and patented many of his own inventions, of which his most famous was dynamite. This revolutionised mining, road building and tunnel blasting because it gave engineers a manageable form of the highly sensitive explosive, nitroglycerine. He also turned his fertile mind to synthetic materials, telecommunications and alarm systems and in his lifetime clocked up the ownership of 355 patents.

But Alfred Nobel was more than an inventor. He was a pioneer in the swift industrial exploitation of his discoveries and the founding of multinational companies. His ultimate total was 90 factories and compa-

nies in 20 countries, on five continents around the world. At the same time, he did not neglect his Russian interests and entered into partnership with his brothers, who by this time were successfully exploiting the Baku oilfields and became known as the Russian Rockefellers. The Nobels also had a reputation as benevolent employers who provided social care and welfare benefits for their employees, a foretaste perhaps of the Swedish style of today.

To the world outside, Alfred Nobel was a

man with a penetrating mind, shrewd in business and with a sceptical idealism. He was also melancholy, slightly self-deprecating, yet with a good sense of humour. Despite his success, he was not a happy man and wrote of his life as "a miserable half-life, which ought to have been choked to death by a philanthropic physician as, with a howl, it entered life." One of his biographers described Nobel in early life as "a prematurely developed, unusually intelligent, but a sickly, dreamy and introspective youth."

Although he had homes in six different countries, his life was that of a vagabond. Paris was close to his heart and so was Bofors in Sweden where he spent his last years. Today, it is the stronghold of the armaments industry he founded.

A lonely man, he never married but in later life developed a strong friendship with Bertha von Suttner, an Austrian baroness. Theirs was a close but platonic relationship, as the baroness was not free to marry. But Bertha von Suttner was a pioneer in the peace movement and her friendship may well have influenced Nobel's thinking about peace. In any event, she was awarded the first Nobel

Peace Prize in 1905.

The real love affair of his life was with an Austrian girl, who was 23 years his junior. But even here, his complex mind seemed unable to forget her social and educational inferiority. Despite that, the liaison lasted for 18 years and one hopes he found warmth and affection, which he must have needed. He tried his hand at both poetry and prose and, in his youth, was so strongly influenced by Shelley's pacifist views as to call war "the horror of horrors and the greatest of all

Left, the Royal Family at Stockholm's Nobel Prize Ceremony. **Above**, Alfred Nobel.

crimes." Despite that, Nobel apparently saw no wrong in profiting from the weapons of war and during his lifetime he amassed a huge fortune.

He was not the sort of rich man who prided himself on his frugality, nor did he wait until he was dead to become a generous philanthropist. His philosophy was always to prefer "to take care of the stomachs of the living rather than the glory of the departed in the form of monuments."

A year before his death in San Remo in Italy, he signed the famous will which, in less than 300 words, stipulated how to convert the major part of his estate into an investment fund. The proceeds were to be used for annual prizes to be awarded to individuals that "shall have conferred the greatest benefit on mankind." There were to be five categories: Physics, chemistry, physiology or medicine, literature and now best known of all—the award for "the best work for fraternity between nations, for the abolition or reduction of standing armies and for the holding and promotion of peace congresses", the Nobel Prize for Peace.

The first four were to be awarded by Swedish institutions. But for the Peace Prize, Nobel went outside Sweden and named a committee appointed by the Norwegian Parliament to make the award.

In 1968, the Central Bank of Sweden added a prize in Economic Sciences to the original categories, in memory of Nobel.

Constant threat: Today, the contradictions of Nobel's complex personality have left a second legacy, quite apart from the Nobel Prizes. Sweden's vigorous armaments industry provides a substantial part of Swedish exports each year, as does the dynamite factory in Karlskoga. In fact, Bofors provides the main employment and, one might almost say, the very lifeblood of the town. Yet it also represents a constant threat to the population. Over the years, Bofors has cost many lives and limbs in accidents, and causes many Karlskogan families to live in constant fear.

It is as though that strange marriage between peace and war that existed in Alfred Nobel continues in his own country today.

NED

TO WORK OR TO PLAY?

A leading Swedish company had the following piece of graffiti written on a wall:
"Who will do the job?

Swedish population	8,100,000
– over 65	1,000,000
= left to work	7,100,000
– under 21	2,900,000
= left to work	4,200,000
– on holiday	350,000
= left to work	3,850,000
– state employees	850,000
= left to work	3,000,000
– on military service	550,000
= left to work	2,450,000
– local authority workers	750,000
= left to work	1,700,000
– on sick leave	700,000
= left to work	1,000,000
– workshy	994,800
= left to work	5,200
– in prison	5,198
= left to work	2

You and me—and I'm tired."

The Swedes, once known for their deeply ingrained Lutheran work ethic, are aware that today more and more people prefer an easier pace and to enjoy life outside office hours. There is a great emphasis on time needed for self-development and to spend with the family. Managers complain about the unwillingness of workers to put in overtime and about union demands for a shorter working week coupled with longer holidays.

Part of the reason for this lack of interest in overtime is that people complain that it is not worth working longer hours if high taxes take away most of the money they earn.

That view is best summed up in the words of one rising executive in a big Stockholm company. "Why should I miss the best years of my family *and* take on extra responsibility for a meagre 50 crowns (£5) a month after tax?" he questioned. Yet in most industrial countries, he'd have been the sort of 'young turk' who put his family well down his list of priorities and his job at the top.

But Swedes do take pride in their jobs. To realise that you only need to glance at the

Left, Volvo's enormous car assembly plant at Goburg is also a tourist attraction, with factory tours in special vehicles.

telephone directory which lists a person's professional status alongside the address.

Nor could anyone accuse the Swedes of being sloppy workers. This small country has produced a list of inventions and industrial successes out of all proportion to its population of eight million. Look at any big Swedish company's map of its world-wide activities, and it is astonishing how many subsidiaries and branch factories it will have in many countries. Swedish firms are also world-famous for high quality goods such as Hasselblad cameras, Volvo and Saab cars, or Electrolux freezers.

Nearly half of the workforce today are in skilled and unskilled blue-collar jobs and, as

one would expect in such an advanced industrial society, the proportion of working class people has declined in recent years, as robots and computers have replaced some menial jobs.

White-collar workers form 35 percent of the workforce, including 7.5 percent in senior management positions, and many claim that Swedish society is middle-class through and through, whatever jobs it performs.

The main employers are the public sector and private industry. Very few Swedes are self-employed, no more than 7 percent. This reflects the fact that it is difficult for a family to set up a small business because high tax rates are not conducive to the amassing of enough money to start a capital intensive operation.

Much of Swedish life is home centred and Swedes will tell you that the struggle in most people's everyday working lives revolves around practical details such as how to get the children to a day care centre or school, and arrange to collect them at the end of a working day. Though most day-care centres or *dagis* also make provision for school-age children to be looked after from the end of the school day to the time one or other parent can collect them, it calls for good organisation.

By international levels, Sweden's unemployment has been low for many years. Though it crept up to over 3 percent (unprecendented heights in Swedish terms) in the early 1980s, it came down again to below 2 percent later in the decade, which in practice means virtually full employment. Everyone is assured of a job, and those who want to change employer generally find it easy to obtain the necessary help or training at the labour market centres, with schemes of grants and loans for retraining.

While unemployment benefits are generous, they are not designed to encourage the workshy. School leavers have to work in hospitals or child-care centres to "earn" their benefits: as Prime Minister Ingvar Carlsson once said: "We don't want our young unemployed people lying in bed until midday."

Swedish employers put a lot of emphasis on personal development at work. Companies send their employees on training schemes and courses, and it is common for Swedes to take further education courses outside the office at adult education centres.

Union organisations, such as the blue-collar union federation LO, encourage their members to take advantage of these training opportunities and show none of the recalcitrant Luddite attitudes of other countries in implementing new technology. The union stance is enlightened and co-operative and aims to use the new opportunities to benefit their members as well as the companies.

The concern for personal development also gives consideration to family relations. It is becoming a common sight to see men sitting in the park with their prams because many more fathers take parental leave or stay at home if a child is sick.

It can come as quite a surprise to foreign businessmen to learn that their contact— "Mr Svensson" at AB Bolaget—is away for three months looking after his latest offspring and the household chores.

To outsiders, the Swedes often appear unambitious on the surface, and their businessmen far from cut-throat. Where else would you come across a senior executive who says he would be happy to take paternity leave "in order to encourage his staff" or a businessman who is willing to sidestep promotion in order to be with his daughter during a crucial part of her early development?

Considerable effort is made to make

Furthermore, there are some work practices which do not encourage effort. Until recently, when it emerged that Sweden's crippling tax system would be reformed, overtime was so heavily taxed that nobody wanted to be paid money for it—instead they would opt for the alternative which is to take double the time off work. So if you worked one day at the weekend, you could earn two days off the next week. One journalist worked so much overtime during the prolonged annual wage negotiations that he earned six weeks off during the summer—on top of his holiday allowance of six weeks.

Most Swedes are entitled to five weeks' holiday a year, which they generally prefer

everyone feel equally important. For example, even the very senior people at the Swedish Employers' Confederation (SAF) have to clock in and out of the office using personal cards at all times—so that nobody feels their bosses are given an easy ride. However, it is sometimes said that their fundamental belief in equality goes a long way towards explaining why Swedes rarely excel when it come to the service sector.

Left, Sweden makes industrial as well as designer glass. **Above**, the twice-daily trip to deliver and collect children at the *dagis* is part of family life.

to take in Sweden during the summer months of June or July when the weather can be glorious, so that for this period the country practically closes down, and Stockholm is given over to visitors. In the bleak cold of the winter months, like the birds, Swedes on holiday prefer to migrate to the south and the sun. They are essentially outdoor people who like fishing, sailing and enjoying nature. A Swedish dream is to spend the summer in the family *stuga*, a small wooden house, painted the traditional red that is a byproduct of copper mining, with white trimmings around the door and windows. They are scattered everywhere, dotted around the islands and the countryside.

Most Swedes are only a generation or two away from the farm and many can go back to what was the family home. But, while the ideal is to own a cottage like this or to build a new *stuga*, many rely on friends or relatives; others may have access to an office *stuga*.

Employers recognise that the only perks worth giving are those which cannot be taxed out of existence, so it has become increasingly common for companies to send an office group on a "conference"—for example, on board a luxury ferry boat to Denmark or for a few days to Portugal. The work aspect is a mere formality—and recognised as such—but the perk is greatly appreciated by employees.

Where Sweden's work system faces real problems today is with absenteeism in industry. Motor manufacturers such as Saab Scania and Volvo have absenteeism rates of about 16 percent and have to rely on pools of extra labour to make up the shortfall, and the average worker takes about 27 days' sick leave a year. This has encouraged more careful thought about the working environment and how to improve working conditions, as well as how to tighten up the monitoring of those supposedly on "sick leave" through a system of inspectors who visit and check up.

Volvo has pioneered a new system for car assembly workers which relies much more on team spirit and builds cars in groups, and other companies have followed this example. Others may arrange sports facilities and saunas for their staff.

The unions play an important part in stimulating such developments and employees are encouraged to hold group discussions on how they feel about issues. Indeed, when an outsider phones in, it can sometimes appear that the entire office is wrapped up in meetings of one kind or another—whether it be to discuss the launch of a bvmarketing strategy, or simply a scheduled "informal" discussion on what each person did for their holiday.

For group participation is the essence in a society which aims at concensus, both when it comes to planning for the future and when enjoying the benefits of success.

Right, one in every five households in Sweden own its own boat.

A century ago, Sweden was divided by a rigid class system. "Poverty, overcrowding, starvation, and sickness were common," wrote historian Åke Elmér. "In contrast, there was an upper class, which in magnificence and wealth stood far above the great mass of people." A small intermediate group of propertied farmers, middle-class merchants and white-collar workers "were objects of contempt to the upper class and envy to the working class."

The elite of nobles, senior bureaucrats, military officers and professors were addressed with the respectful *Ni* (you) and a tip of the cap by common folk and they would respond with the more familiar *du*. Railroad carriages had three different classes and boats four. Industrial workers normally toiled 12 hours a day, while office workers spent a leisurely four or five hours at their job.

"Of the living conditions of the workers, I had no conception," Swedish diplomat Einar Modig recalled in his memoirs describing his youth in an upper-middle class home. "I was only certain that an ill-clad person was a worker; the concepts *worker* and *ruffian* were not sharply distinct."

The situation is quite different in Sweden today. Foreigners surveying the well-dressed crowds and comfortable homes have difficulty seeing any class distinction. Swedes are near the top of the international league of such indicators of living standards as ownership of telephones, television sets and cars. Slums don't exist and the rare cases of individual hardship are widely reported in the newspapers.

Swedes themselves often have trouble identifying the class origins of their fellow citizens. Many of the signposts that denote class in Britain, for instance, are absent in Sweden. Regional or class accents in speech have largely disappeared and the use of *Ni* has been dropped. The relatively uniform high standard of the Swedish press removes

the distinction between the readers of quality newspapers and tabloids that exist elsewhere in Europe. Attending the universities at Uppsala and Lund, Sweden's two oldest learning establishments, does not carry quite the same social cachet as being a graduate of Oxford or Cambridge.

Only 25 years ago, most Swedes still identified with the working class; almost everyone now labels themselves middle-class. One indication of this trend is the rapid change in surnames. People are abandoning

rural family names—those ending in -son (Ericsson or Carlsson) and adopting the Latinised surnames (Beckérus or Glanzelius) of the 18th-century learned classes, to create the impression that one's forebears enjoyed a higher social status. While Karlsson becomes Karnsun, the Swedish nobility, responding to reverse snobbery, prefers to hide their titles rather than flout them. And, although any Stockholmer will tell you that the Östermalm district is upper-class, Norrmalm and Kungsholmen are middle-class and Söder is working-class, the differences are becoming blurred.

There are two main reasons why Sweden

Left, the Swedish dream—a *stuga* (cottage) by sea or lake and a boat tied up alongside. **Right**, Eva Goës, one of the successful Green Party candidates in the 1988 elections.

now possesses fewer class differences than almost any other nation. One is Sweden's rapid spurt of economic growth, the second fastest in the industrial world during the past century after Japan. And although it is relatively easy to spread around the national wealth among a small population of 8.4 million, this has been aided by the policies of the long-ruling Social Democrats.

When the Social Democrats first assumed power in 1932, they eschewed the traditional socialist doctrine of nationalising industry. Instead of pursuing the socialism of production, the government decided to concentrate on what has been called the "socialism of everyday life"—ensuring the even distribu-

this had narrowed to 25 percent. Differences in income are then further reduced by the country's steeply progressive tax rates.

Taxes are important not only as a levelling device but also to pay for Sweden's extensive social welfare system, which guarantees that the disadvantaged, such as the elderly, the sick and the handicapped, will not suffer a fall in living standards. Even the tax system itself is subject to egalitarian principles. Local taxes, which pay for the bulk of social services, do not vary greatly from one region of the country to the other.

Housing and education have been two other areas that have received government attention in its push for egalitarian living

tion of what is produced in the private sector and promoting equality of opportunity if not results. It is a goal that enjoys wide public support. A recent survey found that 55 percent of Swedes value egalitarianism more than personal freedom and thus do not object to strong government interference.

Class differences have also lessened as gaps in income have narrowed. This is partly due to the policy of wage solidarity—equal pay for equal work—which has been championed by the powerful trade unions in their negotiations with employers. In the 1960s, skilled workers were paid 54 percent more than unskilled labourers. By the mid-1980s,

standards. Before World War II, half of all Swedish urban households lived in tiny quarters, consisting of one room and a kitchen. The government embarked on a major construction programme that included rent subsidies to allow low-income families to live in more spacious dwellings. Unfortunately, housing construction has never kept pace with population movements to the cities. Paradoxically, it is central Stockholm's cramped flats, built at the turn of the century to house the working class, that have become the most desirable places to live. For example, Gamla Stan, which 50 years ago was a working-class slum, is now the most chic address in the city.

The Social Democrats also felt that the education system they inherited maintained class barriers since it emphasised streaming pupils into "ability" groups. An American-style comprehensive school system was gradually introduced, making it easier for the children of working-class families to obtain the necessary credentials for admission to university. Sweden now has the highest proportion of working-class youth in Western Europe attending university.

By the late 1960s, with progress made in achieving economic equality, the government turned its attention to promoting sexual equality. A change in the tax rules, to require

sight, a recent government-sponsored study concluded that many "occupations are very clearly divided and evaluated by sex" with women holding mainly low-level and low-paid jobs. It is still a rarity to see a woman in a senior managerial position. More progress has been made in government. About 30 percent of the parliamentary seats and a quarter of Cabinet members are women.

The problem Swedish women face in securing influential positions underscores the fact that Sweden has by no means achieved the perfect egalitarian society. The country's sizeable immigrant population, numbering one million, also has difficulties in achieving the same standards of living as

husbands and wives to file separate tax returns, encouraged the entry of women into the workforce since it penalised one-income households. The percentage of women working has climbed to 82 percent, a development aided by the expansion of day care centres for children.

But the quest for sexual equality has met with mixed success. Although policewomen and female bus drivers are now a common

Left, the start of feminism—a women's sewing co-operative early this century. Above, in many factories robots have taken over the routine and menial jobs.

native Swedes despite government attempts to assilimate them into society. And while income distribution is relatively even, the distribution of wealth is not, with Swedish industry controlled by an oligarchy of family dynasties, such as the great banking family, the Wallenbergs.

In many respects, Sweden may have already reached the apogee of its bid for egalitarianism. Proposed tax reform in the early 1990s will loosen the government's guiding hand over income distribution, increasing the chances for the re-emergence of some class differences. How will egalitarian Sweden face that prospect?

Most immigrants to Sweden have a hobby: it's called Sweden bashing—not in a physical sense, of course, but in words. Every time a couple of people of foreign extraction meet, even for the first time, it's not long before they are complaining to one another about Sweden—the lousy Swedish weather, tasteless Swedish food, high Swedish taxes, unfriendly Swedish people, non-respectful Swedish children and so on. And the diatribes are no less damning for being delivered in not too perfect Swedish.

For some reason, Sweden just seems to have that effect on anyone who lives there for any length of time. Even the Swedes do it. It must be the long, dark winters.

Despite the grumbles, most immigrants stay. It may be because job, marriage, family, or the situation in their home country keeps them there. But, even if they have made it in Sweden, the majority claim they would gladly exchange it for the warmth, and friendliness they left behind—or *think* they left behind. Many, it would seem, are just waiting for an opportunity to go. Others just talk about it, as exiles do everywhere.

Historical upheavals: Although there were colonies of German merchants and craftsmen in Sweden as early as the 13th and 14th centuries, major immigration started from neighbouring Finland in the 16th century. The first non-Nordic wave of foreign immigration can be traced to the arrival of Dutch merchants and Walloon smiths during the 17th and 18th centuries. Their numbers were few by present standards, but even today there are villages, settled by Walloons, where the colouring is darker than average, though their descendants have long since been integrated and become part of the near 100 percent ethnically homogenous Swedish society that existed until recently.

The first wave of modern immigration during the 1930s didn't affect Sweden's homogenous nature as they were mostly ethnic Swedes who returned to escape the Depression in the United States. Also during the 1930s, the number of immigrants began to surpass the number of emigrants for the first time. In only two years since then, 1972 and 1973, has the outflow been larger than the inflow.

In 1950 the number of foreign nationals in Sweden totalled only 1.8 percent of the population, which was then a little over 6.9 million. Between 1944 and 1980, immigration accounted for nearly 45 percent of Sweden's total population growth and one of

every four children born was of foreign extraction. By 1975, the number of foreign immigrants jumped to five percent of the population, which had increased to nearly 7.8 million.

The latest available figures show that over one million out of a total population of 8.5 million are foreign-born or the first generation children of a foreign parent. The foreign-born alone total over 700,000, of which a little over half have become Swedish citizens. Immigration's record year was 1970, when the arrivals peaked at 77,300.

During and immediately following World War II, a different type of immigrant arrived

Left, dressed for the Midsummer celebrations. **Right**, some Swedish schools have pupils from as many as 20 different races.

FINN-FINNS, FINN-SWEDES & SWEDE-FINNS

No two nations are more inextricably linked in past and present than Sweden and Finland. At any given time, there are probably more Finnish immigrants in Sweden than there are ethnic Swedish-speaking Finns living in Finland. The Finns have been immigrating to (and emigrating from) Sweden ever since the 16th century. As a result, the Finns now constitute the largest foreign national group in Sweden, totalling over 320,000. Of these, 190,000 hold Swedish citizenship.

Their life-line is the ferry traffic dominated by the Viking and Silja Lines with the main routes operating between Stockholm and Norrtälja in Sweden to Helsinki and Turku in Finland. These ferries across the Baltic carry more than eight million passengers a year between the two countries, mostly Finns on visits to relatives and friends in Sweden or Finland. The traffic growth over the past few years has turned the ferry into a floating luxury hotel, with berths in cabins for 2,000-plus passengers, and a choice of restaurants, nightclubs and bars to idle away the time.

Finnish domination among Sweden's immigrant population can be traced back to the historical relations between the two nations and, more recently, to the common labour market that allow citizens of the Nordic countries to move from one country to another without the need of a passport or work permit. But the ratio between immigration and emigration for Finns in Sweden is now almost even, with as many people returning each year as arriving; this is because Finland's economy is at least as strong as Sweden's.

For more than 500 years, Finland was a Swedish colony and the Finns were more often than not the foot-soldiers for Swedish generals. The 16th and 17th-century immigrants were usually retired soldiers who helped to settle wilderness areas in central and northern Sweden. Succeeding waves of Finnish immigrants worked in Sweden's mines and forests, then in its factories and hospitals.

Even though this has given the two nations an inter-related history, their differences are significant. This is evident from the three Finnish groups that live in Sweden: Finns with Finnish as a mother tongue (Finn-Finns); Finns with Swedish as a mother tongue (Finn-Swedes); and Swedes with Finnish as a mother tongue (Swede-Finns).

Finn-Finns are the largest immigrant group and are the ones most likely to return to Finland after a period of time. They usually make the trip across the Baltic Sea in the first place because Sweden is where the jobs are. Even if they establish roots in Sweden, they have the security of knowing that Finland is at most a 10 to 12-hour boat ride away.

Finn-Swedes, on the other hand, are likely to stay for a long time. Their Swedish mother tongue is often a hangover from the time when Swedish was the offical language in Finland and used for all bureaucratic purposes. Today, they are a minority in their own country, accounting for less than 10 percent of Finland's total population, and they often have family ties to Sweden.

The Swede-Finns— the fewest in number— usually live along the northern border between the two countries and cannot really be counted as immigrants.

Despite these differences, all Finns living in Sweden unite in common cause at least once every year. They all shout for Finland during the two-day annual track and field meet, held alternately in Stockholm or Helsinki, that pits a Swedish national team against a Finnish national team. More often than not, the Finnish teams, both men and women, come out on top—no small achievement since Sweden has almost twice the population of Finland. It is a sweet victory for all Finns, who have had to put up with a "poor cousin" relationship with the Swedes.

The Finns illustrate this relationship in a story about two Finns who grew up together in a small town in central Finland and, after many years, meet by chance in Stockholm. The newly arrived Matti is upset when his old friend Markku greets him with little enthusiasm. "But Matti," Markku explains, "you must understand, I am now a Swedish citizen."

in Sweden, refugees from the war and supression in Baltic states and central Europe. They also included 122,000 refugees from the other Nordic countries, including 60,000 Finnish children. Those that stayed in Sweden after the war have for the most part become Swedish citizens.

The post-war wave of the 1950s and 1960s were mostly "guest workers" invited by Sweden to work in its factories and help with expanding industrialisation. They came from Italy, the United Kingdom and West Germany. They were soon followed by immigrants from Greece, Poland and Yugoslavia and Turkey. Large numbers of other Nordic country nationals also made the

The latest wave comes from Iran, including a sizeable number of Kurds, and, to a lesser degree, those fleeing the war and terrorism in Lebanon. In 1986 the number of non-European immigrants exceeded the European immigrants for the first time. Sweden now has nearly 25,000 residents of Iranian origin and over 30,000 of Turkish origin. Yugoslavs are still the largest non-Nordic ethnic group and number over 58,000.

The later arrivals from the Middle East are not as welcome as the earlier immigrants. To the Swedes, they appear both too different and too many and liberal Sweden, long the conscience of the world, now has its share of skinheads and other racists. This phenome-

move to Sweden in the late 1960s, especially from Finland, facilitated by the common Nordic labour market that does not require work permits.

When economic conditions began to change in the 1970s, Sweden sought to stem the tide of economic immigrants but still held open its doors to humanitarian immigration and political refugees such as the Chileans, who now number nearly 20,000.

Left, Swedes and Finns get together on the northern border to celebrate midsummer. **Above**, dark heads and fair heads at the Rinkeby Immigrant Festival, near Stockholm.

non is not just a natural development of a too lenient policy that allows easy entry for too many immigrants or political refugees. Latent Swedish racism has surfaced and is growing despite public disapproval.

Today's Sweden has suburban housing projects where the immigrant population far outnumbers the ethnic Swedes. There are schools with students from up to a 100 different nations and there are day-care centres with almost as many different nationalities as there are children.

Creating ghettos is not the intention, and Swedish authorities have made many successful attempts to integrate the new arrivals into Swedish society, including free Swedish lessons which may be taken with full pay during working hours. Paradoxically, many of the latter immigrants, who often come from small villages in Turkey, Syria or Iran, prefer to live together because of language difficulties or to minimise contact with the "foreign" Swedish culture.

Even if they are not naturalised, immigrants have some say in how their lives are run, with a right to vote in municipal and county council elections, but not in national elections, provided they have been residents for three consecutive years. All the political parties try to woo the immigrant vote which can be decisive in some communities.

The percentage exercising the right, however, is far below the national average. This may reflect either that democracy is not something the immigrant population understands or the negative attitude held by many immigrants about Sweden and a hope that their stay is not permanent.

Immigrant contributions: Besides working in factories, hospitals and hotels, immigrants have made several valuable contributions to Swedish society. The one that most affects Swedes and foreign visitors alike is food. Back in the 1950s and 1960s, the choice of restaurants was limited in the extreme. Swedes were not in the habit of dining out

and the restaurants that existed were either the expensive gourmet institutions, like the Operakällaren in Stockholm, or the less expensive establishments, which served food that may have been filling but did nothing for the taste buds. Restaurants with good food in a pleasant atmosphere and at reasonable prices were few and far between.

Then a culinary revolution hit Sweden. Good restaurants started to spring up, first in the big cities and eventually in the smaller towns. Their owners and chefs were often immigrants who were taking the opportunity to move up a step from dishwashing and waiting. The reason for the expansion was also partly the number of Swedes who began to go abroad on holiday, where they learned to like something other than "meatballs". But the main and more significant reason was the attitude of the foreign immigrants to food and dining out.

The Italians naturally led the way, and there is probably not a town of any size in Sweden that does not have at least one pizzeria. Nowadays, the owners are not always Italian but more often that not Yugoslavs. Some Italian restaurateurs have moved on to greater things and now preside over class establishments that make a point not to serve pizza. Several of the most highly rated restaurants in Stockholm—including the traditionally Swedish Operakällaren, Stallmästergården, Riché and Teater Grillen—are now owned by either the son, or two former employee brothers of one of Stockholm's first Italian restaurant-pizzeria owners.

While never as extensive as the Italian, Chinese immigration has nevertheless resulted in a flourish of far-eastern restaurants, almost as numerous as pizzerias. The story goes that the very first Chinese restaurant was in Gothenburg and the owner imported two chefs. After a while the two chefs each started their own restaurant and each imported two chefs. They in turn soon opened their own establishment and so on.

So perhaps the best result of all of over 500 years of immigration is that Sweden now offers a choice of international dining.

Left, boys at the Rinkeby Immigrant Festival. **Right**, the Smörgåsbord (cold table) at Opera Källaren, one of Stockholm's most "Swedish" restaurants, now run by an Italian restaurateur.

THE LAPPS

They call themselves "the people of the eight seasons", the Lapps, who live in Sweden's most northerly province of Lappland. It is Sweden's biggest area, a vast wilderness where nature and the reindeer set the course of the year. For as long as anyone knows the Lapps have lived there, dependent on those seasons and the reindeer.

In the eighth century, a Lombardian monk, Paulus Diaconus, described the reindeer as a strong and hardy little animal that was "not unlike a stag". But that was not the first time that the Lapps and their country were written about. Both the Roman historian Tacitus and the later Procopius had already mentioned Scandinavia. It is unlikely that Tacitus or Procopius visited the Ultima Thule, but perhaps Paulus Diaconus found his way there: he describes the snow-covered mountains, the dress of the Lapps and the skill with which they managed to move along. His writings are also the first to mention the midnight sun and the winter solstice.

The eight seasons of Lappland start with springwinter in April when the covering of snow is still heavy over the plains. In these cruel days, the reindeer have a hard time because they must dig deep through the crust of snow to find their most important food, the lichens—reindeer lichen, beard lichen which hangs so heavily from the branches of the trees, and the tangled horsehair lichen, with its comic name of "nervous wreck".

Hard times: Life is bleak for the reindeer. They are hungry and must wander far to find food. As well, it is a hard-working time for the Lapps who breed the reindeer and must keep the herds in order.

But spring is in the air and soon they will be trekking up the high mountains. The bulls have sloughed off their horns and the cows carry the calves-to-be in their swollen stomachs. The sun arrives in the beginning of May. It is the second season and the cow is ready to calve.

Soon the springsummer is here and the

Preceding pages: Kebnekajse in Lappland, Sweden's highest mountain at 2,123 metres, over 6,000 ft. <u>Left</u>, Lapps in traditional costume at the Jokkmokk winter fair.

mountains blossom with Lapp heath, globe flowers, cloud berries, and all the hundreds of species that grow there. This abundant vegetation gives not only verdant pasture to the reindeer but, as well, a feast for the eye. The region is botanically very rich, and the life of its people provides a rare insight into a unique culture.

Modern ways: The reindeer keeper of today is very different from his ancestors. In the past, even as recently as the early decades of this century, the whole family accompanied the reindeer up into the mountains, the draught-reindeer loaded with all the necessities and paraphernalia required for the summer, not least the *katå*, or cone-shaped hut

that was easy to carry, to provide shelter for these nomadic people. There the family would live out the summer months, making the most of the endless daylight, storing up for the long night of winter.

Today, the family lives in towns and villages and only men care for the animals and follow the herd. To assist them, they have acquired helicopters and scooters, walkietalkies and all the equipment that makes communication easy. But, despite modern life, the reindeer must stay up on the high mountains, where the pasture is rich and a fresh wind blows, very different from the birch woods below where the heat is too

oppressive for the animals. Here too in the cool mountains, they are away from the ever-present insects that sting ferociously.

Summer dream: After the springsummer comes the summer proper, to bring the grazing land that the Lapps dream about in winter. Fresh and clean, the small streams babble and the lakes are rich in salmon-trout, alpine char, white fish and other alpine species. Up here, there isn't a single tree or bush in sight.

Reindeer herding is not easy. The men must mark all the newborn calves with their own distinctive criss-cross sign, and herd the deer, throwing their lassoes with a skill and accuracy that they learned in their childhood games. Today, the lasso is made of nylon and, once caught, the men make a small incision in the calf's ear with a very sharp knife, and thread the small pieces of flesh cut out on to a string or sinew. That way, all the men know how many calves there are in the herd and which belongs to each man.

All too soon the summer is gone and the hardest time of the year looms ahead. Down the mountains the men drive their reindeer herds, into the folds where they will be separated from each other before slaughter.

In the autumnsummer, the reindeer are fat from the fine pastures; the plague of flies and mosquitoes are gone, but heavy storms rage over the mountains and the plains. The knotty dwarf birch will soon shed its leaves but first it goes through a kaleidoscope of yellow, orange, red and brown, turning the mountains into a stunning sight.

The slaughter begins and the ancient scene is like a feast from some primeval rite, full of the strong odours of sweat, blood and dung. The meat that the men do not sell fresh is frozen to become a delicacy—especially when the thin slices of reindeer are fried with onions, mushrooms and heavy cream.

Now it is autumnwinter, the northern lights are blazing and the aurora carries frost in its colours. The days grow shorter and, when mist and storms cover the stars, the nights are black. On the moors, the reindeer huddle together to keep warm along the edges of the birchwoods where the snow is loose and the lichens are still moist and full of nourishment.

Left, in the short northern summer, the ground blossoms with thousands of tiny flowers. **Right**, "Beware reindeer!"

Today, beasts of prey are little danger to the Lapps. The wolf is almost extinct in Sweden, the bear hibernates, and the wolverine no longer lies in wait to lap the fresh blood from the reindeer.

The Fairs: In every way, the life of the Lapps has changed in modern times. Only for festivals and ceremonial occasions do they put on the knee-length costume, trimmed with handwoven ribbons in red and yellow. But the tradition of handicrafts continues strongly and the place to see it is at one of the big market fairs at Jokkmokk. The Lapps make use of any natural materials from tree bark to reindeer horn.

Today, these fascinating people are a scattered remnant of around 40,000 divided between Finland, Norway, the USSR, and Sweden. Yet visitors come not just from Sweden but from all parts of the world to meet the Lapplanders at this traditional fair.

The Jokkmokk fair is unique in that it has only genuine Lapp handicraft, such as the beautifully designed knives, the bowls and baskets plaited from the thinnest root fibres, pieces of carved wood, and ribbons and woven fabrics.

In Jokkmokk, you can also taste all the delicacies associated with the reindeer—the pure Lappland *lappkok*, a casserole made of marrow bones and shredded liver to form a substantial and tasty broth. Another speciality is *renklämma*, a thin slice of unleavened bread shaped into a cone and filled with slices of smoked reindeer.

The fairs take place in August and February, but all over Lappland there are delicacies to taste and Lapp handicrafts to buy and to view at the museums.

During the year 1732, the famous botanist Carl von Linné made an expedition to Lappland, and some years later a copper engraving was made of him in Lapp dress, with the frock, bottle-nosed boots, and the typical Lappish accessories. In his hand he holds a drum with mythical signs, today regarded as one of the most precious possessions by any Lapp.

But the mythical signs are another story— a tale from ancient times, from the very special religion that belongs to the Lapps.

Left, a Lapp woman sells her wares at Jokkmokk. The fair is so popular that you need to book nearly a year in advance to be sure of finding a bed.

In Stockholm, if you are somebody or if you want to meet anybody, you do the art gallery rounds on Saturday mornings. There, in front of the works of "these terribly modern types", fashionable Sweden preens and gleans tips about where the best art investments are to be made. As the country's "ocelot ladies and their camel-haired husbands" wander from the right openings to the "must" showings at the city's highly competitive auction houses, Sweden's culture industry booms.

This may be culture spelled with a small "c" but it is highly popular culture with a vast and varied segment of the Swedish population. Appreciation of art (and its financial ramifications), whether it be homely folk carvings or a Watteau watercolour, has fleshed out the Swedish art market into one of the most vital in Europe. Finding a Clia, or a Litchenstein or one of those new "Foto-Konzept-Kunst" artists from Germany is easy. Simply stroll along the boulevard called Strandvägen in Stockholm, or Avenuen in Götenborg, and you will quickly spy your desired prey ensconced in a gallery display.

Well-fed vultures: Culture spelled with a capital "C" is also inordinately popular. Following every announcement of the winner of the Nobel Prize for Literature, the country's book shops are flooded with the author's works in the original language as well as Swedish. Sell-outs are the rule. The government encourages the culture vultures by subsidising the established arts such as the state opera and state theatre, called Dramaten, with enormous grants. As a result, tickets are among the cheapest on the continent.

What is more, the Social Democrat government fosters the broad view of culture and gives generous support to many activities, from the restoration of 17th-century castles to the baking of flat bread in the distant prov-

inces. Sweden, therefore, is one of Europe's most culture-saturated countries.

Broad-view culture is serious business here. Even the smallest communities set aside considerable tax funds for sponsoring heritage farms where local ladies' guilds weave and card and sew while the menfolk harrow, plough and sow just the way their grandparents did at the turn of the century. The Industrial Revolution came late to Sweden. In 1910, 90 percent of the population was employed on the land. Today, that

figure is just three percent, making ties to granny's farmstead very strong and deeply personal. Back-to-the-farm and nature romanticism constitutes a major part of Swedish culture.

In practical terms this has fostered revival extravagances such as the rebirth of linen production. Just a decade after the last government subsidies were withdrawn from the lagging industry, the fields on the west coast are flushed bright blue with flax flowers producing the raw materials for the looms of Klässbol Linen Mills in Värmland Province. Antique brocade and damask patterns have been rejuvenated there with such exactitude

Preceding pages: Dalahest (Dalarna horse) hand-painted at Nusnäs; National Day celebrations. **Left**, "Bather," by Anders Zorn. **Right**, traditional craftwork.

that the Swedish royal family complements its dinner napkins and table cloths with these newly-woven linens. Sweden's best inns, such as Grythyttan near Örebro and Hook's Manor in central Sweden, proudly advertise their "properly cold-mangled 100 percent linen bed-clothes."

Since a goodly part of the country is forested, woodcrafts are widely produced and broadly appreciated in Sweden. In Dalarna Province, called the Heart of Sweden, communities along the banks of Lake Siljan have turned the local carving tradition into a thriving tourist industry. Dozens of small family-run mills whittle, for example, large wooden spoons and forks with intricate rococo-based

tlingly beautiful baskets, cradles, carry-alls and even snow boots. Such creations demand skill, hours of concentration and subsequently high prices. Typically, the usually penurious Mr. Svensson gladly dishes out a week's wage on a good piece of *näver* work or ironmongery or hand-woven textiles done in traditional patterns.

Patterns for everything from wood joinery to tweed weavery, methods of production such as nature-based wool dyes and the dipping of honeycomb candles—in other words, nearly all the traditional cottage industries of Sweden—are carefully catalogued and preserved by nation-wide organisations such as "The Friends of Handi-

designs, once the prescribed engagement gift from swain to maiden. Such modern reproductions are standard house presents as well as gifts to visiting foreigners.

Although commercialised, the Swedish handicrafts industry is closely associated with the national identity. Nothing is more Swedish to a Swede than a rucksack woven of *näver*—that is, the soft inner bark of the birch tree. *Näver* is harvested in the brisk northern forests in early spring, then cut into narrow strips and left to cure. The snowy winter months in the northern provinces provide the enforced leisure time for weaving this glove leather-like material into star-

crafts" (Handarbetsvänner) and the "Home Industries Association" (Hemslöjdsförening). They also actively promote handicrafts via sales in their shops found throughout the country.

Folk dancing and music also hold a prominent position in the Swedish heart. Polkas, mazurkas, Morris and square dancing are not just the exercises of school children but the serious concern of hundreds of folk dance clubs and fiddlers' guilds. Towns of all kinds usually boast one or two such groups which compete for radio and television time on the national monopoly media.

The country's many bands of fiddlers and

concertina players become a national concern as interest builds every year to a climax at the "Music on Lake Siljan Festival—nine days, early each July. There, hundreds of Sweden's most accomplished "bowmen" show off their talents, new compositions and finely sewn folk outfits. Instruments vary widely from antique violins to rough-hewn farm fiddles. Zithers, dulcimers and half harps hold their own among an enthusiastic public.

Throughout the warm months, the tones of these folk groups can be heard wafting across village greens all over Sweden, especially at the summer solstice, called *Midsommar*, when huge maypoles are raised to the springing boards of the largest farms' threshing floors. That is a sight to make a Swedish expatriate pine; musicians and dancers, brilliant in their folk costumes, swirling through the long hours of a Nordic twilight.

In Sweden, every province and most districts and villages have their particular variation on the national folk costume of embroidered waistcoat, knee breeches and felt hat for the men and flared skirt, apron, waistcoat and bonnet for the women. Fancy needlework and various home-woven fabrics set off each costume. Specific floral patterns on a girl's waistcoat indicate her place of birth and, to the initiated, her marital status.

The folk costume is so firmly established in

beat of traditional songs and the musicians are decked in wreaths of wild flowers. In the cities, folk music takes on the form of well publicised (and often sold-out) concerts, but in the villages these fiddle jams sessions can be as spontaneous as a friendly get-together on the verandah of a pub. In mountain country or in the far north in Lappland, music is always accompanied by dancing on the

Far left, concertina player at folk festival. **Left**, Queen Silvia wears national costume for National Day. **Above**, typical Swedish glassware.

Sweden, it is accepted as formal wear. The wife of a former prime minister regularly appeared in her aprons and ribbons at the Opening of Parliament and royal state dinners. The prime minister opted for the less traditional black and white evening gear. Her Majesty Queen Silvia, as a former West German citizen, has adopted Stockholm's costume and wears it in public on the national holiday, the king's birthday and on official walkabouts through the country—to the enchantment of the people.

A Swedish specialty which swings between craft and industry is glass-making, concentrated on the county of Småland, though other areas have their glass blowers. Even Stockholm has an example of a traditional glass workshop in Skansen on the island of Djurgården.

Although Swedish glass-making is big business, it has all the mores of a craft industry, with single pieces of glass made by one glass blower to the inspiration of one designer, as well as large ranges of standard tableware.

While the culture of the countryside is alive and well preserved, urban culture thrives in many a Swedish metropolis. Return to Stockholm or Göteborg or Malmö or Norrköping on a Saturday morning and the day begins with a peek into the shelves of the

international quality oils by Anders Zorn and Carl Larsson can be had—at a price. For the very up-to-date, Gallery Contur, also on Östermalm, specialises in the latest from the art centres in New York and Frankfurt as well as the most daring local talent.

Since Sotheby's began selling Scandiavian art from the turn of this century for record breaking prices, the Swedish art market has gone through the roof. As one gallery owner puts it, "people are buying anything done in oils and absolutely everything that is signed." High quality works from the beginning of the century are suddenly being pulled out of exile in attics and cellars, dusted down, and shipped to sales in London or Stock-

auction houses. In Stockholm, Auktionsverket, the oldest functioning auction firm, draws thousands of bidders to twice weekly clubbings of everything from Chinese "familie rose" platters to used furniture and fur coats. After that comes the rounds of the art galleries. This might mean National Galleriet for its anti-establishment installations—a year ago the National Galleriet created shock waves with its Anti-Coke installation mounted as a protest against the National Museum's exhibit, "Coke is the World."

For fashionable Sweden there is Gallery Olsson on Stockholm's Östermalm, where

holm.

This all started a few years ago when Sotheby's curator for 19th-century art, the alert Alexander Apsis, included a few turn-of-the-century Scandinavian works in a London auction as an experiment. The international art world went wild. Here was a whole realm of interesting, even excellent, painters and sculptors to be had for a fraction of what their French and English equivalents go for. Carl Larsson's homely *art nouveau* oils, Bruno Liljefors' impressionistic hunt scenes and Anders Zorn's Whistleresque gilded portraits of the beauties and magnates of the Golden Age suddenly burst from their shell of quiet local interest into international celebrity. Prices quickly followed suit.

The motive behind much of this buying is a diffused idea of investing to beat the tax collector. Another gallery owner says: "Most of my buyers are young, well-paid professionals looking to protect part of their income from Sweden's high income taxes. Their first painting is usually something of interest on the international market (the idea is to resell high). The work has to have snob value as well as financial growth potentials. But after they have signed for their third work they are goners—they've been bitten by the collecting bug. Swedish cocktail parties these days seem to be becoming art

canvas, *The Dying Dandy* by Nils von Dardel, realized 13 million Skr. to the unbridled joy of several prospective Roos protégés.

Several important art collections have been established within the last two decades in Sweden. The oldest of these is owned by senior industrialist Carl-Eric Björkegren who has concentrated his collecting on the established names from the early 20th century—Matisse, Leger, Picasso, Bonnard as well as comparable Swedes; Grünewald, Amelin, Dardel and even the moderns such as Allan Cullberg with his bombastic blobs and smears of colour. Björkegren plans to hang his collection in central Stockholm

appreciation discussions."

Despite its convivial forms, art in Sweden is big business. Fredrik Roos, a genial stock exchange dealer in his mid-thirties, has just sold off 28 early 20th-century Swedish paintings, including heavyweights such as Hjertén, Schjerbeck, Kylberg, GAN and Jolin. The manoeuvre freed funds for "cultivating the artists who will be names at the beginning of the next century." A single

Left, characteristic interior by Carl Larsson. **Above**, Ingmar Bergman directing *Fanny and Alexander*.

and, in a typically Swedish move, open his private collection for the public's enjoyment.

Finance guru Robert Weil, just entering his mid-forties, is presently building up a permanent collection of 1980s art in Stockholm. "Aesthetics interest me," he says. "This project is an extension of that interest and my curiosity about design. And it's great fun creating something with an underlying feeling of quality." This collecting is going on in a converted warehouse, listed on the national register as "of national interest to the harbour architecture in Stockholm." Weil and his partner, New York gallery owner David

Neuman, have simply called their "museum" Magasin 3 after the warehouse's address. At least one piece from each show will end up in the Magasin's permanent collection. To date, the works of Joel Fisher, Lynda Bengalis, Mel Keendric, John Chamberlain and Robert Therrien have been featured at Magasin 3, covering all the major post-war trends except minimalism.

Weil has now remedied that lack with a show by Walter de Maria, the Godfather of the American minimalists. His works are usually media events, as they spread over large areas of desert landscape or stick boldly out into tropical bodies of water. Best known of his historic installations are "The

Borken Kilometer" and "The Earth Rom" *(sic)*, on permanent display in New York. In Europe, the Pompidou Centre and the Stadtgalerie in Stuttgart have shown de Maria. Magasin 3 has found room to feature three of his important works, "Large Rod Series", "Cage II", and "13, 14 and 15-sided Open Polygon". These are the first de Marias to be shown in Scandinavia.

Equally daring is the collection of Fredrik Roos in Malmö in the south of Sweden. "I had collected so many canvases, I'd run out of wall space. The logical thing was to buy a big space and hang a show. That idea has turned into the Rooseum," explains Roos.

More culture in Sweden? Of course! This is the world capital of church music. Choirs abound. On a recent first Sunday of Advent, six interpretations of Mozart's Requiem were offered in Stockholm alone. Ricardo Muti thinks enough of the Swedish Radio Choir to have contracted it to record with him at La Scala, and with the Berlin Philharmonic.

There are more than ecclesiastical notes to be heard. Barber shop quintets and sextets are ubiquitous as are the choirs of the student unions, police corps, fire brigades et cetera, et cetera. Best of all this music is offered year round and is often free. In summer, concerts are offered in the Royal Palace in Stockholm, on the grand staircase of the National Museum and in many of the castles thickly dotting the landscapes outside the major cities. On historic Gotland Island, pianist Staffan Scheja has set up the Gotland Chamber Music Festival during July. The old House of the Nobility, Riddarhuset, is also open for an annual summer series of concerts and recitals.

On stage: The Swedish theatre scene is active, experimental and inexpensive—and in Swedish. So try a musical, from *Cats* to *Starlight Express*. They arrive here soon after opening in New York or London. The Swedish "Folk Opera" is a must. Its *Turandot* received rave reviews from the London *Guardian* and the *New York Times* while touring abroad. But if even more pronounced period pieces are your fancy, try to get tickets to the Drottningholm Theatre productions of late baroque plays and ballet. The theatre is part of the royal family's permanent residence, on an island in Lake Mälaren. Theatre tickets or not, this is a palace well worth visiting.

Finally, what *is* Swedish culture? It is indeed the raising of maypoles by swains and maidens in fancy dress. It is also a visit to one of Stockholm's 50-odd museums and also a car-tour through Sörmland—castle hunting. In Sweden the broad view of culture has created a varied and delectable menu for many tastes.

Left, bust of August Strindberg. **Right**, summer outdoor production of *Hemsöborna*, by Strindberg, a free entertainment in a Stockholm park.

One of the least densely populated countries in Europe, Sweden has room to breathe, and when they get the chance many Swedes love to step outside their front doors, draw a deep breath of fresh air and wander off into the great outdoors. Not surprisingly, walking is a popular pastime but, a day's walk is rarely sufficient to satisfy one's commune with nature, and there is always a demand to take part in much longer treks.

Throughout the country, there's an excellent network of waymarked footpaths. Some of the best, like the Kungsleden (Royal Route) which runs for more than 300 miles (500 km) from Abisko to Hemavan, are found in the more scenically outstanding areas like the national parks. These areas are often well away from towns and villages and as a result many of them have a chain of mountain stations set a comfortable day's walk from one another along the footpaths, providing shelter for walkers.

Most of the mountain stations are well-equipped to serve the needs of hungry and tired walkers, and often have cooking facilities, a shop, and comfortable beds. Some even have a self-service restaurant and that most Scandinavian of institutions, a sauna. They are not hotels but simple accommodation designed to provide a haven at the end of the day for tired walkers.

Heavy load: Not all areas, though, are so well off for comfort and a tent becomes a necessity. Along with a sleeping bag, cooker and food, it can mean a walker has to carry 40 lb (18 kg) of gear, or more. Though there are no camp sites in the Swedish wilderness, camping out is never a problem, thanks first of all to a plentiful supply of fresh water from the many lakes and streams, and secondly to *Allemansrätt* or Everyman's Right. This is an ancient law that basically permits someone, within reason, to camp anywhere for a night, or to walk, ski or paddle his canoe anywhere.

One of the attractions of walking in Sweden is the opportunity of being close to ,

creatures of the forest such as bears, wolves, lynx and elk. The walker has little to worry about with such animals, apart from maybe the odd bear that might be tempted to raid unguarded food, but there is one beast that the walker fears, a beast that will attack the ill-prepared walker in large numbers and leave him a quivering wreck: the mosquito.

Insects galore: The forests are full of mosquitoes in summer and all that walkers can do to combat them is plaster themselves with liberal quantities of insect repellent. Though they haven't been able to eradicate the problem itself, Swedish repellents seem to have a magic ingredient that is quite effective, and it is usually better to wait and buy your insect repellent when you get there.

When the snows come—and in the north of the country that can be as early as October—walking becomes difficult and therefore much less of a pleasure. Away, then, go the walking boots and out come the skis.

Swedes get used to the idea of skiing from an early age. Even before they can walk, they're towed behind their skiing parents in a kind of pram-sledge, and once they've mastered the art of walking it isn't long before they start to get to grips with skis of their own. Practically everyone in Sweden owns a pair of cross-country skis. Frankly, it makes getting about in winter so much easier. But it also opens up further opportunities to enjoy the countryside, or even city parks. Winter doesn't mean a shut-down of the great outdoors. It just requires a different approach.

Whereas in summer the wilderness trails attract walkers, in winter they are covered by the parallel lines of skiers. Of course, the paths themselves are not visible, but to make sure people don't get lost, the paths are marked by red crosses mounted on poles. And to make sure one cross can be seen from another in the height of a blizzard, they are spaced fairly closely together. On a clear day they make a strange sight, hundreds of crosses disappearing across a white expanse to the horizon.

So far, downhill skiing hasn't made the same kind of impression on foreign visitors that it has in the Alpine resorts, despite the efforts of slalom champion Ingemar Stenmark to put Sweden on the international skiing map. Nevertheless, Swedish downhill resorts like Åre and Björkliden are developing apace. Åre has even played host to competitors in the world championships, though for the time being at least, it's mainly the indigenous skier who is attracted there for recreational skiing.

Some people find that even skis can't get them around a snow-covered landscape quickly enough, and snowmobiles and snow scooters—sort of motorbikes on caterpillar tracks—are now taking their place in garages in increasing numbers. Swedes who live in more remote areas use them as a serve fuel. There aren't many petrol stations in the wilds, not even on the roads.

Their great disadvantage is that they're hardly environmentally sympathetic and for that reason they are banned in some areas. They're extremely noisy machines and can be heard miles away across open country. Unless there is a good covering of snow they can damage the undergrowth, and they're smelly. Apart from that, they're great fun.

Water sports: Also fun, but much more in keeping with the spirit of the great outdoors, is canoeing. A country that has something like 100,000 lakes and countless miles of rivers is bound to be in favour with canoeists, and there can be no denying the popularity of

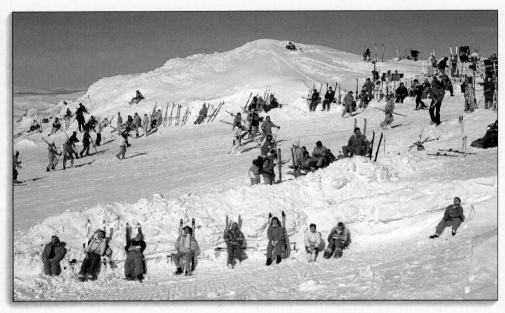

matter of course, but they are also used with trailers to carry food, equipment and spare fuel for holiday touring in areas like Lappland. There, the same people even use them to herd reindeer.

With their automatic gearboxes, snow scooters are easy to ride. Push the throttle and the machine accelerates; pull on the brake and it stops. No licence is needed, you just have to be over 16.

Snow scooters are capable of speeds of up to 80 miles an hour (130 kph), though most riders tend to keep below 20 mph (32 kph), not only to reduce wind-chill and make a bumpy ride more comfortable, but to con-

the sport in Sweden.

There are canoeing centres all over the country, though the district of Värmland offers canoeing waters that are difficult to better. There are so many lakes with interconnecting rivers and creeks in Värmland that it's quite a simple matter to work out a circular route avoiding the need to portage.

Because it is ideal for tours of the waterways, the open Canadian canoe is by far the most common. It's a stable craft capable of carrying two people, but, just as important, it will take all the equipment they need for a week-long trip.

Some people can keep their equipment

down to the absolute minimum, with just some food, a couple of pots, matches to light a fire for cooking, a sleeping bag, and a shelter provided by their up-turned canoe. Most though, prefer to have a few more home comforts around them, and perhaps a tent for shelter.

Not so popular is the kayak, the enclosed type of canoe preferred for white water canoeing. Kayaks require a great deal of skill in handling, particularly over rapids, but they are also used on the coast. A favourite area for sea kayaking is around the Stockholm Archipelago.

These days white water isn't only the domain of kayaks. Rubber dinghies are also company has hit on the idea of charging people to build rafts out of the logs and spend a few days on board drifting down river.

It takes a couple of people several hours to build a raft, using ready cut logs lashed together in three or four layers. One or two layers isn't enough because the logs don't have sufficient buoyancy to support the crew and equipment they need. When all is complete, camping equipment and provisions are placed on board and the crew paddle out to mid-stream to pick up the current. It's not a strenuous task because the current provides most of the power.

Then follow five days of idyllic unwinding. The raft drifts along at a languid two

making an appearance for the latest in heart-stopping excitement, white water rafting. Suitably clad in waterproofs and life-jackets, crews of half-a-dozen people or more descend raging torrents in large inflatable rubber dinghies. It can be a very bumpy ride, but despite appearances isn't really dangerous.

Down on the Klarälven River though, there is a much more sedate form of rafting. The Klarälven is the only river in Sweden where logs are still floated down from the forests to the sawmills, and one enterprising

Left, skiing at Åre, one of Sweden's best ski areas. **Above**, white water rafting.

kilometres an hour; its passengers relax on deck, fish or watch for shy beavers nosing through the water. The slightest sound and the beavers slap their broad tails and dive for cover beneath the surface. Occasionally a little effort is called for, to paddle the raft out of the lazy gyrations of a small whirlpool, or to reach the shore to tie up for the overnight halts.

Finally, for the passengers, the journey ends. The equipment is removed, the raft is dismantled and the logs continue the last few miles down the Klarälven to finish up at the sawmills at Skoghall, where they're turned into pulp for paper.

It has all the makings of a Hollywood movie. Lone-wolf schoolboy from the frozen backwoods of northern Europe beats a tennis ball against a garage door from morning until night, battles his way to Wimbledon, sweeps to victory against all odds, and retires at the age of 26, a multi-millionaire in Monte Carlo.

Recognise it? Of course you do: it's the Björn Borg story. And for tennis fans the world over, Borg's astonishing career represents a golden era for the sport that will probably never be repeated.

For since 1983, when the quiet, willowy Swede with the steely eyes, the long, blonde locks and devastating two-handed backhand abruptly disappeared from the world's centre courts, there's never been anyone quite like him.

"It was obvious right from the start that Björn was something special," recalls Christer Hjärpe of the Swedish Tennis Association. "He was simply one of a kind. I doubt if there will ever be anyone to take his place."

Borg's successors: But what about today's Superswedes of tennis—the Wilanders, the Edbergs, the Jarryds, *et al*? Admittedly, they may lack a bit of Borg's famous charisma— the icy cool, the sexy stride, the hair and the headband (very chic, back then), the three-day stubble (now even more chic) not to mention the Rolls-Royce, the bodyguards and the lusty hordes of female admirers.

But let's be fair. Stroke for stroke, Sweden's current top players have got what it takes. With incredible regularity (some would say monotony) they deftly dominate just about every international tournament going, from the Grand Prix Circuit to the Davis Cup, and continue to rack up victories like pin-ball machines. The difference—in comparison to Borg—is that Wilander & Co are destined to be replaced at the top of the tree the moment they begin to lose their edge.

For Sweden's current stars, despite their outstanding talents, are merely the cream of the first generation post-Borg children.

Left, Börn Borg, inspiration for Sweden's tennis youngsters. **Right,** Stefan Edberg playing in the Davis Cup at Båstad.

Behind them, and only just, are dozens of second generation players, poised to step into the big boys' trainers.

These highly-talented juniors are the continuing product of Borgomania, the phenomenon that turned Sweden into the most successful tennis nation in the world.

After Borg won his first Wimbledon title in 1976, (he won it five times in a row) the Swedish tennis scene erupted. The game that had previously been widely dismissed as a "snobsport" suddenly shot to the top of the

popularity polls, second only to ice-hockey.

Facilities everywhere: Tennis was "in". And just about everyone wanted to have a go. To cope with the surge in demand for facilities, sports associations, local authorities, and clubs up and down the country began pumping money into the game. The national tennis association beefed up its operations. Individual club membership soared and a string of new tournaments, got under way.

Sweden also began to provide heavily-subsidised training schemes for the thousands of youngsters who were queuing up, Borg-type rackets and head-bands at the ready, eager to emulate their new idol. Today, on the surface, there is little sign of Bor-gomania. But underneath, the legacy is un-mistakable. Just about every community in the country boasts a modern tennis centre with indoor and outdoor courts. These are open to anyone, regardless of social position or income, and at an average price of 40 kronor an hour (about £4).

At the last count, Sweden has some 400,000 regular players—which, for a coun-try of only eight million inhabitants, is an as-tonishing 5 percent of the population. And of these, about 120,000 are under the age of 15.

There are 956 clubs with more that 170,000 registered members. One of these, in Vallentuna, a suburb of Stockholm, is

housed in the Björn Country Club—an ex-clusive facility to which the great man lent his name.

The Borg legacy: But perhaps the best illus-tration of "the Borg effect" is the rise and rise of the Donald Duck Cup, the biggest junior tournament in the country for kids aged 11 to 15. It was Borg's first trophy. He won it at the age of 14 against a field numbering 1,000. In 1977, the year after he won Wimbledon, the number of competitors leapt to 8,000. And in 1988, no less than 13,000 took part.

The Donald Duck championship is held in Båstad, an attractive holiday resort on the southwest coast. And here, on finals day, the

atmosphere is more charged than at many a Grand Prix contest. The youngsters fight tooth and nail. Tempers flare, tears are shed, hopes are dashed—and the joy on the face of each new champion is often overwhelming and always irresistible.

Yet in spite of all the emotion, the Swedes maintain that they deliberately discourage their young hopefuls from developing a hard-headed, single-minded will to win.

"We don't pressure our children to win like they do in the USA or in the Eastern bloc countries," the Swedish Tennis Association proclaims. "That's not the Swedish way."

Playing cool: Mats Wilander, himself a for-mer Donald Duck champ, elaborates. "It's a game! The idea is to have fun! Sure, winning is great, but it's not the end of the world if you lose. Swedish kids are taught not to take it too seriously, to enjoy themselves and to control their emotions".

Perhaps that's precisely what makes the Swedes such formidable opponents, Björn and Mats included. That, coupled with the considerable financial support given to the sport and the well-organised training.

Sweden officially spends about 60 million kronor (£6 million) on tennis each year. With sponsorship from private enterprise it's a good deal more. About half of this goes to supporting the juniors.

The main events of the year—the Stock-holm Open (a Grand Prix tournament in the autumn)—and the Båstad Open—(an inter-national round-robin in late summer)—are immensely popular and draw bigger and bigger crowds.

The centre court at the Stockholm Open, for example, seated up to 16,000 spectators in 1989 when it moved from Kungliga Ten-nis Hallen (the Royal Tennis Club) to the Globe Arena, a new and fascinating dome that looms above the skyline on the south side of the capital.

All in all, if Sweden isn't banking on the birth of another Borg, it is certainly deter-mined to cultivate an ever-lasting crop of élite players. Experts predict that at least five of the world's top 30 in the 1990s will be Swedes. Under the circumstances, it would be surprising if it turned out to be fewer.

<u>Left</u>, training starts young for Swedish hopefuls. <u>Right</u>, Mats Wilander.

118

Q: What's the best way to catch a taxi on a rainy November day in Stockholm?
A: *Throw out a line with a baited hook.*
Q: What do Rome and Stockholm have in common?
A: *Horrible traffic.*
Q: What are the differences?
A: *A Roman driver will stop his car to admire a beautiful girl. A Stockholm driver will stop his car to admire a beautiful salmon.*
Q: Why does Swedish foreign policy smell fishy?
A: *Because fishermen store their catches along the wall of the Foreign Ministry.*

Those questions and answers are not just the start of fishing stories. They are all true—well, as true as any fishing story will ever get. Where else in the world but Stockholm can you step out of your city office, or take a few steps from the central railway station, or walk out of your hotel lobby, or stand on the pavement beside the Prime Minister's office, and cast a line for some of the world's most beautiful salmon?

And it's all free. No licence, permits or papers are required.

This is just the Swedish capital's taste of one of the great attractions of this country: sports fishing. No matter where you travel in Sweden—from Lappland in the north to Skåne in the south, along the Baltic on the east coast or the Kattegat or Skagerrak on the west coast—you will never be more than a lure's throw from excellent fishing waters.

In 1636, Queen Kristina (portrayed by Greta Garbo in the 1934 Hollywood film and commemorated by name in so many Swedish cities) signed a decree which stated that any Stockholmer had the right to fish in waters adjoining her palace. That ruling remains in force.

Despite that, this right was of little practical use for most of this century because pollution drove away the most desirable fish, salmon and sea trout. Then, as Stockholm tidied up to host the 1972 United Nations Conference on the Environment, the city

halted the dumping of sewage remains into local waters and fishing enthusiasts started to restock with salmon. Sure enough, it succeeded and city centre fishermen can now pull up beauties that would make Queen Kristina proud.

Tourists, more accustomed to seeing sardines (or whatever they are) pulled out of the Seine by those gallant Parisian fishermen, cannot believe their eyes when they see Stockholm fishermen pull out fighting salmon, of 10 lbs (five kg) or more—as

traffic rushes by, right in the very heart of the business and Government centre near where the lake boats have their terminal.

Oddly enough, relatively few fishermen take advantage of this amazing opportunity. Perhaps there is something that just does not gell: a bustling, busy city scene and salmon fishing. Only on a weekend in late October or through November, when the fish are running best, do you see anything resembling a crowd of fishermen along Strömmen, the fast-moving channel which links the central Swedish lake of Mälaren with the Baltic Sea. But the rushing waters of this narrow stretch are ideal for salmon and at the height of the

Left, next to skiing, fishing is Sweden's first sport. **Right**, a fine catch.

season Stockholm newspapers are full of pictures of triumphant anglers holding up large specimens, all caught for the price of their fishing equipment plus the bonus of hours of pleasure. Other less dedicated anglers sit quietly, their feet and line dangling over the edge of a harbour wall.

Swedes obviously prefer to fish out in quiet, peaceful nature, rather than surrounded by city traffic. And out there, in river, sea, or lake, they have lots of choice..

Along the west coast, you'll find the usual North Sea salt-water fish—cod, mackerel, shark, to name a few. On the east coast, along the Baltic, with its brackish waters, there are pike, cod, perch, perch-pike, whitefish, sea

more than three times a week at the workers' tables. They were also often part of a worker's wages. In view of the hard times and lack of food and jobs in those days, this could be just another fishing story. Pike are far more common. Indeed, there are pikers who specialise in going after only pike over 10 kg. Anything less is child's play, left for the amateurs. These pike specialists generally carve their own wooden lures, a foot (30 cm) long or more, big enough to frighten away the small fry.

One of the great things about sports fishing in Sweden is that it is easy to get at. Recent legislation made all Baltic coastal waters and the nation's three largest lakes open for free,

trout—and, of course, salmon. Naturally, Swedes claim that Baltic salmon is the world's best eating.

In rivers, streams and lakes there is a great variety: pike, perch, trout, salmon, and a long list of other game fish. Bass fishermen are less well catered for: only a couple of private lakes have stocked this popular game fish. Swedes generally prohibit the introduction of new species.

Salmon is common, but not as common as it once was. Contracts for household servants and farm labourers in the 1800s are said to have stipulated—at the employees' insistence—that salmon could not be served

unlicensed fishing. The same free rule had applied earlier to west coast waters. This means, in effect, that a fisherman can drive or walk, or take a bus or train to the coast or to the shore of the three lakes, park, stroll to the shore or launch a boat, and go fishing.

However, unlike Sweden's much admired *Allemansrätt*—the unwritten law giving free public access to all forest and open land—streams, rivers and lakes are private as far as fishing is concerned. This means you need licences or permits. Every county or municipality has publicly-owned waters, for which fishermen can buy licences. These are very modestly priced; indeed, they are one of the great bargains in high-cost Sweden. For example, a licence for fishing in the 45 lakes in Stockholm Kommun costs only 40 kronor a year and only 10 kronor for youth under 17. *(1988 prices)*

Fishing has none of the snob value that you find in some of the rivers of northern Europe, especially Scotland, where permits for famous pools can cost hundreds of pounds for a single day. Nor is there nearly so much emphasis on the importance of fly-fishing, which in many other countries is part of the angling mystique.

Although some waters are designated for fly-fishing only, most anglers use medium or light-weight spinning tackle. With all this

important annual event. Abu-Garcia makes a line of lures that are a must in every Swedish fisherman's tackle-box, including the classic Toby spoon.

Information about fishing is readily available from several sources. The National Sports Fishing Federation (Sportsfiskarna) publishes a handy guide to the nation's fishing waters. Known as *Svenska Fiskevatten*, it is published in Swedish only, but should not be too difficult for a foreigner to figure out. The guide includes phone numbers of county and local fishing offices. (Sportfiskarna, P.O. Box 11501, S-10061 Stockholm, tel: 08-743 07 90.)

Stockholm has several shops specialising

wonderful fishing, it wouldn't be Sweden without at least one internationally-known fishing tackle maker. It is Abu-Garcia, which produces a line of multiplier and spinning reels at a plant in Svängsta, in southeast Sweden. The factory is a few steps from the Mörrum River, one of the nation's most famous salmon rivers.

Opening day results at Mörrum are faithfully reported in the nation's press. It is an

in fishing equipment. Staff are always happy to meet visitors, sell licences, provide information and tips, sell tackle, and, of course, swap stories—all of them absolutely true. Best-known shops are Fiskarnas Redskapshandel, St. Paulsgatan 4, tel: 08-41 82 14 (near the Slussen subway station), and Utters, Kommendörsgatan 11, tel: 08-62 27 05, in the Östermalm district.

Information about organised fishing tours and other fishing information can be obtained at Stockholm Information Service, Sweden House, opposite NK department store—just a short walk from some of Europe's most amazing salmon fishing.

Left, Mälatorget—pure water allows fishing in the heart of Stockholm, or (above) in one of the country's remote lakes.

Sweden can be assured of international attention at least once every year: when the Nobel Prizes are awarded. These prizes, the world's most prestigious, are presented on 10 December, the day of Alfred Nobel's death. Although it is logical to Swedes that they commemorate Nobel's death—after all, without his will and testament there would be no prizes—others might think his birthday and life achievements would be more worthy of honour. For not only did Alfred Nobel invent dynamite, safety fuses and smokeless gun-powder, his business empire was to become a model for modern industrialisation. Nobel created the world's first modern multinational concern, and herein lies one of the keys to the success of Swedish industry.

Whether getting inspiration from the world's most famous Swede, or simply doing what was logical, Swedish industrialists very early went international and multinational. In the 1880s and 1890s, Swedes came up with a long list of inventions and developments that were to form the basis for world companies and to become giants in their fields. Corporate centennial celebrations have become run-of-the-mill: ASEA, electrical equipment; L.M. Ericsson, telecommunications equipment; Alfa-Laval, centrifuges and dairy equipment; Skanska, construction, just to name a few.

There will be more in a few years' time: SKF, bearings; AGA, industrial gas; C.E. Johansson, measuring equipment. Still to come are some of the other, more modern, world-famous Swedish companies' centennials, such as Tetra Pak, the world's largest liquids packaging company; IKEA, the world's biggest furniture retailer; and Hasselblad, the sole remaining European camera maker of any size.

An industrial superpower: What exactly is behind all this? What led to the Swedish industrial success? How could this small

Preceding pages; steel manufacture at Sandviken's works at Sandvik. **Left**, training for motor mechanics at a gymnasium. **Right**, Sweden's lack of oil does not stop the production of oil platforms at Gothenburg.

nation on the northern periphery of Europe create such a star-studded array of multinational companies which have competed successfully on the world scene for so many years despite the handicap of distance?

It is not only the old, established companies, but a long list of relative newcomers, including Volvo and Saab-Scania. Indeed, how can Sweden create not only one, but two, strong motor manufacturers? How can Sweden be the world's largest exporter of heavy trucks? How can it support an aero-

space industry making world-class jet fighters? Just who do these eight million Swedes think they are: an industrial superpower?

Well, yes, they do. First, Swedes have historically looked beyond their own borders for markets. Vikings were more traders than warriors. In the 1600s, with its rich deposits of copper and iron ore, Sweden was a world power. Later, its forests provided wealth: Swedish lumber and pit-props supported the British coal mining industry.

One explanation of the Swedish industrial success is that it is based on this nation's long history of scientists and inventors. This created something of a psychological greenhouse for generations of technicians and engineers. This tradition goes a long way back: Christopher Polhem invented scores of mining machines in the early 1700s; Anders Celsius, the physicist, developed the centigrade thermometer in 1734; C.W. Scheele, an 18th-century chemist, discovered scores of minerals, including tungsten (that's Swedish, by the way, meaning "heavy rock"); and J.J. Berzelius, a 19th-century chemist who developed the system of chemical symbols.

Engineers and inventors: There were also engineers like John Ericsson, inventor of the screw propellor (and designer of the American Civil War battleship *Monitor*); G.E.

Or perhaps the explanation is much simpler: in those long, cold, dark Swedish winters, in the days before television, there just were not many more interesting things to do than tinker in the workshop.

Tinker they did. Gustaf Dalén invented the "sun valve" for automatic switching on and off of lighthouse beacons, and created the industrial gas giant, AGA. Gustaf de Laval invented a continuous milk and cream separator which is the basis for Alfa-Laval. C.E. Johansson invented the "Jo-Block" measuring system that Henry Ford credited with making possible his auto assembly lines. Sven Wingquist invented the self-adjusting ball bearing and created the world's largest

Pasch, who invented the safety match in 1844; and Alexander Lagerman, who in the 1860s designed automatic match-making machinery, said to be the very first automated production system.

All these inventors and scientists, and many, many more, were highly respected and honoured. Other nations have their war heroes; Sweden has been at peace since 1812. Against this background, with a plentiful supply of metals, machinery and power, combined with a natural determination to make a better gadget, it's no wonder that Swedish technicians have created this incomparable industrial empire.

bearings company, SKF (an American from Philadelphia, where the American subsidiary is based, drove past the SKF headquarters in Gothenburg and commented "Oh, you have an SKF branch in Sweden").

Jonas Wenström, an electrical genius who died young, invented a number of devices including the three-phase alternating current system, which lead to the creation of Asea. Uno Lamm developed the high-voltage direct current transmission system, which ASEA stubbornly worked on for 25 years before getting a commercial contract. Birger and Fredrik Ljunström were inventor brothers with hundreds of patents, including double-acting steam turbines, which were the basis for Stal-Laval (now ABB Stal).

Balzar von Platen's high-pressure presses created the world's first man-made diamonds, L.M. Ericsson developed the desk telephone, which led to the formation of the multinational telecommunications giant that bears his name. The list goes on and on.

Production genius: Sweden's two largest companies today are not the result of engineering or technical developments, but more the creation of production genius. Volvo was formed in the 1920s by SKF engineers, who felt they could build a Swedish car and who convinced SKF to put up some seed money. After all, if it succeeded, it would certainly

ing genius who headed the firm in the 1920s made the name synonymous with carpet-sweeping in scores of countries. Balzar von Platen and a fellow student, while working on a master's thesis, invented absorption refrigerators (which work on gas, rather than by electrical compressors, and are used in trailers, boats and cabins), and sold the invention to Electrolux. This got the company into appliances. Today, Electrolux is the world's largest.

In recent years, some analysts maintain that an important factor behind modern Swedish entrepreneurship is the tax system. Everyone knows that the Swedes are the world's most heavily-taxed people, and this

be a good market for SKF bearings.

Yet when Gunnar Engellau, the marketing and production expert who built Volvo into today's giant motor-manufacturer, told Government officials he planned to start exporting to America in the 1950s, he was laughed out of Government House. Today Volvo is the largest-selling European car in North America.

Electrolux, the home appliances giant, did not invent the vacuum cleaner, but a market-

Left, Scania trucks ready for the road. Above, one of the world's largest underground iron ore mines at Kiruna in the north of Lappland.

of course, leads to the obvious consequence: a continuing hunt for loopholes, dodges and shelters. The best are to be found in private business; better still, they can be legal.

This means that bright, enthusiastic, young developers, inventors, and entrepreneurs are willing to leave jobs in large companies and set up on their own to take advantage of all kinds of tax benefits. If successful, they can build up a valuable business. There is really little risk: at worst, if the business fails, the entrepreneur can easily find a job in a country like Sweden that is chronically short of labour.

In any case, his or her spouse is undoubtedly working, too. The Swedish tax system favours and encourages investments by companies. In this respect, as long as money stays within the company, Sweden is a business paradise, although hell for the individual taxpayer.

Union co-operation: One generally-overlooked factor behind Sweden's industrial success and growth are trade unions. Sweden's unions are strong: about 95 percent of blue-collar, and about 80 percent of white collar workers are organised. These unions bargain collectively from a position of strength against equally well-organised and strong employers' associations. The system of central bargaining, which dates back to a famous agreement of 1938, has helped maintain labour peace for decades, although there are new demands for changes in the system.

Unions agree with employers that strong, profitable, competitive companies are the best job insurance. They also agree that companies compete best if they are exposed to competition at home and abroad. This means that Swedish unions, and the Social Democratic Party that has been in power since 1932 (with the exception of six years, 1976-82), have always supported free trade. But they have effectively opposed foreign control of major Swedish companies, raw materials and resources.

This is not new, however, but dates back to the early part of the century. Swedish law limits foreign ownership of publicly listed corporations to about 20 percent, and prohibits foreign ownership of energy, minerals or forests.

An example of trade union interest in international competitiveness was seen in the 1960s, when unions gave full support to automation and rationalisation. One fascinating spin-off of this was that Swedish companies were pioneers in the development and application of industrial robots. Today, ABB Robotics, a subsidiary of Asea Brown Boveri, is the world's largest robot producer. ("Local trade unions are my best salesmen," said one robot marketing man. "Our robots handle the dirty jobs the workers and their unions don't like.")

In the early 1970s, when industrial democracy was hot, Sweden brought in some revolutionary laws which required companies to allow unions to name two members to corporate boards of directors. Although there were

initial fears that this would put the union board members in an untenable position—representing two different sides—the system has generally worked without major problems or disagreements.

Top management and the board get first-hand views from the labour side, while union representatives can directly influence corporate decisions.

A clue to the Swedish character is that several multinational corporate boards hold meetings in English, out of deference to foreign board members who do not know Swedish. Faced with this, union representatives, many of whom have little more than standard school education, did not insist on

meetings being held in Swedish. Instead, they took English lessons.

Everything in place: Foreign visitors to Swedish companies are generally impressed with the prevailing order and neatness, not only in executive suites and conference rooms but throughout the manufacturing or assembly plants. This is symbolic of Swedish mentality, and one more key to industrial success: long-term goals, concentration specific products and niches, orderly, almost pedantic planning and organisation, and a stubborn "stick-to-it" philosophy.

Take this example: Hasselblad, the famous camera-maker, saw the surge of Japanese 35mm single-lens reflex cameras sweeping the world in the 1960s. Viktor Hasselblad, the company founder and owner, instructed his designers to come up with a 35mm model that might compete. But he never produced it. He stuck resolutely to his medium-format, six cm by six cm camera. Experts predicted that the Japanese would wipe him out, even in his own market niche.

But Hasselblad stuck to the same basic camera model, retained the Zeiss lenses from West Germany, and continued production in Sweden. He refused to be bulldozed into fancy electronics. The best-selling Hasselblad today is the model 500C, introduced

first on the New England region. Most experts say this will not work: a truck-maker must have local US production, as Volvo and Mercedes-Benz have. Saab-Scania's response is: "It took us 25 years to conquer the Australian market. We can do the same in the US."

Scania is the world's most profitable heavy-truck maker. One of the reasons for its strength is that it must compete at home and on many foreign markets with Volvo. Here, we have classic economic theory thrown out of the window: Sweden, with only eight million people, is far too small to support one—never mind two—manufacturers of heavy trucks, not to mention passenger cars.

in 1957. Today, the firm is a profitable and publicly-listed company—and Europe's only remaining major camera producer.

Another example: Saab-Scania introduced its Scania heavy trucks into Australia 30 years ago. They faced competition from well-established British, American and local makes. Little by little, Scania grew to become the largest truck company in Australia. Now it has started to sell Swedish-made trucks in the United States, concentrating at

Left, futuristic office building at Frösundsvik. **Above**, 10 percent of Sweden is covered in water and hydro-electric power is important.

Or take IKEA, the world's largest furniture retailer. Ingvar Kamprad, now in his sixties, started selling pens through mail order at the age of 17. He expanded into furniture, with simple wooden kitchen chairs, in the 1950s. He opened a low-priced, cash-and-carry outlet in south Sweden, and successfully battled the established furniture retailers who tried to persuade suppliers to halt deliveries to the price-cutter. Kamprad opened large outlets elsewhere in Sweden, then in Norway, and slowly in other European countries, in Canada and Australia. His sales philosophy is good design, good quality, self-service, knock-down furniture (buyers assemble most items themselves at home), lowest possible prices.

Kamprad expanded into new markets carefully, never over-extending, always paying his own way, never borrowing. He waited until the mid-1980s to tackle the United States, and was an overnight success there in his first outlet. Kamprad is expanding slowly—only six outlets a year worldwide—but surely. In 1989, IKEA had close to 90 outlets in 20 nations, sales near $3 billion, and some 13,000 employees.

Kamprad's next ventures will be in Eastern Europe. The first outlet will open in Hungary and a piece of land has been designated for an outlet outside Leningrad. But before tackling the huge Soviet market, IKEA will have to invest in the modernisation of 30 Soviet furniture plants, to provide local furniture and components. This will be Ingvar Kamprad's biggest challenge. But no-one who has followed his remarkable career doubts that he will succeed.

Swedish modesty: Although Sweden has its share of Porsche-borne yuppies—especially those linked to the stock market (Sweden's market climbed a phenomenal 800 percent in the 1980s)—industrial executives are far from the yuppie breed. Ingvar Kamprad, one of Sweden's richest men, always flies tourist class, as do his executives. Like many wealthy Swedes, he lives abroad, in Switzerland. Hans Werthén, chairman of Electrolux and Ericsson, shares a secretary, answers his own phone and drives a modest Volvo.

Executive jets and private chauffeurs are rare. Most top executives' wives hold full-time jobs—but despite that, in egalitarian Sweden few women are top executives.

Back in the 1960s, most large companies were run by engineers. It was a good background. Those were the days of growth through production expansion and rationalisation. Today, most top executives have business degrees, although you will still find plenty of engineers among the elder statesmen on corporate boards.

Hans Werthén, chairman of Electrolux and Ericsson, is an electronics engineer and worked on Sweden's first television system; Curt Nicolin, chairman of ASEA Brown Boveri, is an aeronautics engineer who lead the team that developed Sweden's first jet engine; Lennart Johansson, chairman of SKF, is a technical high school graduate who worked his way up through production ranks.

These companies—Electrolux, Ericsson, Asea Brown Boveri and SKF—are all in the so-called Wallenberg sphere, and herein is one more key to Sweden's industrial success. The Wallenberg banking-industrial empire was founded in 1856, when A.O. Wallenberg created Sweden's first modern commercial bank. He was a merchant marine officer, who learned the banking business after jumping ship in Boston in the 1840s. His sons financed some of Sweden's early industrial companies, and his grandsons and their descendants carried on the tradition and business.

In the early part of the century, the family had become as interested in industry as banking, and in the following years created a financial-industrial empire unique in the Western world, comparable only to the great Zaibatsu of Japan. As a result, no other single family in Europe or the industrial West exerts so much control over, or influence on so large a proportion of a nation's industry and banking.

Great bankers: The Wallenbergs, whose bank is Skandinaviska Enskilda Banken, the largest commercial bank in Scandinavia, do not generally hold majority stakes in their companies, but they do hold strong minorities. Marcus Wallenberg, who died in 1982, exerted control through his forceful personality, extensive international contacts, thorough knowledge of his companies and their businesses, and through his loyal, talented executives. One of his real skills was in spotting bright, young managers and giving them challenging responsibilities that would lead them to top executive positions.

The Wallenberg federation—that's how it is best described, since there is no single corporate parent company of the group—is now headed by Marcus Wallenberg's son Peter; the next generation of Wallenbergs, now in their early thirties, are taking places on company boards and in bank positions.

The Wallenberg companies list reads like a *What's What* of Swedish industry: Asea Brown Boveri, electrical equipment; Atlas Copco, rock drilling; and a long list of others. Scandinavian Airlines System could very well be included: it was formed by Marcus Wallenberg, and Curt Nicolin, a long-time Wallenberg executive, is board chairman.

Marcus Wallenberg, who, with his brother, Jacob, headed the family federation for 50 years, was an old-fashioned industri-

Left, new buildings are going up everywhere. **Above**, Marcus Wallenberg, the founder of the Wallenberg banking and business empire.

alist. He was primarily interested in product development, production and international trade. The stock market was of little interest to him.

In the post-war decades, the Stockholm Stock Exchange was one of the quietest in the world. That changed in the 1980s. Marcus Wallenberg would have abhorred today's financial wheeler-dealing on Wall Street and London, and would certainly have made sure there was no comparable business on a mini-scale in Stockholm. But one thing he would have approved is the Swedish companies' surge of international expansion, through acquisition, especially in the European Community.

Buying in: Sweden is not a member of the European Community. Lack of enthusiasm for joining by the ruling Social Democratic Party, which uses Swedish neutrality as a convenient excuse, means that membership, if it ever comes, is a long way off. Thus, in the face of 1992's open EC market, Swedish companies have been acquiring European firms as if they were soon to be rationed.

At one point, there were almost daily announcements of buy-outs, take-overs and mergers, most of them largely unnoticed. Others were spectacular, such as Electrolux's purchase of Italy's Zanussi, Asea merging with Switzerland's Brown Boveri; Mölnlycke buying France's Peaudouce; Scancem acquiring Castle Cement Ltd.; Svenska Cellulosa buying paper mills in France, Italy and Germany; Skåne Gripen acquiring Poggenpohl, the famous German kitchen maker; Swedish Match buying Wilkinson Sword; and on and on.

In Alfred Nobel's day, the best way to expand abroad was to create companies and start local production. Now it is faster and more feasible to expand through acquisition. Naturally, this rapid growth outside Sweden worries Swedish trade unions and politicians. After all, if production expands abroad, how will companies be able to continue to expand in Sweden?

Although time will tell, it seems certain that as long as Sweden continues to have its long, cold winters, and as long as Swedes retain their natural stubborn instinct to make things better, there will always be new, expansive companies. After all, if the absurd tax situation has not driven out Swedish entrepreneurs by now, nothing will.

SWEDEN'S NUCLEAR DILEMMA

Technical ingenuity and political pragmatism are two of the many things of which Swedes like to boast. But when it comes to nuclear power, Swedish technical ingenuity and political pragmatism react like, well, a meltdown.

Sweden has some of the world's most advanced, safest, best-performing nuclear reactors. These provide about 50 percent of the nation's electricity. This cheap, reliable power is essential to a large part of Swedish industry, exports and jobs. To top it all off, Sweden has the world's first and only specific operating system for handling spent fuel and nuclear waste and a definite plan for final disposal.

The political absurdity is that Parliament has decided to shut down all of Sweden's 12 reactors by the year 2010, the first one out by 1995, the second by 1996. This may sound good for the environment, except that nobody knows how the lost power will be replaced.

To understand this situation—which would be comical if it weren't so threatening—one must go back to 1945, all the way to Hiroshima and the atom bomb. In the immediate post-war years, Sweden was a technical, industrial power. As a neutral, it had escaped the ravages of war or occupation. In the Cold War years, the Swedish Government backed research into nuclear weapons. Sweden had full technical and industrial competence to build its own bomb. It even has plentiful domestic uranium.

In the early 1960s, Parliament took a definite decision not to develop nuclear weapons. But as a spin-off of military research, the Government had supported work on peaceful nuclear application. By the late 1950s, Sweden could start building its first power reactor, Ågesta, in the Stockholm suburb of Farsta. This reactor, built in a cavern in a granite hillside, operated for 12 winters to provide some electricity to the city network, but mainly hot water to heat the suburb, which had a population of 25,000.

Ågesta was a Swedish-designed heavy water reactor that could utilise domestic uranium. A second reactor, also heavy water, was built at

Marviken, on the Baltic coast, but was never put into operation. The Government feared that it wouldn't be safe without the investment of more money to rebuild it, and took a brave political decision not to fund it further.

The boiler and turbines were converted to oil, while the nuclear parts were put to valuable use in an international research project for full-scale destructive testing of components and systems.

Swedish industry came up with its own designs. Atomenergi AB, later known as Asea-Atom and now ABB Atom, became the world's only reactor-maker with its own boiling light water designs.

In the 1960s and early 1970s, Sweden embarked on a spree of nuclear reactor building. Nuclear power had the solid support of the ruling Social Democratic Party, and an overwhelming majority in Parliament backed nuclear energy. The nation saw this as a way out of its dependence on imported oil.

For years, hydropower had provided low-cost electricity, but now there was strong opposition to the building of more dams on rivers. Sweden had no coal. Nuclear was the answer.

In 1970, the first commercial reactor, Oskarshamn-1, on the southeast coast, went into operation. This was followed by reactors at the Ringhals station, on the west coast, and Barsebäck on the south coast. In retrospect, this was a foolhardy site, only about 12 miles (20 km) from Malmö, Sweden's third largest city, and about the same distance across the straits to Copenhagen, the largest city in Scandinavia. A fourth station was started, at Forsmark, about 60 miles (100 km) north of Stockholm, and plans were made to pipe hot water from the station to heat the capital city.

But there was growing opposition too, inspired by opposition in the USA. This opposition mounted into a huge wave, which helped topple the Social Democratic Government in 1976, after 44 years in power.

The anti-nuclear, pro-environment Centre Party, originally an agrarian party, headed the new non-socialist coalition Government. The nuclear programme was delayed.

Then, in 1980, the Three Mile Island accident in the USA gave the Social Democrats a chance to reverse its long-held opposition to a nuclear referendum. Following a heated campaign, the referendum vote backed the Social Democratic and Liberal Party line. This called for the building of a maximum of 12 reactors and their phasing out as soon as alternative energy could be devised to replace them. The phase-out year was eventually established at 2010, and the final five reactors came on stream in the early 1980s.

Now, Sweden has the world's largest nuclear programme *per capita*, and the Western world's fifth largest programme in electrical capacity, surpassed only by the USA, France, Japan, West Germany and Great Britain. Its reactors (three of which are Westinghouse pressurised water reactors, and the other nine Swedish boiling water reactors) are consistently among the world's best performers. The Barse-bäck reactors have been equipped for some years with unique filters to trap radioactive particles in case of an accident; other reactors have newer, smaller, but as effective filter systems.

Two Swedish reactors have been built in Finland. ABB Atom has a growing export business in fuel components.

Above all, Sweden has the world's only complete system to deal with waste. A special ship was built and put into service to haul spent fuel from reactors to a central underground storage facility, to undergo decades of cooling. Medium and low-level radioactive waste—such as cleaning material and tools from reactors, as well as waste from medical radiology—is stored in a new, underground facility. Swedish scientists and engineers have demonstrated a method for the final encapsulation of cooled spent fuel in solid copper blocks to be buried deep in Swedish granite.

Ironically, the day before the formal dedication of the underground spent fuel storage facility, Chernobyl blew up. Sweden was hit first and hard by fall out. The Social Democratic Government, which had returned to power, said it would not wait until 2010; the first reactor would be "out" in 1995, a second in 1996.

The tough, humourless Minister of Energy, Birgitta Dahl, who was also given the title of Minister of Environment, demonstrated the party's determination. She devised a "thought control"

bill, dutifully passed by Parliament, which made it a criminal offence for a Swede to plan or design a nuclear reactor intended for Sweden. That, she believed, would muzzle any pro-nuclear activity by industry.

The policy effectively killed any further work on Swedish design for an inherently safe reactor, one that would automatically shut down if something went wrong.

But despite the new anti-nuclear tone and oratory, the Social Democrats did not prevent the rise and growth of the environmentalist Green Party. And despite the Green Party's naive economic programme—it would like Sweden to eliminate foreign trade and turn the country into a self-contained, agrarian, handicraft society without heavy industry—it did manage to get into Parliament in the 1988 elections. It was the first new party in the Swedish Parliament since the Communists won seats in 1918. But the Social Democrats and their trusty supporters, the Communists, who are totally anti-nuclear, still retain control.

The Government does not want oil or coal to replace nuclear power and talks instead about energy conservation and the importing of natural gas from the Norwegian North Sea or the Soviet Union.

Meanwhile, the Soviet Union is operating at full blast a Chernobyl-like station at Ignalina, in Lithuania, just across the Baltic from Sweden. Poland and East Germany also have reactors on the Baltic.

But perhaps the most astonishing thing of all is the report that the Soviet Union is planning a huge new nuclear station just across the border from Finland. To many in Sweden, this business arrangement seems much like a Milo Minderbinder deal in *Catch 22*: Sweden would import natural gas from the Soviet Union, which is building new nuclear reactors to enable it to export natural gas to Sweden, which is closing down its nuclear reactors because it is afraid of the same nuclear power which the Soviets are building.

Come to think of it, Sweden's nuclear situation is more like one of Ingmar Bergman's less accessible films: it isn't always clear what is going on, few know exactly what it means, and nobody can guess how it is going to end.

CONSERVING THE GREEN "LUNGS"

The Swedish countryside is beautiful enough to bring tears to your eyes. That is what many Swedes believe—and quite a lot of visitors too. Nowhere is there greater determination to keep it that way because love of the land and affection for their country is deeply rooted in Swedes.

Even the national hymn *Du gamla du fria* does not concentrate on glory, honour, warfare, or any such nonsense, but on a land of high mountains, silence and joyfulness.

From the air, you get a picture of virgin territory with miles and miles of woods, forests, and the twinkling eyes of many lakes—almost 100,000, great and small. Everywhere, it is a diverse landscape, from the fertile areas of Skåne to the tundra on the mountains of Lappland. In between is a land of small hills and valleys, rolling fields, small farms and clusters of cottages.

Along the coasts the sea rolls in with a long waving motion over friendly sandy beaches where bathing is good, or breaks with foaming force against the wild cliffs of Bohuslän, and its unique archipelago, unlike any other in the world.

No trespassing: The "Everyman's Right" (*Allemansrätt*) is an ancient Swedish tradition—not law but a right that no other law forbids. It means that you are allowed to pass over any grounds, fields or woods, to whomever they belong, though Swedes are scrupulous in not using this right to cross a neighbour's garden close to a house or to stride over cultivated agricutural land. This means there are no laws of trespass as there are in many other countries.

You may also travel by boat over any water, and gather wild flowers, berries and mushrooms. But the idea is to use commonsense when making use of Everyman's Right: do not do to others what you would not like done to yourself. Even though you may pick up fallen branches, be careful and do not cause any damage.

There are roughly 20 national parks in Sweden, all owned by the State. The aim is to set apart areas of natural value and beauty that will give the visitor experience of a

Left, Skytta Lake at Tiveden National Park.

specific environment and a visual impression. Most parks are in the north.

Padjelanta is the biggest national park in Europe. The name comes from a Lappland word that means "the higher mountain".It lies along the timber line and the flora is particularly interesting because of the bedrock which is rich in limestone. In this soft, undulating mountain landscape, you come across many small streams, which the Lapps call *jokkar*, and it has always been an important pasture for the Lapps and their reindeer herds. Here, it is safe to drink the water anywhere, and to enjoy a stream's own special, clean taste.

At the opposite end of the country and on

many more rare species to delight the birder for hours.

The greatest proportion of Sweden is virgin country and for anyone from a densely populated and polluted area, from north to south the whole country seems like "a green lung"—a place where you can breathe.

In this untouched countryside, you can stroll mile after mile along tracks without coming across another human being. You can drive a car on serpentine gravel roads and never have to turn aside for another vehicle, or cycle through untouched land on the special bicycle trails.

But how do Swedes themselves approach nature and the environment? They are dedi-

a very different scale is Norra Kvill in Småland, one of the smallest but also one of the wildest reserves, true virgin forest round a small tarn. Here you can find pine trees hundreds of years old and enormous firs. It is no wonder that this park is an El Dorado for the lover of mosses and lichens.

Rich birdlife: If you want to study the herbaceous flora and listen to the birdsong, Dalby Södereskog is at its best in the spring, while Store Mosse in Småland is worth a detour for the birdwatcher. This is the biggest national park south of Lappland, a huge flat peat moss with a very rich birdlife which includes whooper swan, marsh harrier, cranes and

cated to nature and everything out of doors. Many families save for years to get a *stuga* (cottage) in the countryside or along the endless stretches of the coast. Others are lucky enough to have inherited their little spot in a meadow.

Almost all Swedes are only a generation or two away from rural life and many have relatives who still live in their original home districts. As soon as the younger generation has any spare time, they head for the family's traditional home.

The Swedes do not just enjoy the countryside and its fruits, they make use of them. At the first sign of spring nettles, the Swede rushes out, gloves on hands, with a pair of scissors and a paper bag to collect the nettles. For, despite their stings, nettle broth is a fine start to a meal even at a first-class restaurant, and nothing beats the first nettle broth of spring, made from nettles picked with your own hands.

After that come sweet gale, and the tiny leaves of blackcurrant which Swedes use to spice the Christmas aquavit. Then summer arrives with a rich harvest of wild berries—raspberries, cloud berries, wild strawberries, blueberries and, towards autumn, lingon berries, rose hips and blackberries. To Swedish families, no cultivated fruit can compare with the wild ones they have picked them-

very seriously: there are organised excursions to look for mushrooms and berries, and classes to tell people what they can and cannot eat. Even then, it is not the filled freezer that gives the biggest thrill, but the delight of picking your own natural fruits out in the woods and fields.

Strange plant: No wonder that the Swedes are worried about dangers to the environment such as acid rain, which has already killed off some plants and over-encouraged others, and also damaged many of the fishing lakes. Particularly in the west, they lie there, clear, beautiful, and totally empty of any water life, except for a strange white lichen-type plant on the bottom. Many of the fishing

selves, even if they have had to fight off the mosquitoes to do so; and it is positively fashionable to appear in Stockholm on a Monday morning with the stain of berries still dark on your fingers.

The mushroom season begins with turbantops—now slightly suspect—followed by baskets of chantarelles, ceps, edible agarica, ringed boletuses and all the rest of the mushroom family which the nature-conscious Swede can find. Swedes take their funghi

societies have taken an active part in trying to save these "dead" lakes and, with government cooperation, have organised programmes of liming the water. But this is no more than a palliative which they have to repeat at regular intervals.

Millions of Swedes fish in their spare time, and all along the coasts and in the big lakes fishing is free from land or boat, with rod and line, though amateurs are expected not to disturb the activities of the professional fishermen.

Strict laws protect the rarer mammals such as the bear, wolf, wolverine, lynx, musk-ox (a late immigrant from Norway), arctic fox,

Left, Redshank—birdlife is plentiful and protected. Above, the end of a day's berry picking.

otter, or whale. In any case, it is difficult to catch sight of them. But other animals are very common—roe deer live in the forest and only in Scandinavia will you see the traffic sign which means "Danger, Elk". This is no joke: traffic accidents involving animals have increased as the number of cars has grown, especially at dusk and dawn when the elks are crossing the roads between the forests.

The Swedes have many regulations to protect birds, particularly the more endangered species. A hundred years ago, the peregrine falcon was so common that the landlords near Lake Vättern at Omberg sent out peasants to collect their eggs to make omelettes; recently peregrine numbers have dropped so fast that strict conservation laws have been enacted to save the birds.

The human predators: There have also been rescue operations for the eagle owl, the guillemot at Stora Karlsö, and the black guillemot along the coasts of Bohuslän. Despite the importation of birds from the Faroe Islands, the black guillemot of Bohuslän has not been saved, and others have disappeared from the lists of Swedish fauna. No-one has seen a middle spotted woodpecker since the beginning of 1980. As in many other countries, Swedish ornithologists are also faced with the menace of those human predators who collect eggs and young from the nests of the rarer birds of prey and sell them for profit.

The very variety of the countryside offers suitable habitats for many rare plants, from the alpines of the high mountains to the rich orchid flora of the limestone areas. The months of May and June in particular bring out an army of botanists—but always just to look, never to touch. For Sweden began to protect its plants as early as the beginning of this century.

If any further proof were needed of the interest the people of this "green lung" take in their environment, you only have to switch on Radio Sweden. Where else would you find a national broadcasting service that regularly employs bird calls as its interval signal? A new one is used each week, and described by a well-known ornithologist every Sunday morning.

Left, if you get lost, remember ant hills always face south.

Sweden may not have the great international gastronomic reputation of, say, France or Italy, but visitors to the country can certainly expect to eat very well.

Perhaps the best testimonial to the high standards of Swedish cuisine is the sight of all those healthy-looking tanned Swedes you see in the summer, who certainly do not appear to have succumbed yet to the junk-food culture.

The secret is probably that the Swedes make the most of their natural resources when it comes to eating. Gathering mushrooms and wild berries is a national preoccupation in the autumn, while favourite meat dishes include reindeer, venison or elk from the mountains and forests. Above all, the Swedes are great eaters of fish, both from the sea and from the rivers and the 96,000-plus lakes (no-one is sure of the number).

A meal in itself: Sweden is probably best known abroad for its unpronounceable *smörgåsbord*. Translated literally, a *smörgås* is simply a slice of bread and *bord* is a table, but it is definitely a misnomer to describe it as a "bread and butter table".

Going back 200 years, an "aquavit buffet" was the prelude to a festive meal in Sweden and it was laid out on a separate table in the dining room. Guests could indulge in a modest snack of herrings, sprats and cheese before getting down to the serious business—accompanied, naturally enough, by a few sharpeners of aquavit.

This buffet became more and more lavish over the years as hosts and hostesses vied with each other to provide the best spread, culminating in the giant *smörgåsbord* which had its heyday in the 19th century and even then was still regarded only as the prelude to a "proper" meal. Nowadays the Swedes are gourmets rather than gourmands, so the *smörgåsbord* is a meal in itself; but the groaning table can still present a pretty daunting picture to the foreign visitor.

The secret of smörgåsbordmanship is to take things gradually and not to overload one's plate. Start with a few slices of herring

Left, the first skål of many during the evening—a boat party off Bohuslän.

prepared in all kinds of mouth-watering ways—in a mustard or horse-radish sauce, maybe—accompanied with a hot boiled potato. If you're lucky, you may encounter *gravad lax*, thinly-sliced salmon cured in dill—although scurrilous rumours abound that it is more likely to be trout these days.

For the main course (or courses), you graduate to a bewildering choice of cold meats or fish and salad, or a typical hot dish like Swedish meatballs or "Jansson's Temptation" (a popular concoction of potatoes, onions and anchovies) before rounding off the meal with a refreshing fruit salad.

The *smörgåsbord* is not such a dominant trend in Swedish gastronomy as it once was, but it still prevails down in the south in Skåne, where the good-living tradition is maintained most faithfully. You also still find hotels that make a speciality of a lunchtime *smörgåsbord*, particularly on Sundays.

Perhaps the best value for visitors is the breakfast served in most Swedish hotels, which is really a mini-*smörgåsbord* in its own right. You will usually find several kinds of cereal, cheeses, herrings, boiled eggs, jams, fruit, milk and different types of bread (including the ubiquitous *Wasabröd* crisp-bread). Sometimes you may even find some scrambled eggs and sausages or bacon on the hot-plate.

Best bargain: You can certainly stoke up for the day with a hearty Swedish breakfast—which could be a pity because the best-value eating out is to be had at lunchtime rather than in the evening. Particularly in the cities, you'll find many restaurants offering a *dagens rätt* ("dish of the day") for about 40 kronor, which includes a main course, salad, soft drink and coffee, and helpings are usually generous.

Eating out in the evening is generally much more expensive and you should reckon on paying 150 kronor for a two- or three-course meal without wine. The price of alcohol in Sweden is prohibitive, so you may prefer to stick to mineral water (Ramlösa is the best-known local brand).

The budget-conscious will find plenty of cafés and cafeterias in the larger cities, as

AN EDUCATION IN THE SKÅL OF LIFE

The British and the Germans are mocked for their stuffy formality, but they have nothing on the Swedes when it comes to the rigorous protocol which surrounds social entertaining and, particularly, the drinking of toasts (or *skål*ing).

A visitor is more likely to be asked to a Swedish home for a casual meal than invited to a very formal dinner party but, even then, there are quite a few social rules to be borne in mind. First, it's necessary to look at the etiquette for a formal party because it provides the basis for the more informal occasions.

To start with, arrive on time—or at least within about 15 minutes of the stated time. The casual approach to social time-tables which the Latin races have developed to a fine art is not appreciated in methodical, organised Sweden. Take some flowers or a box of chocolates for your hostess and, if there are a number of other guests, introduce yourself to them.

Once seated, you may find that a glass of schnapps or wine is already poured out; but on no account take a sip till the host has raised his glass for the first "skål" to welcome the guests (he may make a little speech as well). This first toast can also be a kind of "communal *skål*" in which you exchange greetings with your fellow guests, particularly those just opposite to you and those on your immediate left and right.

The most important part of *skål*ing, whether in a formal or casual environment, is that you must establish eye contact, glass raised, with the other party or parties not only before you take your sip but also immediately after.

On a formal occasion, each male will "*skål*" the ladies, starting with the one on his right, then the one on his left. Men will also *skål* fellow guests at random throughout the meal, but if there are more than eight guests at the table it is considered polite not to *skål* your host or hostess, on the basis that an input of schnapps on that scale might well have dire consequences. Incidentally, the normal routine is to *skål* with schnapps but not with wine.

The rules are naturally much less rigid if you are invited for an informal meal with Swedish friends. But again the rule holds good: wait for your host to *skål*.

The *skål*ing tradition does not seem to have been especially affected by Sweden's tough laws against drinking and driving. Most people attending an evening party either take a taxi or one partner (guess which one) "volunteers" to stick to the mineral water and drives home.

When the meal is over and before you retire to the drawing room for coffee and liqueurs you must do what every Swedish child is taught to do at an early age and say to your hostess: "*Tack för maten*" ("Thanks for the food", literally). On a formal occasion, one or two of the guests may make a short speech of thanks as well.

If it's a good party and the conversation carries on late into the night, your hostess will probably disappear quietly into the kitchen and re-emerge with a tray of tea or beer, snacks and sandwiches. This is a tactful signal that the evening is coming to an end—although by the time you've knocked back your beer another hour will probably have passed all too rapidly.

Someone—at a formal party it will be the guest of honour—will eventually make the first move to depart, sparking off the ritual exclamations of "Is it that late?".

There then starts a round of farewells in which each guest shakes hands with the host and hostess and says "*Tack för i kväll*" ("Thanks for this evening"). All the guests will likewise shake hands with each other with mutters of "*Tack för trevligt sällskap*" ("Thanks for your pleasant company") or "*Det var trevligt att träffas*" ("It was nice to meet you").

By the time all these farewells and "*tacks*" have been exchanged, another half-hour has probably elapsed—so if you want to catch the last tram you need to start making your first moves early.

But you haven't quite finished with the ritual yet. It's the done thing to telephone or write to your hostess the following day—or certainly within a week—to say "*Tack för i går*" ("Thanks for yesterday") or "*Tack för senast*" ("Thanks for last time"). It all sounds quite exhausting. But if you just remember to say "*skål*" and "*tack*" in the right places you won't go far wrong.

well as fast-food outlets such as Wimpy or McDonald's. For something more typically Swedish, try the *korvkiosk*, the nearest equivalent to Britain's "chippy"; it specialises in fast-food items like grilled chicken, hot dogs or sausage with French fries.

Cuisine in the larger cities is increasingly international with Swedish overtones, and many of the up-and-coming chefs have been influenced by immigrant owners and by the *nouvelle cuisine* trend for small portions, beautifully cooked and presented.

It's better to head for the rural regions if you want to experience the more typical Swedish home cooking known as *husmanskost*, which produces strange combinations

shellfish are boiled in water, dill, salt and sugar and left to cool overnight and are then served with hot buttered toast and caraway cheese, accompanied by the odd schnapps and beer.

The Swedes themselves will admit that the negative aspect of their gastronomy is the high cost of alcohol, which arises from punitive taxes and excise duties. Beer comes in three grades—Class I (light beer), Class II (ordinary beer) and Class III (export)—with prices ranging between 10 and 40 kronor a bottle. The best-known brand is probably Pripps—acceptable enough, but not up to Carlsberg or Tuborg standards.

A bottle of Italian wine can be bought in

like pea soup with pancakes, traditionally eaten for dinner on Thursdays. The traditional drink to accompany this is a lethal and deceptively sweet alcoholic drink called *punsch*. Another favourite is *Pytt i Panna* (literally, "Put in the Pan"), a gigantic fry-up which is a good way of coping with the leftovers from the previous day.

If you are in Sweden in August, you may be lucky enough to be invited to a crayfish or *kräftor* party. These delicious freshwater

the State-controlled "Systembolaget" stores for a little over 30 kronor. But a three-fold mark-up will push the price to around the 100 kronor mark if you're having a restaurant meal.

It's worth splashing out on the odd aquavit, if only to assess which type is worth buying at the duty-free shop on the way home. Skåne is the best-selling brand, but many connoisseurs prefer O.P. Anderson, which is flavoured with caraway, aniseed and fennel seed and goes well with herring dishes. Devotees of vodka will prefer to take home Absolut, a 100-year-old brand now sold all over the world.

Sweden can hardly be described as a religious country. Church-going is a minority pursuit, but the vast majority of Swedes remain nominal Christians, even if they go to church only to be baptised, confirmed, married and buried. So perhaps it is not so surprising after all that the pattern of festivals and folk traditions throughout the year is still determined very much by the church and its calendar.

Despite that, many have more than a whiff of the old pagan festivals, connected with the seasons. The dark days of winter coincide with the traditionally gloomy time of Lent and although Catholic practices were outlawed in Sweden at the time of the Reformation, many people still keep up the tradition of eating heartily on Shrove Tuesday, just before the season of fasting.

Lent leads up to Easter, which is really a sneak preview of spring, when many Swedes head for the mountains to ski. Both Good Friday and Easter Monday are public holidays and a long weekend is a welcome break after the rigours of winter. But there are still plenty of traditions at Easter-time, like the eating of decorated hard-boiled eggs.

Witches' brew: Maundy Thursday, in Swedish folklore, was the day that witches flew off on their broomsticks to pay their respects to the Devil, returning on the following Saturday. Good law-abiding citizens used to protect themselves from all this evil power zooming through the skies by lighting bonfires, letting off fire-arms and painting crosses on their doors.

Nowadays Swedish youngsters still dress up as hags and pay visits to their neighbours on Maundy Thursday or Easter Eve, leaving a decorated card in the hope of getting sweets or money in return. Bonfires and fireworks are still set off in some areas.

The real start of spring is celebrated on 30 April, the Feast of Valborg, better known in English as Walpurgis Night. The wildest celebrations are in the university towns, particularly Uppsala, where thousands of

students process through the streets in their white caps and sing traditional songs before dancing the night away and seeing in the first dawn of spring. In many parts of Sweden, Walpurgis Night is marked by large community bonfires, and in some areas the spring celebrations are on 1 May although, as in many European countries, this is now a public holiday for Labour Day rather than a true spring festival.

Ascension Day is a public holiday in Sweden, even though it is a festival more

often associated with the Catholic countries. Appropriately, many people still mark the day by getting up early and going out into the countryside to hear the dawn chorus.

Whitsun is another religious festival still marked in Sweden, with the Monday as a public holiday. It is a popular time for weddings and many young people are confirmed on Whit Sunday.

Waiting for the sun: Sweden has a National Day on 6 June but it is not celebrated with nearly as much style and gusto as the comparable day (17 May) across the border in Norway. In Sweden, 6 June is a normal working day, although there are parades in

Preceding pages; folk dancing at Österby Bruk. Left, St. Lucia's Day in December. Right, children dress up as witches for Easter.

most towns and the flag is hoisted everywhere. The reason for the low-key celebration of National Day is probably that Midsummer is only just round the corner, and that has special significance in a country which is so influenced by the whims of the sun and its long dark winters.

Midsummer Day is a slightly moveable feast because it was decided in the 1950s that the celebrations should be on the weekend nearest 24 June, the Feast of St John the Baptist, but in many parts of the country people still observe the festival on 23 June, whatever the official calendar may say.

On Midsummer Eve Swedes decorate their homes and churches with garlands of

flowers and branches and most communities hoist the maypole during the afternoon. Everyone dances round the maypole and the dancing goes on right through the night—outdoors if the weather is fine.

Like Maundy Thursday, Midsummer has all kinds of supernatural connotations. Young Swedes traditionally used to pick many different varieties of flowers and place them under their pillow in the hope of dreaming about their future bride or bridegroom.

After Midsummer, Sweden tends to pack up for a couple of months as people head off to the countryside or the coast for the summer and there are no more public holidays

until All Saints' Day at the beginning of November. This is not a particularly joyous occasion because it is the time for families to lay flowers on the graves of their loved ones; but it can be a moving sight to see the graveyards at dusk glowing with the candles and lanterns of the relatives.

December rounds off the year with a hectic bout of festivities. More people probably go to church on Advent Sunday than at Christmas itself, and Advent is also the time when houses and streets are decorated with trees, garlands and lights for the whole of the long Christmas season.

St Lucia's Day—the Festival of Light—is celebrated on 13 December, a throwback to the days when it was mistakenly regarded as the longest and darkest night of the year. In the present-day Lucia celebrations, a young girl dressed in a white gown and wearing a crown of lighted candles—a distinctly hazardous-looking pastime—brings in a tray of coffee and ginger biscuits and maybe mulled wine (*glögg*) for the assembled guests, accompanied by girl attendants also dressed in white and boys wearing tall conical paper hats and carrying stars.

Christmas traditions: This festival is celebrated in Swedish homes on Christmas Eve rather than on the day itself. The festivities resemble Christmas elsewhere in Europe, with the traditional tree and the giving of presents, but after dinner there is a visit from the *tomte* or Christmas gnome, a benevolent sprite who was supposed to live under the barn and look after the livestock in bygone days. The *tomte* comes into the house loaded down with a sack of presents as a kind of substitute Santa Claus.

New Year's Day is a lower-key affair; most Swedes celebrating at home with a few friends, but families tend to have a lavish meal on Twelfth Night (Epiphany), another public holiday.

The last fling of the Christmas season is one week after Twelfth Night in the form of "Knut's Day" when the Christmas tree is finally dismantled and there is probably a party for the children. The year's festivities may be over, but Shrove Tuesday and Lent are not far away.

<u>Left</u>, a concertina encourages dancing to celebrate midsummer. <u>Right</u>, the start of the crayfish season in August.

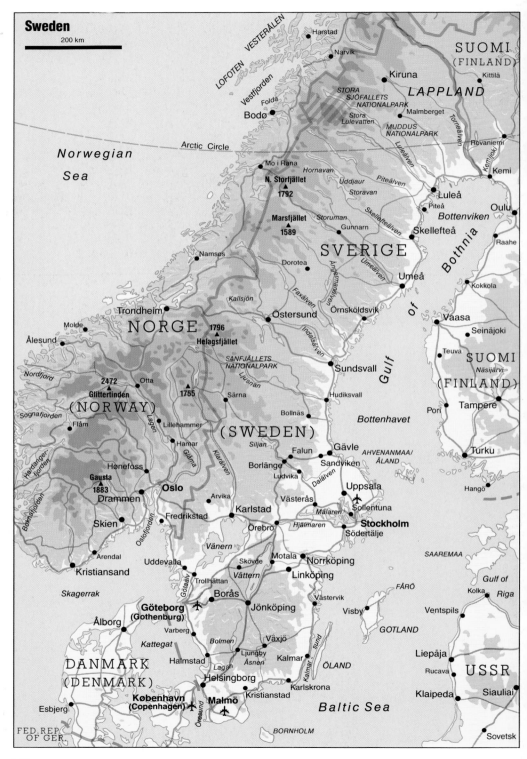

Sweden

200 km

LOFOTEN

VESTERÅLEN

Harstad

Narvik

SUOMI
(FINLAND)

Kiruna

Kittilä

LAPPLAND

Vestfjorden

Folda

STORA
SJÖFALLETS
NATIONALPARK

Malmberget

Bodø

Stora
Lulevatten

MUDDUS
NATIONALPARK

Rovaniemi

Kemijoki

Kemi

Arctic Circle

Norwegian

Sea

Mo i Rana

Hornavan

Uddjaur

Piteälven

Luleälven

Luleå

N. Storfjället
▲
1792

Storavan

Piteå

Oulu

Marsfjället
▲
1589

Storuman

Gunnarn

Skellefteälven

Skellefteå

Bottenviken

Raahe

Namsos

Dorotea

SVERIGE

Umeälven

Umeå

Kokkola

Kallsjön

Faxälven

Ångermanälven

Örnsköldsvik

Trondheim

Östersund

Indalsälven

Vaasa

Seinäjoki

NORGE

1796
▲
Helagsfjället

SANFJÄLLETS
NATIONALPARK

Sundsvall

Gulf

Teuva

SUOMI
(FINLAND)

Näsijärvi

Molde

Ålesund

Nordfjord

2472
▲
Glittertinden
(NORWAY)

Otta

Ljusnan

Särna

▲
1755

Hudiksvall

of

Bottenhavet

Pori

Tampere

Bothnia

Sognafjorden

Flåm

Lågen

Lillehammer

Klarälven

Bollnäs

Turku

Hardanger-
fjorden

Hamar

Glåma

Siljan

Falun

Gävle

AHVENANMAA/
ÅLAND

Hangö

Gausta
▲
1883

(SWEDEN)

Borlänge

Sandviken

Hønefoss

Ludvika

Dalälven

Drammen

Oslo

Arvika

Västerås

Uppsala

Sollentuna

Stockholm

Boknafjorden

Skien

Fredrikstad

Örebro

Hjälmaren

Mälaren

Södertälje

Oslofjorden

Karlstad

Vänern

Arendal

Kristiansand

Uddevalla

Göteborg
(Gothenburg)

Trollhättan

Götaälv

Skövde

Vättern

Motala

Norrköping

Linköping

SAAREMAA

FÅRÖ

Gulf of

Kolka

Riga

Ventspils

Skagerrak

Borås

Jönköping

Västervik

Visby

GOTLAND

DANMARK
(DENMARK)

Ålborg

Kattegat

Varberg

Bolmen

Halmstad

Lagan

Ljungby

Åsnen

Växjö

Kalmar

Kalmar sund

ÖLAND

Liepäja

Rucava

USSR

Helsingborg

Kristianstad

Karlskrona

København
(Copenhagen)

Malmö

Øresund

Klaipeda

Siauliai

Esbjerg

FED.REP.
OF GER.

BORNHOLM

Baltic Sea

Sovetsk

160

If you could pivot the whole of Sweden on the southernmost city of Malmö, it would stretch as far as Rome. This long, narrow country is both the largest and most prosperous in Scandinavia, but its population of only eight million makes it one of the least crowded countries in Europe.

To fly over Sweden is to discover a land of forest where lakes glint among the trees. Even Stockholm, which covers a much wider area than you might expect for its 300,000 population, is a city of sea, lake and open spaces, and never far from the thousands of islands that form its archipelago, reaching out towards the Baltic. If you arrive by boat from Western Europe, Gothenburg's magnificent west-coast harbour is the first view. This is Sweden's second city, noted for its wide avenues and canals. The third main city, Malmö, in the extreme south, is also a port; the gateway to Denmark is just half an hour or so away across narrow straits.

As well as these three principal cities, there are the two university towns, Lund, near Malmö, and Uppsala, north of Stockholm, which goes back to the days when it was the ancient capital of Uppland, the cradle of Sweden and the home of the old pagan ways.

Outside the main centres, Sweden has miles and miles of road through endless forest, a coastline spiked with rock and smoothed by beaches, and unspoilt northern mountains ideal for summer walking and winter sports. The southern provinces of Skåne, Blekinge, Halland (plus Bohuslän on the west coast) were for centuries part of Denmark and even today in Skåne the accent is faintly Danish. Much of south central Sweden is dominated by the great lakes, Lakes Vänern and Vättern, the heart of a network of waterways that make it possible to cross this widest part of Sweden by boat along the Göta Kanal, which links Stockholm to Gothenburg.

Further north, the geographical centre of Sweden holds Dalarna, often called the Folk County, where old customs linger. At the end of the long road or rail route north are the mountains, many with a covering of snow all the year round. This is the land of the midnight sun, where you can play golf at midnight in high summer. It is also the home of Scandinavia's second race, the Lapps or Samer, whose wanderings with their reindeer herds take little account of national boundaries.

Preceding pages: summer in Skåne; the Tjörn Runt race for keel boats; reindeer cool their feet in July; summer in Härjedalen.

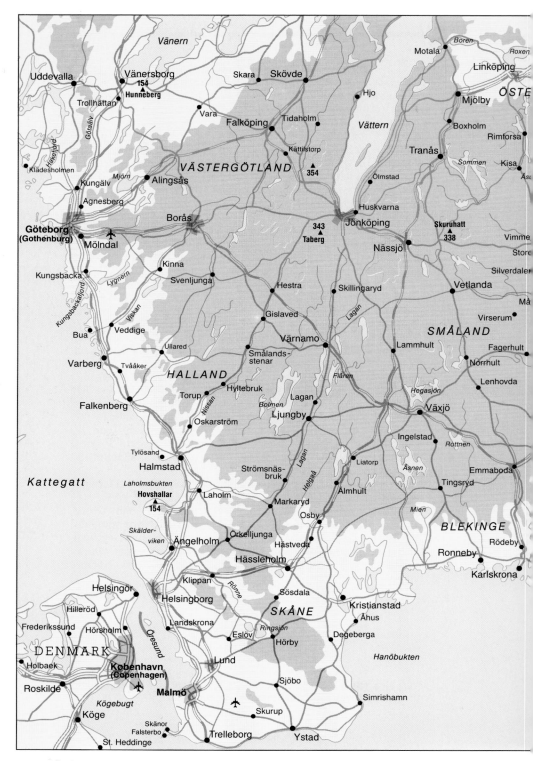

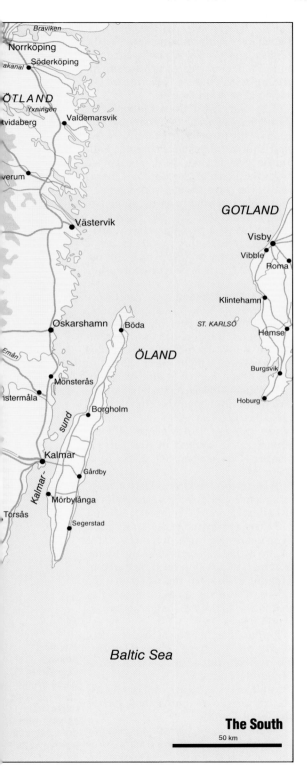

Baltic Sea

The South

50 km

SOUTHERN SWEDEN

Skåne is Sweden's most southerly county, so close to Denmark across the narrow sound that even the accent is faintly Danish. This isn't surprising because for centuries Swedes and Danes fought over this area, along with the counties of Halland and Blekinge, until Sweden established its sovereignty in 1658.

Skåne is often called Sweden's food store because of its rich farmland, mild climate and good fishing. Although many think of the landscape as flat, there is in fact a lot of variety. Along the coast it is undulating and lush and especially spectacular in the southeast corner, **Österlen**. Inland, there are three large ridges, **Söderåsen**, **Romeleåsen** and **Linderödsåsen**, with lovely walks and a number of lakes. **Ringsjön** is the largest, known for its birdlife, as is **Krankesjön** to its south.

History goes back a long way in Skåne: Stone-Age burial chambers can be found at **Glumslöv**, north of Trelleborg, at **Tågarp** and north of **Kivik**. The King's grave at **Bredarör** dates from the Bronze Age and is famous for its rock carvings, different from any found in Sweden and the other Nordic countries from the same period.

Great wealth: The affluence of Skåne is obvious when you consider the number of castles and manor houses. There are said to be 240 in the county. Most are still in private ownership and not open to the public, but it is usually possible to walk round the gardens.

Among the most interesting are **Vrams Gunnarstorp** near Bjuv, **Vittskölve** between Degeberga, and Åhus, **Christinehof** in north Österlen, **Marsvinsholm** near Ystad, **Bosjökloster** by lake Ringsjön and **Övedskloster** by lake Vombsjön. **Sofiero**, outside Helsingborg, was built in 1857 and Gustav VI Adolf used it as his summer palace until his death in 1973. He was a keen botanist and made the gardens a real attraction.

Each year, 25 million people cross the

sound between Denmark and Sweden, most coming through Helsingborg and Malmö. Ystad and Trelleborg are the ports for traffic to and from Travemünde in Germany.

Malmö is Sweden's third city, with a lively population of just under 250,000. In the 16th century, Malmö competed with Copenhagen to be Scandinavia's leading capital, but in those days it was an important port on a major sailing route, not far from rich fishing grounds.

Today, the harbour is still busy with crossings to Denmark and other traffic, and many of the old buildings remain. **Malmöhus**, the dominating castle built by King Christian III when Skåne was still part of Denmark, is now a museum and, from the same period, the Town Hall is set in Stortorget, one of the largest squares in Scandinavia. Malmö also has a network of pedestrian streets, with many places to shop and coffee houses to sit awhile.

Military historians should make for the **Commander's House museum**, full of relics of a turbulent era, con-

stantly fought over by Sweden and Denmark. **Pildammsparken** is the largest landscaped park in Sweden and houses Pildammstheater, a huge amphitheatre with summer performances of music, dance and drama.

Travelling west from Malmö, visit **Lund** before joining the coast road. It is a university town with a beautiful cathedral and an interesting museum, **Kulturen**. Along with the University of Uppsala, north of Stockholm, Lund is one of the two ancient Swedish universities, both with their own traditions and unique customs. Having joined the coast road, you pass **Barsebäck**; apart from a 14th-century castle, it has a nuclear power station, which the nuclear-free Danes have repeatedly asked to have shut down.

From **Landskrona**, you can take a boat across to **Ven**, a small island most famous for having been the home of the prominent Renaissance astronomer, Tycho Brahe. He built a castle called Uranienborg which burnt down: a model of it is kept at Malmö Museum.

Glumslöv offers memorable views. From the hill above the church, on a clear day you can see 30 churches and seven towns: Helsingborg, Landskrona, Lund, Malmö in Sweden and Dragör, Copenhagen and Elsinore in Denmark.

Råå, on the outskirts of Helsingborg, is a picturesque fishing village with an excellent inn.

Potters and artists: Helsingborg itself is an interesting town, dominated in the centre by the remnants of an old castle, **Kärnan**, and with a bustling harbour. **Höganäs** is a town full of potters and artists. There are always a number of exhibitions and the large pottery is worth a visit.

On the side of the bay of Skälderviken is the small fishing village **Torekov**. From there, you can get a boat across to **Hallands Väderö**, a nature reserve. **Båstad**, near the border with Halland, is the home of tennis tournaments such as the Davis Cup.

Southeast from Malmö are **Skanör** and **Falsterbo**, once important towns but now summer idylls. Travel through

Malmö's Annual Equestrian Week brings show-jumping to the main square, plus dressage and trotting in the park.

Trelleborg to **Ystad**, famous for its Tudor-type houses. Follow the coastline through **Simrishamn** to **Kivik**, whose market days in July are a magnet. The sale of horses and cattle used to be accompanied by freak shows, circuses and all kinds of entertainment. These days, a lot of the entertainment has disappeared, but the horse and cattle trading still goes on. **Kristianstad** is the birthplace of the Swedish film industry, which started around 1910. The old studio is intact and is now a museum where you can watch some of the old films on video.

Blekinge is a tiny county with lovely sandy beaches along the coast and Sweden's most southerly archipelago. It was here, just outside Karlskrona, where the first Russian submarine was sighted a few years ago and hit the international headlines. Today, parts of the archipelago are restricted areas, and in years past the forest land to the north made an excellent refuge for outlaws during the wars with Denmark.

Blekinge is excellent for sea fishing

of all kinds, from boat or shore. There is peaceful angling in some of the lakes or good sport for salmon in the Mörrum River. Canoeing is also popular along the coast and on the rivers, and you can move from lake to lake by connecting canals.

Driving to Blekinge from Skåne, you first reach **Sölvesborg** where the narrow streets and old buildings show its medieval origins. There is a small **Museum of Fishing** and you can see the ruins of the 13th-century **Sölvesborg Castle**. From Sölvesborg you can also catch a ferry across to **Hanö**, an island with one of the tallest lighthouses in northern Europe and an English cemetery dating from the Napoleonic wars.

Mörrum is famous for salmon fishing. You can visit the **Salmon Aquarium** and see salmon and trout at different stages of their development. On an island in the river you can also visit Elleholm church and castle.

Karlshamn is an old seafaring and market town with thriving industries. But it was not always so and the Emmi-

Kalmar Castle, Småland.

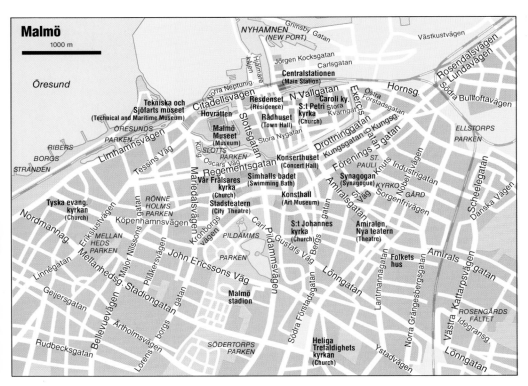

A TOUCH OF GLASS

It's reassuring in a way that vandalism isn't just a 20th-century phenomenon. They even had the problem in 16th-century Sweden, when King Gustav Vasa's courtiers used to round off an evening of feasting and carousing by smashing as many expensive Venetian glasses as they could lay their hands on. The King, adopting a fatalistic attitude towards this medieval delinquency, invited Venetian glassblowers to his court, commenting that it would be cheaper in the long run to break home-blown glassware rather than the expensive imported variety.

The first glass was melted in Sweden in 1556, although history doesn't record whether Gustav Vasa's courtiers abandoned their expensive pastime. But it was to be almost another 200 years before glassmaking really became established as an industry in Sweden.

The oldest works, Kosta, was founded in 1742 by Anders Koskull and Georg Bogislaus Stael von Holstein, two generals in the army of King Karl XII, who rewarded them for their efforts on the battlefield by appointing them as provincial governors in Småland. Eager to make a little money on the side, they decided to set up a glassworks, taking the first two syllables of their respective surnames to create "Kosta".

The location was ideal because the dense forests between Växjö and Kalmar provided vast supplies of timber to keep the furnaces going. The only problem was that, despite Gustav Vasa's patronage 200 years earlier, there were still very few skilled glassblowers in Sweden; so Kosta had to import the first craftsmen from Bohemia.

Those early craftsmen founded the Swedish tradition of fine glassware and there are still a number of craftsmen at Kosta who are direct descendants of those first immigrants from Bohemia. Kosta has been a pioneer in the production of full lead crystal glass with what is claimed to have the highest lead content—up to 30 percent—of any produced in Sweden (to qualify for the "crystal" description, there must be at least 24 percent lead oxide in the glass).

The second oldest glassworks is Rejmyre, founded in 1810 by Johan Jakob Graver. But it has moved with the times by specialising, since 1972, in the production of heat-resistant glass which is exported all over the world.

One of the best-known Swedish glass manufacturers is Orrefors, a relative newcomer which has been producing glass only since 1898.

Orrefors started in the glass business by producing the more mundane products like window-panes and bottles, but in 1913 the works was taken over by Johan Ekman, an industrialist from Gothenburg. It was he who set the company on the course of producing top-quality tableware and decorative items.

Ekman was one of the first to involve artistic talent in the design of glass, and during World War I he recruited two artists who were to transform Orrefors into one of the world's most renowned glassworks: Simon Gate, a portrait and landscape painter, and Edvard Hald, a pupil of Matisse.

They were followed by new generations of designers. It is their creative flair, coupled with the centuries-old skills of the glassblower, that has put Sweden in the forefront of worldwide glass design and production.

Only in comparatively recent years have the glassworks of Småland come to appreciate the importance of tourism but now it is reckoned to account for 10 percent of turnover. Most glassworks are open every weekday between 8 a.m. and 3 p.m. and visitors are free to wander round and see the whole process from the initial glassblowing to the final engraving. Most of the works also have shops.

An old glass-country tradition—the *hyttsill* ("glassworks herring") evening—has been revived in recent years for the benefit of tourists. In bygone times the glassworks was not just a place of work but also a social centre where the locals would gather for a chat and bake herrings and potatoes in the furnace, with music provided by an accordionist or fiddler.

During the summer some of the leading glassworks—including Kosta, Orrefors, Bergdala and Pukeberg—are now running updated *hyttsill* evenings for visitors to Småland. Reservations can be made on the spot.

grants' Monument "Karl-Oskar and Kristina" is a reminder of different times, when thousands of Swedes left for a new life in the New World. Karlshamn has an interesting cross-timbered **town hall** and the beautiful **Carl Gustav Church**. On the way to Ronneby, visit the **Eriksberg Nature Reserve**, where there are herds of deer and European buffalo.

During the 19th century, **Ronneby** was a popular spa, receiving summer visitors from all over Sweden and Europe. Now it's Sweden's largest conference and recreation centre. It has a number of museums, among them a **Cultural Heritage Museum**.

From Ronneby, you can get a ferry across to **Karö**, which is always a surprise: an island with almost sub-tropical vegetation. Around Ronneby there are a number of interesting historical burial grounds at **Hjortsberga** and **Hjortshammar** and also the **Björketorp Stone**.

From **Almö**, drive across to **Hasslö** and then island-hop by ferry before going to **Karlskrona**, the biggest town in Blekinge. Karlskrona, built in the 17th century, is a naval town, with wide streets and impressive buildings. **Björkholmen** is a part of town where you will find neat cottages built by ships' carpenters.

At **Hästhallen** in **Möckleryd** are fascinating rock carvings from the Bronze Age. Torhamn Point is well known to ornithologists as the path of migratory birds and an excellent observation point.

On the east coast of Blekinge is the village of **Kristianopel**, once a Danish stronghold on the border with Sweden. You can see the restored defensive wall and step-gabled church. These days it is more famous for its smoked herring.

Öland's attractions: Travelling north along the coast from Blekinge, you reach Kalmar where the **Öland bridge**, the longest in Europe, connects the island with the mainland. On the northwest coast of the island are the ruins of **Borgholm Castle**, once a splendid residence dating back to the 12th century.

Left, making Kosta Boda's world famous glass. **Below**, Kalmar Castle, Småland.

During the summer it is a venue for open-air concerts.

Solliden Palace, just outside Borgholm, is the king's summer residence. Öland has many ancient burial places and there are remains of 16 fortified dwellings from earlier times. The most interesting is **Eketorp**, which has been partly restored.

Öland is also interesting to the botanist. Its flora is reminiscent of that of the tundra and there are 30 types of orchid.

During the late 19th and early 20th centuries, Sweden's population exploded, and many families could no longer eke out a living on the land. So began the great years of migration to North America. Of the million or so who left, the majority came from Småland. Today, one of the most popular places is the **House of the Emigrants** in **Växjö**, opened in 1968, which tells the story of the exodus.

Because of Småland's 17 major glassworks, it is known as "The Kingdom of Glass." King Gustav Vasa introduced glass-blowing from Bohemia in the 16th century and nowadays famous names such as Orrefors, Kosta Boda and others have turned the craft of making glass into glass sculpture. Many glassworks are open to visitors, who marvel at the blowers' skill as they twirl the glowing red bulbs of molten glass. As well as glass, the industrious Smålanders are famous for paper, furniture, matches and sewing machines.

Kalmar, one of Sweden's oldest cities, was of great importance in the Swedish-Danish wars. It has an impressive 12th-century castle which is also the last resting place of all that remains of the royal ship *Kronan*, which in 1676 sank with a crew of more than 800 men. A team of divers rediscovered the wreck in 1980; since then, treasures such as cannon, the ship's bell, wooden sculptures and the ship's compass have been painstakingly recovered, making an evocative display.

From **Oskarshamn**, a ferry plies across to Öland—or Gotland, a bit further out. **Västervik**, further north, is a picturesque summer resort.

Camping at Lunegård in Öland offers more than a tent.

West from Kalmar are **Emmaboda** with its glassworks, **Lessebo** with its paperworks, and the busy town of **Växjö**. North of Växjö is **Lake Helga**, a birdwatchers' haunt. In **Värnamo** visit the **Homestead Museum** and at Smålandsstenar the **Judges' Circles**, the site consists of five circles formed by between six and 20 raised stones. The circles, probably 2,500 years old, were used for ancient court sessions.

The wild west: As a contrast, **Anderstorp** has become famous as the venue for international car races. Near it is the **High Chapparral** ranch—the Wild West recreated in the Swedish forest.

Continue north to **Jönköping**, where the manufacture of matches began in the middle of the 19th century and made the town known all over the world. It is also the centre of the teetotal movement and several religious sects.

At **Gränna**, by **Lake Vättern**, you can buy rock and visit the nearby medieval village of **Röttle**. There's also a splendid view across the lake to the island of **Visingsö**.

Östergötland, with its rich farmland, shows signs of habitation very early on in history: remains of villages have been found dating back 4,200 years. The famous stone at Rök is from A.D.800 and its 800 runes have yet to be decoded.

North of Gränna is **Alvastra**, site of Sweden's first **Cistercian monastery**, which was founded in 1143. The well-preserved ruins contain the chapel, chapter house, refectories, abbot's house and infirmary.

Strand, built in 1919, was the home of Ellen Key, a feminist writer well-known for her suffragette activities nationally and internationally; it has attracted famous women visitors from all over the world.

Lake Tåkern is one of Europe's finest bird sanctuaries where over 250 species have been observed. **Vadstena**, a medieval town, has an **abbey**, a **monastery** and a **castle**, and **Vas Vitreum** has a modern glassmaker's workshop specialising in crystal.

The Göta Kanal: Crossing the Göta Kanal at **Motala**, you come to **Övralid** where the beautiful home of the poet Verner von Heidenstam, built in 1925, is open to the public. The view of Lake Vättern is magnificent. **Stjärntorp**, by Lake Roxen, was a 17th-century castle and is still an imposing ruin. Nearby **Linköping**, once a military city, is now better known as a centre of technology, though **Gamla Linköping** (Old Linköping) takes you back to past centuries with its well conserved houses. Also near the city are two interesting castles, **Bjärka Säby** and **Ekenäs**.

The biggest municipality in Östergotland is **Norrköping** where you find rock carvings from 1500 to 500 B.C. as well as museums and interesting buildings. Just north of Norrköping is Europe's biggest safari park, **Kolmården**, with more than 100 kinds of animals.

Keen cyclists head for Östergötland, particularly along the banks of the Göta Kanal where the tow paths make ideal cycling tracks. You can hire bikes at several places, and the most popular route for cyclists is between **Berg** and **Borensberg**.

High
Chaparell,
near
Anderstorp,
the Wild
West in
Sweden.

GOTLAND

Islanders in general have a reputation for being independent in outlook and not taking too kindly to edicts from a distant central government. This is certainly the case with the 56,000 inhabitants of the island of **Gotland**, who like to think of themselves as something apart from the rest of Sweden.

Gotland is the largest island in the Baltic, about 75 miles (120 km) long by 35 miles (56 km) at its widest part, and it has been inhabited for 7,000 years. The island's position 50 miles (80 km) off the west coast of Sweden makes the Soviet Republic of Latvia its nearest neighbour to the east, but its history has been more concerned with commerce than with politics. Today, its air and sea connections with mainland Sweden are excellent and it is a favourite holiday spot for Swedish people.

Fear of piracy: In the Viking Age the island and its wharves were busy trading posts while later Visby, the principal centre of population, became a prosperous Hanseatic town. It had strong links with the German Hanseatic League and, in particular, with Lübeck, in order to protect the Baltic trade routes from piracy, which was widespread.

Despite its concentration on trade, Gotland could not escape involvement in the wars between Denmark and Sweden which ranged over the whole of the south of Sweden. In 1361, the Danish King Valdemar Atterdag conquered Gotland but, after some further changes in ownership, in 1645 it eventually became and remained Swedish.

Visby, with a population of 20,000, is called "the town of roses" because the climate is so good that roses bloom even in November. The town is one of the best reasons for visiting the island. First of all, it is unlike any other Swedish town; in parts, its architecture is much more reminiscent of Germany or Austria, no doubt a result of its Hanseatic League associations.

The other island towns are small. Even **Hemse**, the second largest, is more a grand village than a town.

The 280 miles (450 km) of coastline are a mix of sand or shingle beaches, cliffs, or meadows stretching down to the water. There's a good beach south of Visby, at **Tofta**, and another at **Sudersand** on Farö. Some of the most impressive limestone stacks (or *rauker*) in the whole of Gotland lie off **Hoburgen** at the southernmost tip of the island. They were formed by the action of the sea and many parts of the island coasts have similar natural monuments.

Most popular attraction: Two miles (three km) of the medieval limestone city wall remain virtually intact, interspersed with 44 towers and numerous gates. The oldest part is the sea wall that once protected the richly-laden Hanseatic ships, and the powder tower, but the entire wall is one of Europe's best preserved structures from the Middle Ages.

Within the walls, the town has many step-gabled houses and a network of little streets and squares, all of which contribute to its unique atmosphere.

Preceding pages: Almedalen at Visby, Gotland, once the Hanseatic Harbour now a park. Left, medieval remains on Gotland.

Gotland

25 km

FÅRÖ
Farö

Kappelshamn
Lickershamn
Lärbro
Farösund

Visby
Slite
Källunge
Gothem
Roma

GOTLAND

Klintehamn
Lojsthajd
▲ 83
Ljugarn
Stånga

ST. KARLSÖ

Hemse
Ronehamn
Havdhem
Kattlunds
Burgsvik
Faludden

Baltic Sea

Hoburg

The original Hanseatic harbour, **Almedalen**, is now a park, while **St Maria Cathedral** is the only medieval church in Visby that is still intact and in use. By contrast, only the ruins remain of the old Gothic **Church of St Catherine**, next to the market square.

One of the most interesting buildings to survive is **Burmeistershaus**, the house of the Burmeister, who was a German merchant. Today, it is the tourist office. The town also has a particularly fine museum, the **Fornsalen** (Historical Museum).

Tourism is vital to Gotland and during the relatively brief but hectic summer season, the normal population of 56,000 is swollen by more than 300,000 visitors. In early August, Visby holds a medieval week when, as you stroll in the town, you are likely to rub shoulders with people dressed as Hanseatic merchants, monks and craftsmen.

Once the summer season is over, Gotland is quiet and reverts to its island owners. The brevity of the season has little to do with the climate, which is milder even than southern Sweden and is claimed to be mild throughout the year. This kindly climate (and the limestone, perhaps) is why 36 species of orchid make their home in Gotland, together with many other rare plants.

Limestone has also created one of the island's major attractions, the **Lummellundagrottorna**, impressive caves to the north of Visby, with magnificent stalactites, something not to be missed.

Defence area: The northern end of the island is picturesque and, just past **Bunge**, there's an open-air cultural and historical museum with a collection of preserved old buildings. Beyond is **Fårösund**, where there's a ferry over the sound to the island of **Fårö**.

Unfortunately, this northern end of the island plus Fårö is part of the Swedish defence zone, which means that foreigners need special permission to stay there. You can spend up to 72 hours in the community of Fårösund and its immdiate area, but you may visit Fårö only during the summer for a day trip organised by Gotland's three major

A mild climate makes the island famous for roses and orchids.

travel agencies. Even then, unless you obtain permission to travel independently, you must follow the set programmes.

Another claim to fame enjoyed by this northern part of Gotland is that it is the only area of Sweden where oil has been found. On either side of the road the pumps—"nodding donkeys"—move monotonously up and down to extract fossil fuel from the earth below.

Further south on this eastern coast, you come to an area which is largely and sadly overlooked by visitors. Typical is **Ljugarn**, with its seaside villas and *pensions*. The whole coastline provides good opportunities for birdwatchers.

Wild ponies: Inland, the island consists largely of a limestone plateau (*alvar*) which reaches a maximum height of only 255 ft (78 metres) above sea level. It is a mixture of moorland and forest, barren in some places, and inhabited only by a breed of small semi-wild pony, which the islanders call *Russ* because the ponies are supposed to have come from Russia. The strange thing about this breed is that the animals have two toes instead of a hoof.

The predominant livestock of the area are sheep. The farms have a more down-at-heel and untidy appearance than the neat and orderly properties of the mainland.

All over Gotland you come across medieval churches, more than 90 in all. There are many other relics of the past, including some of a much earlier age, such as runic stones and burial mounds. In the centre of the island is **Romakloster**, a ruined 12th-century monastery. At some point in its long history, Gotland must have been a religious centre, but even the names of the men who built the many churches are largely lost.

Today, Gotland is a small, peaceful isle which comes alive for a few short summer months; but, as you wander round the ruins of so many medieval churches and past the giant walls and other relics of the past, you find yourself wondering how many people worked and worshipped there in its commercial heyday.

Thatching party on Fårö, off the northern coast of Gotland.

GOTHENBURG

Preceding pages, Álvsborg Bridge at Gothenburg; the Tall Ships enter Gothenburg waters. Left, Masthuggs-kyrkan and Sjöfartstornet, near the harbour. Below, Korsgatan, one of the many pedestrain streets.

Second cities have a lot in common. They like to think they have the largest, biggest and best of almost everything. Call it the second city syndrome.

Gothenburg, Sweden's second city, is no exception. Situated at the mouth of the Göta River on the Swedish west coast, this accessible city of not quite 450,000 has had to play a secondary role to the capital, Stockholm, ever since it was officially given its charter by King Gustav II Adolf over 350 years ago. Striving to do and be more has been a way of life for Gothenburg. Its claims to greatness often go beyond Sweden's own borders; being number one just at home does not always satisfy.

Realism does, however, prevail. Aware that it can't always be the biggest in the world, Gothenburg makes do with being number one in its own backyard, northern Europe, as often as possible.

A favourable geographical position

almost equally distant from the major population centres of Stockholm, Copenhagen and Oslo has helped Gothenburg become Scandinavia's largest seaport, now handling over 14,000 ships a year. Being in the centre of things, where else would you expect to find Scandinavia's largest stadium (**Ullevi**) and amusement park (**Liseberg**)? The latter even ranks as one of the largest tourist attractions in Europe with over 2.9 million visitors a year and it just happens to have Europe's longest roller-coaster as well as Sweden's largest dance restaurant (**Rondo**).

Gothenburg used to have northern Europe's largest indoor arena, **Scandinavium**, but lost this honour to Stockholm in 1989 with the completion of the Globe Arena. The second city's other attractions take up the slack by having northern Europe's largest covered shopping centre (**Nordstan**), permanent antique market under one roof, botanical garden and fish market.

Sickening statistic: Gothenburgers do, however, have the dubious distinction of being ill more often than other Swedes. In 1987 they had an average 29 days' sick leave—six days more than the national average. The reason may be because Gothenburg claims to have Sweden's longest summer (144 days, lasting from 13 May until 4 October) and they want more time off to enjoy it.

With an infrastructure geared for largeness, it is no wonder that the city stages most of the top events in northern Europe, ranging from rock concerts (Bruce Springsteen attracted 126,856 fans for two concerts in 1985), to sports events (the annual Gothia Cup is the world's biggest football tournament, with some 16,000 young boys and girls from over 30 countries participating).

In 1988 Gothenburg even hosted the very first professional American National Football League game ever played on continental Europe. It was an exhibition game between the Chicago Bears and the Minnesota Vikings. The match venue was appropriate since Gothenburg and Chicago are sister cities. This did not prevent most of those attending the game to revert to Swe-

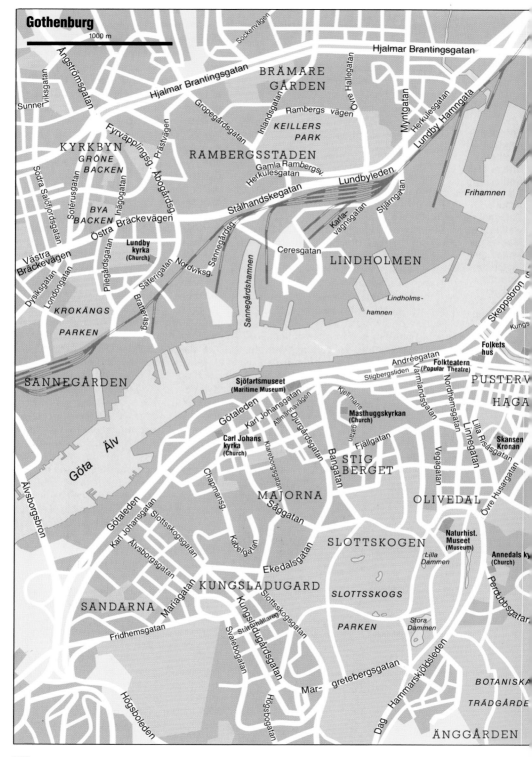

Gothenburg

1000 m

Ångströmsgatan
Sunnerviksgatan
Hjalmar Brantingsgatan
Sockenvägen
BRÄMARE
GÅRDEN
Hjalmar Brantingsgatan
Gropegårdsgatan
Inlandsgatan
Ramberg vägen
Övre Hallegatan
Myntgatan
Herkulesgatan
Lundby Hamngata
Hjalmar Brantingsgatan
Fyrväpplingsg. Åbogårdsg.
Prästvägen
KEILLERS
PARK
KYRKBYN
GRÖNE
BACKEN
RAMBERGSSTADEN
Gamla Rambergsv.
Herkulesgatan
Lundbyleden
Frihamnen
Södra Salöfjordsgatan
Söterusgatan
Inägogatan
BYA
BACKEN
Bräckevägen
Östra
Stålhandskegatan
Sannegårdsg.
Karla-
vagnsgatan
Stjärngatan
Lundby
kyrka
(Church)
Västra
Bräckevägen
Pilegårdsgatan
Säterigatan
Nordviksg.
Ceresgatan
LINDHOLMEN
Dysiksgatan
Londongatan
KROKÄNGS
PARKEN
Bratterasg.
Sannegårdshamnen
Lindholms-
hamnen
Skeppsbron
Kungs
Folkets
hus
SANNEGÅRDEN
Andréegatan
Folkteatern
(Popular Theatre)
PUSTERV
Sjöfartsmuseet
(Maritime Museum)
Stigbergsliden
Värmlandsgatan
Nordhemsgatan
HAGA
Älv
Götaleden
Karl Johansgatan
Allmänna
Djurgårdsgatan
Kjellmans
Masthuggskyrkan
(Church)
Fjällgatan
Linnégatan
Lilla Risåsgatan
Skansen
Kronan
Göta
Carl Johans
kyrka
(Church)
Klareborgsgatan
Bangatan
STIG
BERGET
Vegagatan
Övre Husargatan
Älvsborgsbron
Götaleden
Chapmansg.
Kabelgatan
MAJORNA
Såggatan
OLIVEDAL
Karl Johansgatan
Slottsskogsgatan
Älvsborgsgatan
Ekedalsgatan
SLOTTSKOGEN
Naturhist.
Museet
(Museum)
Lilla
Dammen
Annedals ky
(Church)
Mariagatan
KUNGSLADUGÅRD
Kungsladugårdsgatan
Slottsskogsgatan
Starrahällareg.
SLOTTSSKOGS
Stora
Dammen
Perdubbsgatan
SANDARNA
Svalebogatan
PARKEN
Fridhemsgatan
Högsbogatan
Mar-
gretebergsgatan
Dag Hammarskjöldsleden
BOTANISKA
TRÄDGÅRDE
Högsboleden
ÄNGGÅRDEN

den's past and cheer on the Vikings.

However, not everyone really understood the game. A leading Gothenburg sports writer even criticised American football as being too violent. He apparently forgot the much more violent game of ice hockey, which is Sweden's second most popular national sport after football (soccer).

Bigness on the commercial side is closely related to Gothenburg's being a seaport. Consequently, it is the home base for Sweden's largest and most internationally well-known manufacturing enterprises: Volvo cars and trucks, SKF ball bearings and Hasselblad cameras.

Being the home of Volvo, it is only fitting that the **Gnistäng Tunnel** under the Göta River is the world's widest motor vehicle tunnel through rock, being 62 ft (19 metres) wide and 2,330 ft (712 metres) long.

Gothenburg has also become the venue for some of northern Europe's biggest fairs and exhibitions, which are naturally held in Scandinavia's largest Fair Centre. The Swedish International Travel and Tourism Fair (TUR), for example, attracts over 60,000 visitors, a third more than those attending a similar fair in Copenhagen which has nearly three times the population.

This emphasis on bigness and largeness should not put one off from visiting what is truly an attractive, often interesting and even entertaining city.

Gothenburgers like to think that they are more humorous and generally enjoy themselves more, weather permitting, than other Swedes. To understand this on a visit during the summer months, do as the natives do: take a stroll up and down **Kungsportsavenyen**, more commonly known as just "**Avenyn**". This is Gothenburg's answer to the Champs Elysées or how the Via Veneto used to be.

The Avenyn, about 160 ft (50 metres) wide and just under a kilometre long, is a boulevard lined with trees, restaurants, pubs and sidewalk cafés as well as street musicians and peddlars of fruits and trinkets. To many a Swede, both Gothenburgers and others, it is almost like not being in Sweden. It is one of the few opportunities a foreign visitor has to see and experience a more open side of the Swedish character.

Like other famed boulevards, the Avenyn has been invaded by the local McDonald's franchise and young people monopolise many of the watering holes and restaurants. A certain tradition does prevail, as many of the establishments along the Avenyn have been the gathering place for successive generations of Gothenburgers. The beat has changed somewhat, but it goes on.

At the top of the Avenyn is Gothenburg's cultural centre, **Götaplatsen**, with the imposing Poseidon fountain by the Swedish sculptor Carl Milles. Götaplatsen is flanked by the **Art Museum**, with the largest collection of Scandinavian art in Scandinavia; the **Concert Hall**, which is home of the acclaimed Gothenburg Symphony Orchestra; the **Municipal Theatre** where major productions such as a revival of *West Side Story* are performed; and the **Municipal Library**, which has more than 400,000 volumes.

The **Stora Teatre**, at the other end of the Avenyn, is Scandinavia's only theatre specialising in light opera, musicals and ballet.

Historic Gothenburg: Unlike its sister city in America, Gothenburg does not have any towering skyscrapers or, for that matter, a subway system. It's not that it doesn't want the former or need the latter. The city just happens to be built on top of a bed of clay up to 400 ft (120 metres) thick and said to have the consistency of microscopic cornflakes—not the most suitable of foundations.

Even the Dutch engineers who built the city for Gustav II Adolf back in 1621 were well aware of the unstable sub-soil and advised against having any structure more than two or three storeys high. Gustav II Adolf was, nevertheless, reported to be pleased with his choice for the city since the same clay would prevent his arch-rival, Denmark's King Christian, from assaulting the city with his heavy cannon.

Stora Teatern specialises in light opera and musicals.

The Dutch builders naturally gave Gothenburg a typical 16th-century Dutch style with canals and moated fortress, though some of the former have now been covered over. The Dutch immigrants even held 10 seats on Gothenburg's first city council, which also included seven Swedes and one Scot.

The centre of Gothenburg retains this distinctive "Dutch" character, even though two of the canals were filled in long ago and are now called **Östra Hamngatan** and **Västra Hamngatan**, Most of the moat and Grand Canal still exist and now serve as the route for the flat-bottom boat *Paddan* sightseeing tour. It takes about 55 minutes and passes most of the city's historical buildings as well as some of the action in the inner harbour.

Gothenburg has nothing to compare to Stockholm's Old Town; five major fires over the years saw to that. The city's historic centre within the confines of the moat, grand canal and the Göta River is an architectural hodge-podge of styles and periods. This concentra-tion places Gothenburg's historic attractions, for the most part, within easy walking distance of each other and most hotels, which makes it very manageable even without a car. Also, the city's famous tram network is well-used.

The first town called Gothenburg was actually on the other side of the Göta River from the present-day city centre in an area now called **Hisingen**. It was founded by King Karl IX. In one of the fierce internecine wars that broke out regularly among the Scandinavians, the Danes and Norwegians destroyed it in 1611 and cut Sweden off from the sea. A ransom of one million Rikdsdaler, equal to an entire year's grain harvest at that time, was eventually paid for the return of the Old Älvsborg fortress and an outlet to the sea.

To make sure it didn't happen again, King Gustav II Adolf enlisted the aid of Sweden's first guest workers: the Dutch, who were more experienced than the Swedes at building defences and sea trade. The statue of Gustav II Adolf in the square of the same name

Below: left, the *Paddan* sightseeing boat on Gothenburg's canals; right, the Fish Church, now an indoor fish market.

points to the place where he wanted his new city to be built.

The day the King signed the Gothenburg city charter, 2 June 1621, is not celebrated by Gothenburgers. Instead they honour the day he died, 6 November 1632 during the Thirty-Year War at the battle of Lützen, by eating small cakes with the King's image made of marzipan. It is a fitting Gothenburg answer to the Napoleon pastry since both were warrior kings or emperors, as the case may be.

Architectural remnants of Gothenburg's earliest days are few and include only the **Kronhuset**, in the centre of town, the **Bastion Carolus Rex** at Kungsgatan and two small forts, **Skansen Kronan** and **Skansen Lejonet**.

Kronhuset is Gothenburg's oldest secular building, dating from 1643, and was originally the town armoury. In 1660 it was briefly converted to the House of Parliament so the five-year-old Crown Prince could become King Karl XI and succeed his father King Karl X Gustav, who died suddenly while visiting Gothenburg. It is now the **City Museum**. In an adjacent newer building, a little over 200 years old, is the **Kronhusbodarna**. It once housed various craftsmen's workshops and has now been restored into a living museum of turn-of-the-century shops and a handicrafts centre.

The other 17th-century structure open to the public is the fortress **Skansen Kronan**, now the Military Museum. Situated on a hill in the city's **Haga** district, it also offers from its ramparts a fine panoramic view of Gothenburg and the harbour. Haga was Gothenburg's first suburb back in 1640 and as the city expanded it eventually became the "workers" district during the 19th century.

Examples of the wooden houses from that period are found along **Västra Skansgatan**. A typical 19th-century working class family home at Bergsgatan 19 is open to the public.

Gothenburg became an economic force largely through the early efforts of

Grocer's shop at Kronhusbodarna—old workshops now restored as a living museum.

the great merchant fleets and traders. Most notable is the Swedish East India Company, which brought great wealth into the city as early as the mid-1700s. Evidence of this wealth exists today in the buildings along the **Stora Hamnkanalen** (the Grand Canal).

The East India House itself is now three museums: the **Archaeological**, the **Historical** and the **Ethnographical**. The latter has an especially interesting collection from South America that includes many of the best Peruvian Indian textiles and artefacts found outside Peru.

Most of the city's more historic structures are now used by the local government, either as offices or for official functions as well as museums. Along the Norra Hamngatan side of the canal is the **Sahlgrenska Huset**, built in 1753 and, among other things, the office of the Municipal Secretariat for Trade and Industry as well as the Gothenburg Region Promotion Office.

Across the canal on Södra Hamngatan is the **Residenset** built in 1650 for Field Marshal Lennart Torstensson, although its present appearance dates from an extension in the 1850s. It is now the official residence of the Governor for Gothenburg and Bohuslän.

In the square around the statue of city founder Gustav II Adolf, which faces the canal, are several historic buildings all with official uses. The **Rådhuset** (Town Hall) built in 1672 and extended in the early 19th century, is now partly used as a court house. Next is the **Wenngrenska Huset**, with the first two floors dating from 1759 and the top floor from 1820. Originally the home of a city councillor called Wenngren, it has come almost full circle and is now used as offices for the city councillors.

The **Stadshuset** (City Hall), built in 1758 as an armoury, was later used as a guardhouse and barracks for the city militia. It now houses the City Council and City Administration Department, which also has offices next door in **Börshuset** (the Former Stock Exchange), which dates from 1849. The city also hosts official banquets and receptions in Börshuset.

If you arrive in Gothenburg by ship, you can't help noticing the **Nya Elfsborg Fortress** on an island at the mouth of the Göta River. It was built in the mid-17th century to protect Sweden's western gateway against the Danes. Nya Elfsborg witnessed its last taste of fire against the Danish fleet led by Norwegian Peder Tordenskiold in 1717 and again in 1719. It was last used officially as a prison during the 19th century and now serves as a venue for meetings and banquets, as well as weddings in the **chapel**. It is one of the few Gothenburg tourist attractions that is not within walking distance or a tram ride from the city centre. For a closer look it can be reached only by a boat.

The green-garden city: If the canal and city centre reflect the early Dutch influence, the many parks give Gothenburg a 19th-century English impression. Sweden's second city has some 20 parks, more than any other city in the country. So inevitably Gothenburg is called the "Garden City" and the "Green City".

As far back as 1746, the noted Swedish botanist Linnaeus called Gothenburg "the prettiest city in the whole land"—and that was before many of its parks were even thought of. Even when it concerns nature, Gothenburg likes to comes out on top.

In the very heart of the city, along the south and east side of the moat, is the **Trädgårdsföreningen Park**. The locals call it "Trängår'n" and it is Gothenburg's answer to New York's Central Park or London's Hyde Park. It is not as large as either, but it does have the **Palmhuset**, a greenhouse for tropical plants that was built in 1878 and recently refurbished. It is claimed to be Scandinavia's largest glass structure. Trängår'n also has a relatively new **Rosarium** which in season has some 10,000 roses of 4,000 different species. No official claim has yet been made to declare it the largest rosarium of its kind, but it must be—at least in Scandinavia.

Gothenburg's other parks of note are all relatively close to the city centre. The largest is **Slottsskogen**, which covers 338 acres (137 hectares) and is a total

recreation centre with sports facilities, zoo, museums and restaurants as well as numerous small lakes and lovely areas for walks and picnics.

Slottskogen is also the setting for a traditional sleep-out. Gothenburgers maintain that by Ascension Day it must be summer and that it must be warm enough for sleeping under the stars, which they do that evening in Slottskogen.

Across the Dag Hammarskjöld highway from Slottskogen is the **Botanical Garden**. It justifies Gothenburg's claim as being one of the largest of its kind in the world by having 13,000 plant species, including 1,500 flower species, in its greenhouses and along 22 miles (35 km) of roads and paths. It also has one of Europe's largest rock gardens, with 4,000 plant species from all over the world. Not surprisingly, the Botanical Garden attracts over 400,000 visitors a year.

A little to the south is the nature reserve of **Änggårdsbergen**, at least twice the size of Slottskogen.

The overwhelming impression of nature encountered in Gothenburg makes it hard to believe that this is also a highly industrialised city with nearly 450,000 inhabitants. Equally impressive is that all of Gothenburg's nature, including the seaside and beaches, is highly accessible by an environmentally friendly system of tramcars.

Even the popular **Liseberg Amusement Park** is more than just rides and games. Some 13 restaurants and nightclubs, six stages and four theatres make it an entertainment centre for young and old in a setting that is both flower garden and sculpture park.

Donation city: Another large park of note is across the Göta River on the Hisingen side. This is **Keillers Park**, which provides a sweeping panoramic view of the entire city and harbour from the top of a 282-ft (86-metre) hill. This park was donated to the city by one of its more wealthy citizens, an engineer named James Keiller.

Gothenburg's leading citizens seem to have developed a habit of bequeathing part of their wealth to the people.

Consequently, the city's attractions are often named after their benefactors. The obvious result is that Gothenburg is also known as the "donation" city. The **Röhsska Art and Crafts Museum** is named after the brothers Wilhelm and August Röhss. The **Fürstenberg Art Museum** is another example. An exception is the **Maritime Museum and Aquarium**, which was made possible by a donation from the ship-owning Broström family.

Education was a popular choice of the civic-minded citizens such as William Chalmers, director of the East Indian Company, who founded the renowned **Chalmers Institute of Technology** in 1829. Merchant James Robertson Dickson gave part of his fortune to establish the **Dicksonska Library** in Haga in 1861. The College that grew to become the **University of Gothenburg** was founded in the 1880s by donors such as industrialist David Carnegie.

The originator of this tradition seems to have been Niclas Sahlgren, who was responsible for the success of the Swed-

ish East Indian Company in the 18th century. When he died in 1776, he left part of his fortune to help the city's poor and sick, which led to the founding of the **Sahlgrenska Hospital** in 1782. It overlooks the Botanical Gardens and is today one of the largest hospital complexes in Sweden.

Other Gothenburg institutions founded by donations include the **Carlander Memorial Hospital** and the **Renström Hospital**.

Maritime traditions: Gothenburg's relationship to the sea was the reason for its coming into being. Its importance during the past century was even proclaimed by Sweden's most famous dramatist, August Strindberg. A character in the 1886-87 drama *The Maid's Son*, was to realise, after seeing Gothenburg's busy harbour for the first time, that Stockholm was no longer the Scandinavian focal point and that Gothenburg had taken the lead.

When Strindberg wrote those lines, Gothenburg's harbour was alive with ships bound for, or returning from the four corners of the earth. The outbound traffic was also human, for at that time the flow of Swedish immigrants to America was still in full swing. For most of the nearly one million Swedes who made their way to the promised land across the Atlantic, the last they ever saw of their homeland was Gothenburg.

Several decades later, Gothenburg was the port for the Swedish American Line luxury liners *Gripsholm*, *Kungsholm* and *Drottningholm* that used to bring dollar-laden American tourists and some returning immigrants to Sweden. These liners eventually gave way to faster, less costly air travel and are most likely now sailing under Greek flags, or as converted cruise ships.

The port of Gothenburg has nevertheless survived as a gateway to Sweden for people and cargo. More than four million passengers a year are carried by Stena Line and Scandinavian Seaways ferries to and from Denmark, Germany, England and Holland. There is no better introduction to Gothenburg than to ar-

190

rive by sea. The American entertainer Bette Midler discovered this inadvertently when she flew into Gothenburg's Landvetter Airport to start a European concert tour: she thought the pilot had gone off course and was about to land in Siberia. "There was nothing but rows and rows of trees and darkness that was every now and than interrupted by a black lake or racing river," she said. "Not a road, not a house, not even a Howard Johnson's to show that there were any people or that any planned to come here. It was beautiful, but disturbing especially since I was to perform before 6,000 people. Where would they come from?" Had Ms Midler arrived in Gothenburg by sea, she would have understood.

In addition to Gothenburg's Maritime Museum, an open-air homage to Gothenburg's seafaring tradition is now found along the Göta River near the city centre. The **Maritime Centre** at **Lilla Brommen** is intended to revitalise the inner harbour with a worthy tourist attraction since it lost much of its atmosphere when the shipbuilding yards closed as competition from the Far East made them no longer profitable.

When completed, the existing **Ship Museum** will be expanded to include 20 historic vessels moored along the dock and will be open to the public for visits on board. The ships include a destroyer, a lighthouse ship, a cargo vessel, several tugboats and the four-masted barque *Viking* among others. A Swedish submarine, the *Draken*, will also be exhibited at Lilla Brommen—but on land.

The Maritime Centre is not intended to be just a static display. The Göta Kanal Steamship Company, which sails the scenic inland waterway up to Stockholm, is to embark and dock its vessels at Lilla Brommen. There are restaurants, shops, boat and helicopter rides, lecture programmes, film shows and exhibitions, all intended to give the Maritime Centre wide family appeal. The *Paddan* sightseeing boats will also take a new route for a riverside view of the vessels moored along the dock.

Gothenburg is Scandinavia's largest and busiest seaport.

THE GOLDEN COAST

They call it the Golden Coast and it is well-named: 250 miles (400 km) of glorious coastline divided in two by the city of Gothenburg. To the south is the county of Halland, where the best beaches lie. North of the city, in the county of Bohuslän, the coast is majestic: all granite rocks, islands and skerries. The Swedes discovered the Golden Coast as a favourite holiday spot early in the century, and its popularity has never waned.

A natural barrier: A ridge running inland from the coast forms a natural border between Halland and the adjoining county of Skåne while the coastal strip throughout the length of the Golden Coast is separated from the hinterland by a man-made border, the E6 highway.

The first town "over the border" into Halland is **Laholm**, which is also the county's oldest town, founded in 1231. But once it had achieved this distinction, Laholm seems to have rested on its laurels as it remains a small and quiet centre with, for its size, a remarkable number of sculptures, mostly by the artist Stig Blomberg. This part of the coast has plenty of sandy beaches, such as those at **Skummeslövstrand** and **Mellbystrand**, while inland if you cross the busy E6, it is quietly pastoral with woodlands, farms and winding rivers and roads.

Halmstad, farther up the coast, is the largest town in Halland, on the river Nissan. There is a 17th-century castle, remains of a city wall and St Nikolai, a church which dates back to the 13th century. The town museum has an important marine section and a large-scale model of the town. More models are to be seen at Miniland which has famous Swedish buildings to a scale of 1:25.

The Riviera: Nearby is **Tylösand**, a popular holiday resort, dubbed "the Swedish Riviera" but in fact it is more reminiscent of Le Touquet than Juan les Pins. It has a predominantly sandy beach, and there are also good beaches at **Östra Strand**, **Ringenäs** and **Haverdalsstrand**. Tylösand is dominated by the massive complex of the Nya Hotel Tylösand which has all the trappings of a major modern holiday centre, from a *crêperie* to a casino. There are plenty of sporting facilities too, including two 18-hole golf courses.

On the road from Halmstad to Falkenberg, the next town north along the coast, is Ugglarp where you will find **Svendinos Bil och Flygmuseum** (Car and Plane Museum). It's a bit untidy but is bursting at the seams with 140 old cars and 31 old and new aircraft which delight the enthusiast and the engineer. The bigger, modern aircraft sit outside, but inside the rest are crammed bumper to bumper and wingtip to wingtip. Treasures include such exotic names as a Bullerbilen car which was built as long ago as 1897.

Salmon galore: Falkenberg is on the **Ätran**, a river famous for its salmon. The British were the first to enjoy the sport of angling here in the 1830s. When English and Scottish immigrants who

had settled in Gothenburg invited friends to join them for hunting and fishing. For many years in the 19th century the fishing rights on the river were leased to a Baron Oscar Dickson, who belonged to one of the best known families in Gothenburg.

A London solicitor, W.M. Wilkinson, was so moved by the quality of the fishing that in 1884 he wrote and had published privately a little book for the benefit of his Swedish and English friends. Called *Days in Falkenberg* it reveals that the going rate for salmon was 3s. 6d. a pound (about 18p for a half-kilo).

The oldest pottery: One salmon smokehouse remains but it is now the local museum. The old part of the town with its 18th-century wooden houses and cobbled streets is centred on the 14th-century **St Laurenti Church**. There is an old toll bridge (*tullbron*) from 1756 and the oldest pottery in Sweden, **Törngrens Krukmakeri**, which has been run by the Törngren family since 1786. More good beaches are found at **Olofsby** (north of the town) and **Skrea Strand** (south of the town).

Road 154 from Falkenberg goes through placid farmland to **Ullared**. Every year this small village of 700 people attracts three million visitors. They come from all over Sweden and even from Norway and the big attraction is cut-price shopping. Ullared is the prototypical out-of-town shopping centre. It all started with one man opening a very basic shopping warehouse— no display, no designer interior—just merchandise at bargain prices. Today a whole range of buildings is stuffed with all manner of goods from glass to shoes. There is a vast car park but, even so, on busy Saturdays eager buyers may have to queue for several hours to get in. Tax-free facilities are available for foreign visitors and the warehouse accepts credit cards.

Varberg, in contrast to the rather restrained atmosphere of Falkenberg, is a bustling sort of place combining spa, resort, port and commercial centre with a ferry service to Grenå in Denmark.

It looms impressively beside the

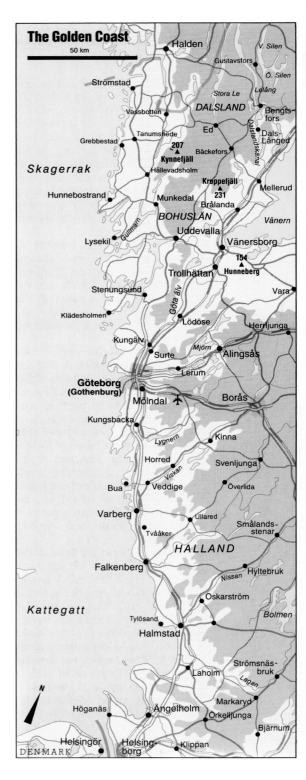

The Golden Coast

water, and houses a museum with 35,000 exhibits. Pride of place goes to the Bocksten Man who demonstrates what the well-dressed 14th-century male should be wearing. He is the only preserved figure in the world to be wearing a complete costume from the Middle Ages. There is also a Museum of Communications in King Karl XI's stables, which has a collection of carriages, boats and—from a somewhat different era—bicycles.

A hundred years ago: Varberg also has two reminders of its late 19th-century development as a Swedish holiday resort—and both are in use today. One is the 1883 **Societetshuset** in the park, an elaborate wooden pavilion which is now a restaurant.

The second is the 1903 bathing section where the visitor could indulge in gentle sea bathing and sun bathing. You cross a little bridge from the shore to a rectangular wooden structure with the sea in the middle. Around the sides of this bathing station are changing huts and sun chairs where, after a quick

plunge in this early version of a seawater swimming pool, the bathers relax over coffee and waffles and enjoy the sun and sea air. More than once it has been suggested that the structure was an anachronism and should be demolished, but happily it still survives.

Around Varberg you will find several more beaches. At **Apleviken**, the beach shelves gently and is safe for children but Träslövlägen's beach is disappointing. But never mind. The island of **Getterön**, three miles (five km) north of the town has both beaches and something for the naturalist in a nature reserve and bird sanctuary. You reach it by a bridge from the mainland.

At **Väröbacka** there is a bulge in the coastline with a fishing village at Bua, but its picturesqueness is overshadowed by the nearby nuclear power station at Ringhalm.

South of Kungsbacka you come to what is probably the most out-of-character building along the entire coast. **Tjolöholm Castle** was built as recently as the turn of the century but in an

Tjolöholm Slot, built to resemble an English Tudor mansion.

English Tudor style. It looks for all the world as if it has been transported lock, stock and leaded lights from some corner of England, stands at the centre of a large park, and has a splendid art nouveau interior.

The original way of cleaning the interior of this architectural aberration was as bizarre as the castle itself. When the dust lay too thick, teams of horses dragged a huge and primitive vacuum cleaner up to the castle, where cleaner, horses and all came in through the windows. Today, the City of Gothenburg owns Tjolöholm, which is open to the public, and the cleaning methods are much more conventional...but less interesting too.

The most northerly town in Halland is **Kungsbacka**. Only 18 miles (30 km) from Gothenburg, it was almost inevitable that it would be reduced to becoming a dormitory town for Big G. Yet, when it was established as a wooden city in the 13th century, Kungsbacka was an entirely separate town with its own identity. In 1676, it briefly knew Royal patronage when King Karl XI made Kungsbacka his headquarters during one of the wars against Denmark that too often raged over the southern provinces of Sweden.

In 1846, fire did what war had not achieved and left only two buildings standing in Kungsbacka, an all too frequent occurrence in Sweden's "wooden towns". The survivors are the **Röda Stugan** (the red cottage) in **Nord Torggatan** and a house in Östergatan. But though the buildings in the market square today are less than 150 years old, they are very pleasant for all that.

Inland from Kungsbacka a high ridge runs parallel with the coast. It is called **Fjärås Bräcka**, and was the result of action by glaciers many thousands of years ago. From the top of the ridge there are good views over the Kungsbacka Fjord. On the other side of the ridge is an equally attractive view of **Lake Lyngern** which is 12 miles (20 km) long. In the distant days before the Ice Age, it was part of the fjord. Towards the southern end of the ridge

Woodlands on Hallands Vaderö, an island nature reserve in the south of the country.

there are some Bronze Age graves and also about 125 *menhirs*—grave stones—from the Iron Age. The most impressive is the **Frode** stone which gets its name from a Danish fairy king who, legend says, is buried there.

Early worship: Where the road reaches the top of the ridge is **Fjärås Church** which was built in 1800 but has a 1596 bronze font, an altar from 1630 and a pulpit from about 1650—all reminders that there has been a place of worship here for hundreds of years.

South of Fjärås Bräcka, at **Askhult**, you will come across a preserved hamlet, a collection of buildings from the 18th and early 19th centuries, grouped around a common courtyard. It is one of the few surviving examples of an undivided hamlet and is now a museum. Not far southwest of Askhult is the 12th-century church at **Gällinge** which has some beautiful 18th-century ceiling paintings.

Take a minor road on your return to Kungsbacka and you can pass **Gåsevadholm**, a pink, privately-owned castle built in 1757 by Niclas Sahlgren, when he was manager of the East India Company.

Towards the coast there are several villages, including **Vallda** and **Släp**, which were home to the "sailing farmers"—men who made a living by combining a smallholding and fishing.

The moment you reach the little seaside resort of **Särö**, you realise the coastline has changed. Apart from some small sandy coves, the beaches have gone and instead, as you near Gothenburg, a more dramatic landscape of rocks, inlets and islands takes over.

Tennis players: As early as the first years of the 19th century, Särö was a fashionable resort and, when it became popular with the Swedish Royal Family, its name was made. Both King Oscar II, and the tennis playing King, Gustav V, liked to spend time there each summer and Gustav was a frequent player on the same tennis courts which you can use today. This was the resort where the wealthier inhabitants of Gothenburg had their summer villas,

Street markets bring colour to almost every Swedish town.

charming wooden houses with verandahs, balconies and an abundance of carved woodwork which still remain.

A little narrow-gauge railway used to connect the resort with Gothenburg but that has now disappeared, although the station building at Särö remains as an attractive restaurant and you can cycle along the former trackbed.

Fortunately Särö has resisted development and remains in something of a time warp with its turn of the century atmosphere. You can walk along the **Strandpromenaden** and through **Särö Västerskog**, one of the oldest oak woods along the west coast. There is one small sandy beach on the south side of the town, otherwise it is smooth granite rocks. The pace is leisurely and summer excitement is restricted to going out in a boat to fish or to watch the basking seals.

The county of **Bohuslän** begins on the north side of Gothenburg and already the coastal scenery has set a pattern which will continue all the way to the Norwegian frontier: rocks, islands and skerries. Off the coast is a group of 10 islands, the **Öckerö**, but these lie within an area semi-restricted for foreigners. You have to go further up the coast to **Marstrand** for the first island with unrestricted access.

Clever craftwork: You reach this island by a short ferry crossing from Marstrand, a town dominated by Carlsten Fästning (Carlsten Fortress) which is unfortunately spoiled by the obtrusive radar equipment on top of its tower. A town without cars, it is a popular holiday resort and, above all, a sailing centre. In summer, this is also the place to find craftwork, for the town is packed with crafts of all kinds.

King Oscar II also gave this town his patronage and his statue stands in front of the Societetshuset. As a link with the past, a quartet often plays in **Paradise Park** in the season. You get the best views of the island from the fortress and Hangman's Hill.

Beyond Marstrand are two major islands, **Tjörn** and **Orust,** and a number of smaller ones. You reach Tjörn over a

Left, Bohuslän's smooth rocks make for good sunbathing. Below, Smögen, one of the west coast's most popular sailing islands, connected by bridge.

bridge near Stenungsund (a town which the tourist literature says, with refreshing candour, "is known for its petrochemical industries"). A second bridge links Tjörn with Orust and a third bridge gets you back to the mainland.

This area is known as the **Bästkusten**, the best coast, the heart of Bohuslän. Tjörn is beautiful with some barren areas inland, but a fascinating coastline. Off the southern corner is **Kladesholmen**, a tiny island, linked by yet another bridge (this entire area is full of examples of Swedish bridge-builders' skills).

Kladesholmen is a colourful jumble of tightly packed wooden houses which seem to cling to the rocky surface. Like the majority of these villages, they are not just pretty places for the holiday-maker but are working fishing villages. Views may be spoiled by industrial-style buildings which are usually connected with fish processing or the repair of trawlers and their gear but this is part of local life. Further round the coast of Tjörn is Skärhamn, another fishing vil-

Bronze Age rock carvings at Tanum.

lage with tight little streets, wooden houses and a small square in the centre.

A magnificent curved bridge, which provides good views in either direction, takes you from Tjörn to **Orust**. This island, the third largest in Sweden, has its quota of fishing villages including Mollösund, Hallerviksstrand, Gullholmen, Ellön and Käringön. Inland from the deeply indented coastline with its succession of rocks and coves, there is farmland and an enjoyable mix of scenery in this fertile area.

As you cross yet another bridge, you have the impression that you are on yet another island but it is in fact a long jagged promontory and part of the mainland. Two more fishing villages are **Grundsund** and **Fiskebäckskil** while from the latter a ferry crosses the **Gullmaren**, Sweden's only genuine fjord, to Lysekil.

Lysekil has been Swedish for 300 years; before that it was Norwegian. In the 19th century it became a summer resort and its popularity has continued to the present day. During the summer it

comes to life and is full of bustle and activity with boat excursions to the other islands and coastal villages and sea fishing trips.

Fishing continues: North of Lysekil on the **Sotenäs** peninsula are yet more fishing villages. **Smögen**, another little bridge-connected island, is particularly attractive with its brightly painted houses near the water's edge. Amongst the amateur sailors with their boats the fishing fleet goes about its daily business. Fresh Smögen shrimps are renowned along this part of the coast. **Kungshamn** is a repeat of Smögen except that it is on the mainland.

As you travel north along this coast of smooth pinkish granite rocks the combination of fishing village and holiday centre is repeated: Hunnebostrand, Tegelstrand, Hamburgsund, Fjällbacka and Grebbestad. The oldest of the fishing villages is Bovallstrand.

There are few major towns in Bohuslän but, going north from Gothenburg, you come to **Kungälv**, an old Viking centre, which occupies a key strategic position on the Göta Älv river. It is now within easy commuting distance of Gothenburg and so, like Kungsbacka, it has become another dormitory town.

Uddevalla, the biggest town of the county was a major shipbuilding centre, but like so many others in Europe, the shipyard closed and has been partially replaced by other industry. If the town has little to interest the visitor, then there is a place on the outskirts which has greater merit. **Gustavsberg** claims to be Sweden's oldest seaside resort and it was mentioned by the noted Swedish botanist Linnaeus in his book *Westgötha Resa,* published in 1746. Like many of the other resorts, it has its Societetsalongen—another of these grand, richly ornamented wooden buildings—which continues as a restaurant. The original spa building is now a youth hostel and this and other buildings are all set in a delightful park which leads down to the water's edge.

Going further north is **Munkedal**, near which is a small **railway museum** and—somewhat more improbable—a

museum devoted to **Elvis Presley**.

Tanumshede, a small town on the E6, lies inland from the fishing village of Grebbestad and has two claims to fame. One is **Tanums Gestgifveri**, an inn established more than 300 years ago by Royal decree. It has been welcoming visitors since 1663. The modest-looking wooden building, painted in the traditional buff colour, belies an interior of cosy rooms and outstanding cuisine. Fish dishes naturally rank high on its list of specialities. The hotel accommodation is in an adjoining building.

Yesterday's newspapers: Tanum's second claim to fame is of much greater historical importance as it is in the centre of Europe's largest collection of **Bronze Age rock carvings**. These were the original tabloid newspapers: all the news in pictures and no text, a strip cartoon that's 3,000 years old. The carvings show battles, ships, hunting and fishing scenes and warriors. At nearby Vitlycke they cover 2,200 sq. ft (204 sq. metres) and a Rock Carving Institute provides further information. Other carvings can be seen at Fossum, Tegneby and Litsleby.

The last town before you reach the Norwegian frontier is **Strömstad**. It is an old-established health resort and one of the first places in Sweden to provide saltwater and seaweed baths. It is also said to have more hours of sunshine than anywhere else in Northern Europe and is known as the town of the prawn. Strömstad prawns are considered by the local inhabitants to be in a class of their own, with a distinctive mild flavour.

A hint of Norway: The Strömstad district has more than a touch of Norwegian about it which is not surprising. In the past, the histories of Denmark, Norway and Sweden were inextricably linked and for many years Strömstad was part of Norway. But at last, at the Battle of Strömstad in 1717, the Swedes finally succeeded in defeating the dreaded Tordenskiold and his Danish fleet. Otherwise, this far northern tip of the Golden Coast could still be part of Norway, not much more than a gunshot away on the other side of the Svinesund Bridge.

Right, sailing into the sunset.

THE GREAT LAKES

Two enormous lakes, Vänern and Vättern, dominate the map of Sweden. The larger of the two is Vänern, a vast stretch of water with an area of 2,156 square miles (5,585 sq. km). It is not only the biggest lake in Sweden but also the largest in Western Europe, and its western shore embraces two countries—Dalsland and Värmland.

Dalsland is a county of modest, neat farms and prosperous small towns and villages, with empty roads running through its birch forests. From bus or car, you may be lucky enough to catch a glimpse of an elk sliding out of the trees, particularly in the early mornings, or late evenings as dusk begins to fall. This gentle countryside with its sprinkling of lakes and rivers stretches from the fertile **Dalboslätten** in the southeast, to the northwest slopes of the **Skogdal**. The nearer you go to the Norwegian border, the more barren it gets. No

county in Sweden can be described as truly "small" but, by the standards of this large country, everything in Dalsland is on a modest scale, to give it the title "Sweden in Miniature."

The major feature in the county is the **Dalsland Canal**. In some ways, "canal" is a misnomer as the waterway is basically a network of interconnected lakes and rivers. Very little of its 158 miles (240 km) has had to be excavated. The canal was designed by Nils Ericsson and built between 1864 and 1868, to provide better transport for the ironworks and saw mills of the area. Today, it is used only for pleasure and is popular for sailing and canoeing.

The most dramatic piece of engineering is the aqueduct at **Håverud**. Made of iron and 108 ft (33 metres) long it carries the canal over the rapids of the river Upperud. Held together by 33,000 rivets, it is still watertight after 116 years. Apart from the aqueduct there are road and rail bridges and locks at Håverud, and the best view of this unusual combination is from the hill above the roadway. Håverud has a small Canal Museum, which tells you about the various sets of locks, and that the canal stretches from Köpmannebro, on Lake Vänern, to Töcksfors, in Värmland, close to the Norwegian frontier.

Dalsland's largest town is **Åmål** on the lakeside. It was founded by Queen Kristina in 1643, and is now a commercial town, with some 18th-century houses in what was the market place and is now a public park.

King Karl's genius: Between two lakes, **Stora Le** and **Lille Le** (Big Le and Little Le) stand the twin villages of **Ed** and **Dals-Ed**, nowadays so close that it is hard to tell where one ends and the other begins. The views of water and forest on either side of the villages are lovely, and this has long been a popular holiday centre, particularly with people who come out from the city of Gothenburg. The area's earlier history was more dramatic because Dals-Ed had links with the last campaign against Norway of Sweden's 17th-century military genius, King Karl XII. In 1718, as his army besieged the border fortress of

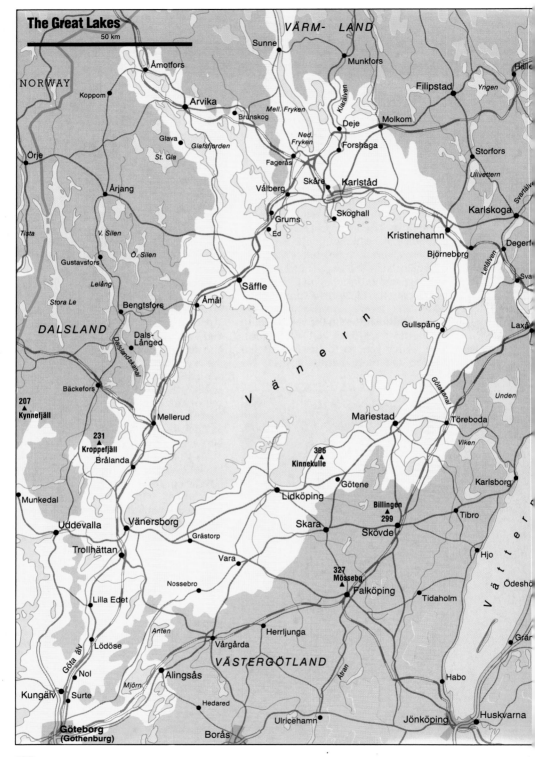

The Great Lakes

50 km

VÄRM- LAND

NORWAY

Sunne

Åmotfors

Munkfors

Hälle

Koppom

Arvika

Filipstad

Yngen

Brunskog

Mell. Fryken

Deje

Molkom

Glava

Glafsfjorden

Ned.
Fryken

Forshaga

Storfors

St. Gla

Örje

Fageräs

Ullvettern

Årjang

Vålberg

Skåre

Karlstad

Grums

Skoghall

Karlskoga

Tista

V. Silen

Ed

Kristinehamn

Degerf

Gustavsfors

Ö. Silen

Björneborg

Leilång

Säffle

Sva

Stora Le

Bengtsfors

Åmål

Gullspång

Laxå

DALSLAND

Dals-
Långed

V ä n e r n

207
▲
Kynnefjäll

Bäckefors

Mellerud

Mariestad

Töreboda

Unden

231
▲
Kroppefjäll

Viken

Brålanda

306
▲
Kinnekulle

Götene

Karlsborg

Munkedal

Lidköping

Billingen
▲
299

Tibro

Uddevalla

Vänersborg

Skara

Skövde

Trollhättan

Grästorp

Vara

Hjo

327
Mössebg.
▲

Ödeshö

Nossebro

Falköping

Tidaholm

Lilla Edet

V ä t t e r n

Anten

Herrljunga

Lödöse

Vårgårda

Grän

Nol

Alingsås

VÄSTERGÖTLAND

Habo

Kungälv

Surte

Mjörn

Hedared

Göteborg
(Gothenburg)

Borås

Ulricehamn

Jönköping

Huskvarna

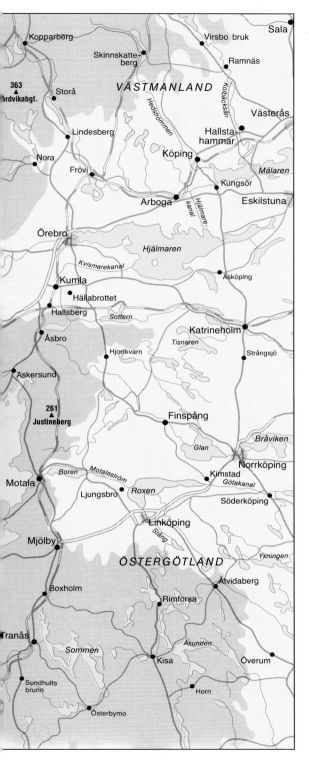

Frederiksten, a mystery bullet killed the warrior King, and the local Dals-Ed Museum touches on the community's involvement in these great events. The museum is housed in the oldest building, which dates back to 1790, a charming wooden structure with verandahs and first floor balconies, with windows facing both lakes. To the southeast is **Kropefjäll**, an upland area which is a nature reserve and popular with botanists.

Dals-Ed should not be confused with **Dals-Långed** which lies to the northeast and is an art and handicrafts centre. Between there and Håverud is **Tisselskog** with its many Bronze Age rock carvings, the county's principal historical attraction. In the opposite direction, on Lake Laxsjön, is **Baldersnäs Manor** in an Edwardian park. The original house was built in 1796 and pulled down in 1910 when the present building was erected.

To the northwest are **Billingfors** and **Bengtsfors**. The former is an area of pulp and paper mills (with a distinctive smell!). Bengtsfors has an open air museum—**Gammelgården**—which is devoted to local history and culture.

An old parish register in Western Värmland states: "Between Sweden and Norway lies Värmland", which shows a certain rugged independence that still asserts itself today, plus a slight Norwegian accent. Värmland also has a timelessness which is difficult to describe—being more a feeling than a fact. It is a region with strong traditions and which has produced a rich crop of writers of both prose and poetry.

Spruce and pine forests cover seven-tenths of the county and are often referred to as "Värmland's gold". Forests, fast running water and the discovery of iron ore all played an important part in the economic development of the county, although the old ironworks are now just a part of history.

Värmland is criss-crossed with long narrow lakes and rivers, and the Klarälven river can claim to be among its most beautiful. It begins turbulently enough near the Norwegian border but gradually becomes broader, winding, and sluggish before emptying itself into Lake Vänern near the county's largest town, **Karlstad**.

The town is 400 years old and stands on the site of an earlier and important trading post called Tingvalla. Karlstad has a cathedral (consecrated in 1730) a school museum in its old grammar school, and a popular park, **Marie-bergskogen**. Near the town is **Alster Manor**, the birthplace of one of Sweden's greatest poets, Gustav Fröding. The house, built in 1770, is now a memorial to the poet and it also holds a permanent exhibition devoted to the history and industry of the region.

From Hammarö, on the outskirts of Karlstad, you can follow the route of the pilgrims of old, up the valley of the Klarälven. They had already crossed Lake Vänern by boat to Hammarö, where they prepared themselves for the next stage of their journey. Then, they set off on the road north, to follow the Klarälven throughout its 168 miles (240 km) on their long pilgrimage to the grave of St Olav the Holy, at Trondheim on the west coast of Norway. For the pilgrims of long ago, the valley must have provided a short respite on their arduous journey. Today, it is a pleasant drive.

At **Ransäter**, on the Klarälven, is a well-arranged heritage village which includes four museums devoted to mining, forestry, agriculture and rural life. Together they provide a fascinating picture of the Värmland of yesterday. There is an inn, a manor house from 1684 and a tilt hammer driven by a water wheel, the only one of its kind still in working order. Ransäter holds an annual festival with a local folk play in the open-air theatre.

Further up river, the 17th-century church at **Ekshärad** has a baroque interior but of equal interest is the adjoining graveyard where in place of headstones there are wrought iron embellished crosses—a reflection of the region's industrial past.

The Klarälven is the only Swedish river which is used to float logs down, an age-old method which has now re-

First build your raft, then sail it down the Klarälven.

sulted in a new kind of holiday. You assemble a raft from logs and then take several days to drift slowly along on the gentle current. This kind of holiday is regarded as a stress reliever and an opportunity for overworked Swedish executives to become adventure-loving children once again. The river also offers wonderful opportunities for fishing, especially for salmon, trout and grayling.

Nobel Prize: To the south, and almost parallel to the river, are two lakes, Övre Fryken and Mellum Fryken, which together are 50 miles (80 km) long. Between the two is the little town of **Sunne** which makes a useful base from which to explore this area. High on the list of places to visit is **Mårbacka**, the manor house home of the Swedish writer Selma Lagerlöff (1858-1940). She was the first woman to receive a Nobel prize (for literature in 1909). Her best known work is probably *The Adventures of Nils Holgersson* and her first major success was *The Story of Gösta Berling*. Through her books she made the Fryk valley and lakes famous and she is regarded as one of Sweden's greatest literary figures. The house is open to the public and is exactly as it was when she died.

On **Mellum Fryken** is **Rottneros Manor** which is claimed, with some justification, to be Sweden's most beautiful park. The 98 acres of parkland have an arboretum and 100 works by famous Scandinavian sculptors, including such luminaries as Milles, Eriksson and Vigeland. Rottneros was Ekerby in Selma Lagerlöff's *The Story of Gösta Berling*. At **Fryksdalshöjden**, on the road to Branskog, you get a bird's eye view of the valley and lakes below.

Midway along **Övre Fryken**, to the west, is the mountain of **Tossebergsklätten**, which gives wide-ranging views across the lake and surrounding countryside. Further to the southwest is another region with a huge patchwork of lakes. This is where you will find **Glaskogan**, a vast area rich in wild life, and with 150 miles (241 km) of marked trails where you can also fish,

Rottneros Manor, Värmland.

bathe, camp or go canoeing. Most of it is unpopulated and its forests are dominated by the **Stora Gla** and **Övra Gla** lakes.

Two other places of interest within this area are **Klässbols Linnerväveri** and **Brunskog Gammelvala**. Klässbols is a small traditional linen and damask weaving mill, the last of its kind in Europe. Among other things, it provides all the table linen for the Swedish diplomatic corps. Visitors are welcome and there is also a shop. Brunskog Gammelvala (the Old World) is a collection of 15 old buildings on a picturesque site by Lake Värmeln. Each summer it comes to life for a brief period, when all the traditional crafts and skills are practised.

The western part of the county is comparatively empty, except for elk (Värmland has Sweden's biggest elk population) but here and there are places of interest. At **Töcksfors**, just short of the frontier with Norway, you will find a hotel with a highly unusual bedroom. The owner found an old World War II bunker beneath his grounds and has converted it into a room for guests who wish to get away from it all. Furnished in 1940s style, it is particularly popular with honeymoon couples.

Early industry: North of Lake Vänern, the bedrock is rich in minerals and this area has long been associated with Sweden's early industrial development. It is dotted with the remains of old disused ironworks, of interest to industrial archaeologists. Many Americans make the pilgrimage to Filipstad, which has the mausoleum of John Ericsson. There are also two cannons from the Monitor, the warship designed by this gifted inventor and engineer. The Monitor's greatest fame is that it is said to have won the American Civil War for the North. Ericsson also invented the ship's propeller, and his brother Nils was almost equally talented. They were born at Långban Herrgård to the north of the town and, after his death, Ericsson's body was brought back from America to his native land.

Putting back the clock at Gammelvala Brunskog—outdoor museum.

212

Björkborn Herrgård, near Karlskoga, was the home of another well-known Swedish inventor, the world-famous Alfred Nobel. Björkborn is now a museum while **Karlskoga** is dominated by Bofors, the armaments manufacturer. To the south is Kristinehamn where a 49 ft (15 metres) high sculpture by Picasso is the most striking navigational feature on Lake Vänern.

Värmland's eastern neighbour is Närke, one of Sweden's smallest counties and **Örebro**, its principal town, is worth a visit. It lies on the plain between Kilsbergen and Lake Hjälmaren (Sweden's fourth largest) and is bisected by the meandering river Svartån. In the centre, on an islet in the river, is the castle. Despite its massive appearance, the castle dates only from the end of the 19th century but there has been a castle here since the 13th century.

Beside the River Svartån is **Wadköping**, a preservation area with a collection of buildings which includes the house of Cajsa Warg, the Swedish Mrs Beeton. For good views take the lift

up the Svampen (the mushroom), a water tower 190 ft (58 metres) high with an observation balcony around the rim.

Karlslunds Gård on the outskirts of the town is a splendidly proportioned country house with 90 preserved 18th and 19th-century buildings ranging from a cow shed to a tavern within its spacious grounds. Örebro itself is well served with four museums. The only other town of note in Närke is **Askersund**, a quiet little place at the northern end of Lake Vättern which was established by that busy lady, Queen Kristina. The Landskyrkan church is impressive.

Lake Vättern, the second largest lake in Sweden, covers an area of 738 square miles (1,912 square km) and the region separating it from Lake Vänern offers rich pickings for the visitor. This is the country of **Västergötland** which extends beyond the lakes, spreading southwestwards until it diminishes almost to a point at Gothenburg. It includes mountain tablelands, which look out over the Västgöta plain, one of

Örebro Slott.

Sweden's finest castles (Läckö) and the weavers' country centred on Borås.

In 1746 the indefatigable Linnaeus said: "Truly no one could ever imagine such splendour as in Västergötland who had not seen it for himself." That's a bit over the top, but nevertheless it is a pleasant county. Almost before you come between the lakes, near Gullspång, is the Södra Råda church, a wooden structure with an interior completely decorated with naive biblical paintings dating from 1323 and 1494.

Along the east coast of Lake Vänern on the river Tida is **Mariestad**. The silhouette of the town is dominated by the spire of the 17th-century Renaissance-style **cathedral**, one of the few churches of this period which remain in Sweden. There are interesting little streets around the cathedral which conform to the 17th-century town plan.

Between Mariestad and **Lidköping** is **Kinnekulle**, which rises up 1,000 ft (306 metres) above the surrounding countryside and is called the flowering mountain. As such it attracted paeans of praise from, guess who?, Linnaeus. There are good views from the top and you can drive virtually to the summit where there is an observation tower.

Porcelain and pottery: Lidköping is the porcelain town and renowned for its pottery. The leading maker is Rörstrand, which has its own pottery museum. Every August the town is filled with artists and eager potters ready for the china festival. They all compete to see who can throw the tallest, widest and most beautiful pot. The original town dates back to 1446 when it was on the east bank of the river Lidan but the present town on the west bank owes its existence to the Earl of Läckö. In 1670 he laid down a grid plan for the streets, an innovation at that time. The dominant feature is the large square with the old town hall in the centre. There is a **Handicrafts and Maritime museum**.

Most Swedes learn at school that the king who first united the Svear and Götar tribes, Olof Skötonung, (994-1022) was baptised in 1008, at Husaby

A potter at work. In August, Lidköping has a china festival with potters from all over Sweden.

Spring, near Lidköping. Some experts dispute the place and date, but other researchers would like to establish Husaby as the cradle of the Swedish state. Husaby Church has an imposing stone tower with three spires and to the north at Flyhov you will find 350 rock carvings from the Bronze Age.

Near the tip of the beautiful **Kållandsö** peninsula, which juts out into Lake Vänern and ends in a fringe of islets and skerries, is **Läckö Castle**. It is one of the most impressive castles in Sweden. Built in the 17th century in baroque style, it has 248 rooms. In recent times it has been completely restored and is now an important attraction in this part of the country. Every summer it holds major exhibitions relating to Sweden's cultural heritage. On the western side of the peninsula is **Hindens Rev** (reef) which is three miles (five km) long. This thin finger stretching out into the lake is a remnant of the glacial era 11,000 years ago.

On the western side of Lake Vättern, **Karlsborg** is dominated by its huge fortress. In 1809, when the Swedes lost Finland to the Russians, they realised that a new defence strategy was required and decided to build two massive fortresses. These were to house the Government and the Treasury and would be more or less impregnable. The first, at Karlborg, was started in 1819 and required 250,000 tons of limestone. It was quarried by prison labour on the western side of the lake and then ferried across by boat. The castle has walls 6.5 ft (two metres) thick and three miles (five km) of ramparts but by the time it was finally finished in 1909, fortresses were out of fashion. The second castle was never built.

The fortress includes **Slutvärnet**, said to be the longest building in Europe at 2,224 ft (678 metres) from one end to the other. There is an interesting museum, and some buildings are still used by the Swedish army.

Further down the coast, the small lakeside resort of **Hjo** has been popular since the turn of the century. It has some preserved wooden houses, a pretty lakeside park and you can tour the town sedately in a horse-drawn carriage, or cruise on the lake in the 1892 steamer *Trafik*.

Troll country: In the north, between the lakes, is **Tiveden**, an area of dark forests and massive rocks and just the place to find a troll (the gnome-like creature of Scandinavian legend). To the south the **Göta Canal** cuts its way from Sjötorp on Lake Vänern to Karlsborg on Lake Vättern, through Lake Viken and flights of locks, which overcome differences in height. At **Toreboda** you can cross the canal on what is claimed to be Europe's smallest ferry—and the cheapest with a five-öre fare.

South of the canal the scenery slowly changes till it culminates in the upland plateau of **Billingen** which is about 1,000 ft (300 metres) above sea level. To the east you look down on the garrison town of **Skovde**, while to the west is the town of **Skara**. It has **Sweden's oldest cathedral** (originally 11th-century) and there is a County Museum and a Veterinary Museum while rail buffs can take a train on the preserved nar-

Wall painting at Habo Church.

row-gauge railway to **Lundsbrunn**.

Skara Sommarland lies five miles (eight km) from Skara on road 49; it is reckoned to be Scandinavia's biggest activity park with over 70 attractions for children, from lunar vehicles to aqualand. The park covers an area of 890,000 sq.yards (774,000 sq. metres) and is well laid out, clean, and efficiently run. Within this triangle formed by Skara, Skovde and Falköping is **Homborgasjön**, a wildlife area with over 100 species of birds. The biggest attraction is the annual mating dance of the crane, a graceful long-legged bird.

It is hard to believe that the little town of **Tidaholm** was once an important centre for Sweden's automotive industry. It was a hive of activity from 1903 to 1934 but all that remains today are some exhibits in a museum housed in the former Vulcan match factory. On the river is the **Turbinhus** (turbine house) built in 1898 and now used for art exhibitions, while there are four preserved workers' cottages, two in 18th-century style.

Southeast of Tidaholm and on the way to Lake Vättern is **Habo Church**, which is not in, or even close to Habo village. It is perhaps the most remarkable timber church in Sweden and was probably built in the 14th century. It was enlarged in the 1600s, and rebuilt in 1723. What makes this church so distinctive is the painted interior, the work of Johan Christian Peterson and Johan Kinnerus, both of Jönköping.

Between 1741 and 1743, Peterson painted the northern half and Kinnerus the southern half. Their paintings illustrate Luther's catechism, with the Ten Commandments on the walls (even numbers north side, odd numbers south side), the Lord's Prayer above the gallery and the Baptism and the Lord's Supper on the ceiling of the nave. There you will also find the Confession and Absolution. The overall effect is outstanding. The church also has a 1731 organ built by Johan Niclas Cahman, a renowned Swedish organ builder, and there is a separate and elegantly proportioned bell tower.

Autumn colours.

To the southwest of Skara and Falköping lies a large fertile plain around Grastörp and Vara which is a major cereal growing area. Flat and rather featureless, you can find light relief every August at **Edsvara** where the annual World Wheelbarrow Racing Championships are held.

Vänersborg and **Trollhättan** lie just within the borders of Västergötland, the former at the southern tip of Lake Vänern while the latter is an industrial town and the headquarters of Saab, which has its own motor museum.

But Trollhättan was famous long before the invention of the motor car because of the magnificent falls of the river Göta Älv. The water level drops by about 105 ft (32 metres) and when the Göta Canal was built an impressive flight of locks was required to give ships access to Lake Vänern. Today the river is diverted to generate electricity and the falls are silent. But on certain days during the summer it is released to follow the old course to provide an impressive spectacle.

Textile territory: The southern part of Västergötland is the heartland of Sweden's textile industry, with the focal point at **Borås**. This is not an elegant town by any yardstick but it does have factory shops, bargain stores and trendy boutiques. In other words, it's fine for shopping.

There is a Textile Museum, while Rydal has a well-preserved mill, together with textile workers' houses. Borås zoo contains about 400 animals in a natural habitat, and covers an area of 750 acres (30 hectares). At Hedared, between Borås and Alingsås, is one of the only remaining stave (wooden) churches in Sweden, probably dating from the 13th century.

Gräfsnäs has the ruins of a 16th-century castle and rail fans have another treat because they can reach it by a narrow-gauge museum railway from Anten. Not far away at **Alingsås** they hold an annual potato festival. Why? Because it was here in 1724 that Jonas Alströmer planted Sweden's very first potatoes.

A peaceful lakeside picnic.

GÖTA KANAL,
THE BLUE RIBBON

The challenge of linking the lakes and rivers through the interior of Sweden from Stockholm on the east coast to Gothenburg on the west coast had exercised the minds of many industrialists, statesmen and kings before Baltzar von Platen actually succeeded at the beginning of the 19th century.

For 22 years, 58,000 men laboured to build this great canal, many of them soldiers who worked with little to help them but steel-reinforced wooden spades. It was a massive undertaking and nothing like it has been built in Sweden since. At the time, the country needed this new artery from east to west to transport timber, iron, food and a range of other goods, and also to build up industry along its banks. One of the advisers to the plan was the famous Scottish engineer, Thomas Telford.

To many, the canal was as important as a booster of the nation's morale, because the period in which it was built was one of political decline and near bankruptcy for Sweden. For several years crops had been poor, the state's finances suffered and the nation's once strong military power was greatly diminished.

As a result of the country's peripheral involvement in the Napoleonic wars, Sweden lost Finland, which had been part of Greater Sweden for hundreds of years, and her Baltic colonies. The King was blamed and lost his throne in a bloodless revolution. In this general atmosphere of despondency, the realisation of the old dream to build the canal generated a glow of triumph and optimism for the future.

A choice of ways: For the visitor there are many ways of seeing the Göta Kanal. By passenger boat all the way from Stockholm to Gothenburg takes four or five days, depending on how much sightseeing you do on the way. It is an enjoyable and leisurely way of travelling—but not cheap. There are also a number of passenger boats which take you along part of the way and small

boats to provide sightseeing trips at various points along the canal.

Many Swedes travel the canal each summer in their own motor and sailing boats. A lot of skill is involved in managing the locks and many a marriage gets to breaking point as the "skipper" in the boat shouts at his wife, "the mate", who is on the edge of the lock busily pulling at ropes as she tries to prevent the boat from hitting the side or other boats in the same lock.

Along both sides of the canal are towpaths, which make excellent cycle tracks. Bikes can quite cheaply be transported across the lakes on the passenger boats and ferries.

Travelling along the canal gives you a whiff of Swedish history. Coming from the east, the first town is Söderköping, a medieval trading town with a number of beautiful churches and a nicely restored town hall. **Söderköping** is now a sleepy small town but it comes alive during the summer months when this small town idyll with its wooden houses and cobbled streets bustles with visitors.

Birdwatching: After you have passed through **Lake Asplången**, keep your binoculars at the ready: this is where the herons nest. **Lake Roxen** is also full of birdlife which can best be observed from the bird tower. After Lake Roxen the canal takes you through 15 locks in two miles (three km), lifting you 120 ft (37 metres).

Along your journey towards **Motala** you will see a medieval church at **Brunneby** near an 18th-century mansion and opposite **Kungs Norrby**. The town lies just before the canal enters **Lake Vättern**. Motala was also founded by Baltzar von Platen, who drew up the town plans and started the now thriving mechanical industry. The Motala Canal and Maritime Museum tells the story of the canal and the history of how it was built.

Lake Vättern, the fifth largest in Europe and the second largest in Sweden, is deep and cold and rich in fish. **Vadstena**, a few kilometres south of Motala, was originally built round a nunnery founded by Holy Birgitta in 1370

and became an important cultural and spiritual centre during medieval times. In 1545 Gustav Vasa built the imposing **Vadstena Castle**, recently restored.

Crossing Lake Vättern, you will see **Visingsö** to the south. On shore, there are bikes for hire, or you can be driven around in a horse-drawn carriage.

From **Karlsborg**, you start travelling down stream and the landscape becomes more dramatic. **Forsvik**, on the way, was once a thriving industrial community but is now partly a museum with a 14th-century watermill.

Sjötorp marks the end of 58 locks and the beginning of **Lake Vänern**, Sweden's largest lake. First, however, visit **Mariestad** with its lovely 18th and 19th-century wooden houses.

At the other side of Lake Vänern, you pass through **Vänersborg** and a few locks before reaching the waterfalls at **Trollhättan**. Once there were 11 locks; today there are only four. At **Kungälv** is **Bohus Fortification**. Then Gothenburg, with its four bridges, lies ahead. You have arrived on the west coast.

Preceding page, the Göta Kanal. Below, Göta Kanal boat William Tham tackles a lock. Right, birdwatching from the canal is firstclass.

STOCKHOLM: CITY OF SEA AND LAKE

The novelist Selma Lagerlöff called Stockholm "the city that floats on water". Nowhere do you see this more clearly than from the dizzy observation platform on top of the Kaknäs television tower, which rises 500 ft (150 metres). Below, Stockholm spreads out in a glinting panorama of blue water and the red of old buildings against the stark white and glass of the new, all cut through by green swathes of trees and grass in a country where space is abundant.

In winter, a white blanket lies over the city, fading the colours to pastel, and the summer ferries and pleasure boats are held fast in the solid ice of bays that cut deep into the heart of Stockholm. At that dark time of the year, only the icebreakers keep the more open stretches free of ice around the wharfs where ships for Finland and Denmark are docked.

Undiscovered treasures: To the east are the thousands of islands of the archipelago, estimated at 25,000—though it varies from 24,000 to 30,000 according to the teller. They are all different shapes, sizes and contours, stuck on the sea like a rough collage. The archipelago is one of Stockholm's undiscovered treasures, at least to visitors, though the hundreds of small boats along the edge of the inlets and islands indicate the passion of every Stockholm family to own and sail a boat.

Fresh and salt water are separated by the island of Gamla Stan (the old city) and the great lock gates of Slussen at the southern end, like an ill-fitting cork in the neck of a bottle. This island barrier is where Stockholm started some time before the 13th century.

Today, half the city is on Lake Mälaren, the other on Saltsjön, which leads out to the archipelago and the Baltic Sea, and the city continues to grow. From its small beginnings as a trading post and fort, Stockholm had no more than 75,000 inhabitants by the 18th century. Then came the late industrial revolution at the end of the 19th century,

bringing Swedes by the thousands into the cities from the land—a process which is still continuing. By 1900, Stockholm had 300,000 city dwellers. Now the population of the city itself has more than doubled at around 700,000, and with Stockholm county has over one and a half million.

The whole area is the powerhouse of Sweden, and accounts for more than one-fifth of the country's employment and a quarter of its total production, with more than 20,000 companies. In many countries this would make Stockholm a noisy, industrial city; but Sweden's wide countryside means that the whole area covers some 2,500 sq. miles (6,500 sq. km) and has space enough for everyone and more.

From Kaknäs, it is easy to understand why the Swedes were a seafaring people, and why the Swedish Vikings went east over the sheltered sea to Russia and down the great rivers to Constantinople rather than face the more perilous routes to the west, and this high vantage point reveals some-

Preceding pages: sailing in the centre of Stockholm; Riddarholmen and Gamla Stan with "Malardrottningen". **Left**, the Royal Guard. **Right**, Stockholm by balloon.

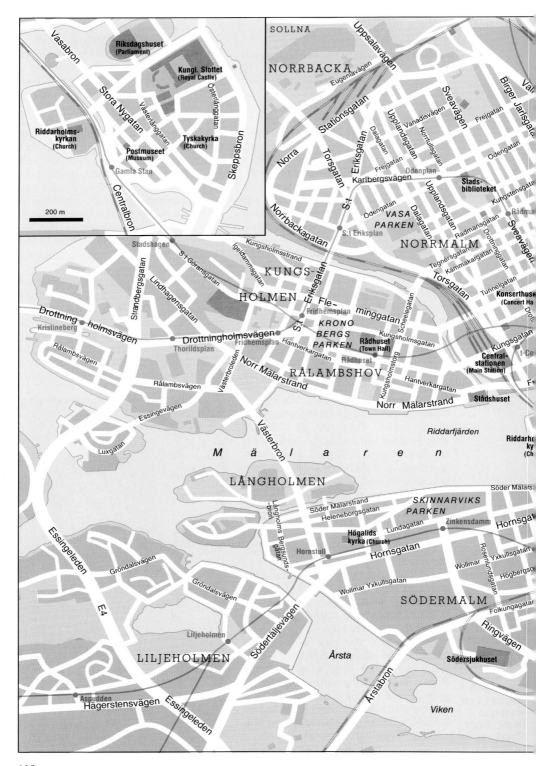

Inset map (Gamla Stan area):

Vasabron

Riddarholms-
kyrkan
(Church)

Stora Nygatan

Riksdagshuset
(Parliament)

Kungl. Slottet
(Royal Castle)

Västerlånggatan

Österlånggatan

Postmuseet
(Museum)

Tyskakyrka
(Church)

Gamla Stan

Centralbron

Skeppsbron

200 m

Main map:

SOLLNA

NORRBACKA

Uppsalavägen

Eugeniavägen

Stationsgatan

Sveavägen

Birger Jarlsgata

Val

Freijgatan

Upplandsgatan

Vanadisvägen

Norra

Torsgatan

S:t Eriksgatan

Dalagatan

Norrtullsgatan

Odengatan

Freijgatan

Odenplan

Karlbergsvägen

Stads-
biblioteket

Kungstensgata

Norrbackagatan

Odengatan

VASA
PARKEN

Dalagatan

Upplandsgatan

Rådmansgatan

Rådma

S:t Eriksplan

NORRMALM

Sveavägen

Stadshagen

S:t Göransgatan

Igeldammsgatan

Kungsholmsstrand

KUNGS-

Tegnérsgatan

Kammakargatan

Drottninggatan

Strandbergsgatan

Lindhagensgatan

HOLMEN

S:t Eriksgatan

Fle-

Torsgatan

Tunnelgatan

Konserthus
(Concert Ha

Fridhemsplan

minggatan

Scheelegatan

Drottning holmsvägen

Kristineberg

Drottningholmsvägen

Fridhemsplan

KRONO
BERGS
PARKEN

Kungsholmsgatan

Kungsgatan

Rålambsvägen

Thorildsplan

Hantverkargatan

Rådhuset
(Town Hall)

Central-
stationen
(Main Station)

Rålambsvägen

Norr Mälarstrand

Rådhuset

RÅLAMBSHOV

Kungsholmstorg

Hantverkargatan

Essingevägen

Luxgatan

Västerbroleden

Norr Mälarstrand

Stadshuset

Riddarfjärden

Riddarh
ky
(Ch

Essingeleden

E4

M ä l a r e n

LÅNGHOLMEN

Söder Mälars

Långholms
bron

Söder Mälarstrand

Heleneborgsgatan

SKINNARVIKS
PARKEN

Zinkensdamm

Hornsga

Långholms Bergsunds-
gatan

Lundagatan

Roslundsgatan

Yxkullsgatan

Gröndalsvägen

Högalids
kyrka (Church)

Hornstull

Hornsgatan

Wollmar

Högbergsg

Gröndalsvägen

Wollmar Yxkullsgatan

SÖDERMALM

Folkungagatar

Liljeholmen

Söertäljevägen

Årsta

Ringvägen

LILJEHOLMEN

Södersjukhuset

Aspudden

Hägerstensvägen

Essingeleden

Årstabron

Viken

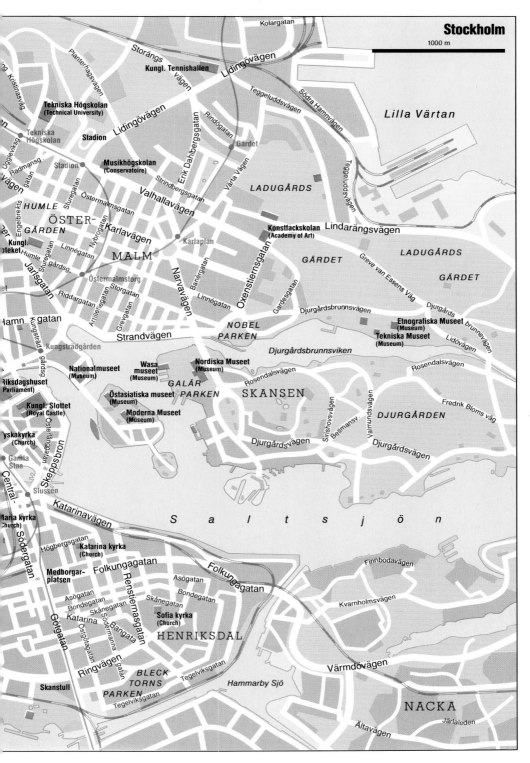

Stockholm

1000 m

Kolargatan

Storängs vägen

Kungl. Tennishallen

Lidingövägen

Teggeluddsvägen

Södra Hamnvägen

Lilla Värtan

Plantorhagsvägen

Kristinasväg

Tekniska Högskolan
(Technical University)

Lidingövägen

Rindögatan

Erik Dahlbergsgatan

Tekniska Högskolan

Stadion

Gärdet

Ugglevikss

Radmansg.

Stadion

Musikhögskolan
(Conservatoire)

Strindbergsgatan

Värta Vägen

LADUGÅRDS

Teggeluddsvägen

vägen

galan

Valhallavägen

HUMLE

ÖSTER-
GÅRDEN

Engelbrekts

Sturegatan

Östermalmsgatan

Nybrogatan

Karlavägen

Karlaplan

Konstfackskolan
(Academy of Art)

Lindarängsvägen

Linnégatan

Kungl.
oteket

Humle Sturegatan

MALM

Östermalmstorg

Narvavägen

Banergatan

Oxenstiernsgatan

GÄRDET

Gärdesgatan

Greve van Essens Väg

LADUGÅRDS

GÄRDET

Jarlsgatan

gårdsg.

Riddargatan

Storgatan

Linnégatan

Djurgårdsbrunnsvägen

Djurgårds

Etnografiska Museet
(Museum)

brunnsvägen

Hamn

gatan

Artillerigatan

Greygatan

**NOBEL
PARKEN**

Tekniska Museet
(Museum)

Lidövägen

Kungsträd

Kungsträdgården

Strandvägen

Djurgårdsbrunnsviken

Rosendalsvägen

Rosendalsvägen

gårdsg

Nationalmuseet
(Museum)

**Wasa
museet**
(Museum)

Nordiska Museet
(Museum)

SKANSEN

Fredrik Bloms väg

Riksdagshuset
(Parliament)

Östasiatiska museet
(Museum)

**GALÄR
PARKEN**

Sirishovsvägen

Bellmansv.

Valmundsvägen

DJURGÅRDEN

Kungl. Slottet
(Royal Castle)

Österlånggatan

Moderna Museet
(Museum)

Djurgårdsvägen

Djurgårdsvägen

yskakyrka
(Church)

Skeppsbron

Gamla
Stan

Central

Slussen

Katarinavägen

S a l t s j ö n

laria kyrka
:hurch)

Högbergsgatan

Katarina kyrka
(Church)

Folkungagatan

Folkungagatan

Finnbodavägen

Södergatan

**Medborgar-
platsen**

Folkungagatan

Asögatan

Rensternasgatan

Bondegatan

Kvarnholmsvägen

Asögatan

Katarina

Bondegatan

Skånegatan

Bangata

Södermanna gatan

Skånegatan

Sofia kyrka
(Church)

Götgatan

Ringvägen

Östgötagatan

HENRIKSDAL

Skanstull

**BLECK
TORNS
PARKEN**

Tegelviksgatan

Tegelviksgatan

Hammarby Sjö

Värmdövägen

NACKA

Järlaleden

Ältavägen

thing about modern Stockholm too. In this city life is still focussed on the water and, though nowadays Swedes may sail for pleasure rather than plunder, the affinity is as strong as ever.

Gamla Stan: Stockholm's history starts in Gamla Stan, the old town, still an almost perfect replica of a medieval city. Its narrow alleys and lanes follow the same curves along which the seamen of old carried their goods, and no-one restores a house or hotel in Gamla Stan without revealing the remains of an old fortified wall or an early workshop. Traces of even earlier times remain. At the corner between Prästgården and Kåkkbrinken, some bygone workmen has casually repaired the wall with a Viking runestone, probably the first stone that came to his hand.

These early years are shadowy, as is much early Swedish history, perhaps because the Vikings were too busy raiding and plundering to spend time writing more than the runes that decorate their memorials. As long ago as prehistory, this small stony islet between Lake Målaren and Saltsjön was used by fishermen and hunters but in the 12th century it became a base for German merchants from Lübeck who had begun to trade in iron, and an early king built a primitive watch tower.

The first mention of Stockholm is in 1252 when Birger Jarl, one of the regents in an age when kings died young and left infant heirs, built strong city walls and enlarged the original tower, which became the Tre Kronor because of the three golden crowns (still a national symbol) above the central tower. The present Royal Palace stands on the same site.

Stockholm was never a Hanseatic town, though one of the landmarks today is the graceful copper-clad spire and the bells of the **German Church** which at four-hourly intervals during the day alternate two hymn tunes. Other reminders of the Germans are **Tyska Brinken** (German Slope) and **Tyska Skolgränd** (German School Lane).

Today, Gamla Stan covers the original island of Stadsholmen, Riddarhol-

Gamla Stan's pedestrian streets.

men (the island of the knights and nobles), Helgeandsholmen which is entirely taken up by the Riksdag (Parliament) and the tiny blob of Strömsborg, all so close that it is sometimes difficult to realise you have crossed from one to another. The best place to start a tour is **Stortorget**, the centre of the original city, from which narrow streets fan out in all directions.

Medieval traders: Today, Stortorget is a peaceful square. In medieval times, it was a crowded, noisy place of trade, where German merchants, stallholders, craftsmen, and young servant girls and boys jostled and shouted. Along one side is **Borsen**, the old Stock Exchange building, and the modern Stock Exchange still occupies the ground floor. On the floor above, chandeliers that once looked down on the glittering Royal splendour of the New Year balls, now preside over the **Swedish Academy**'s weekly meetings. The Academy also meets here to elect the winners of the Nobel Prize for Literature.

In the cobbled square, people laze on benches or sit at one of the outdoor cafés, and it is hard to visualise that in 1520, the cobbles ran with blood during the Stockholm Bloodbath. Despite a guarantee of safety, the Danish King, Kristian II, known as The Tyrant, murdered 82 people, not only nobles but innocent civilians unlucky enough to have a shop or a business nearby. This gory incident triggered the demise of the Kalmar Union, which had united Sweden with Denmark and Norway. The following year, Sweden's first heroic king, Gustav Vasa, put an end to the Union and made Stockholm his capital.

More peaceful memories greet you if you follow **Köpmangatan** at one corner of the square and walk the short distance to **number 11**. Open the small door to the surprise of a gentle courtyard created in 1930 in what had been a dirty huddle of overcrowded buildings. The work was carried out as an example of successful restoration and renewal by the Skt. Erik Association, which has done so much to preserve Gamla Stan.

Back in the square, take the opposite

Stortorget, Gamla Stan.

A City And Its Symbol

From any part of Stockholm that lies south of Lake Mälaren, one building dominates the skyline: Stadshuset, the City Hall. Its position alone, on the water's edge of Ridderfjärden, would have guaranteed that it was spectacular, but the architect, Ragnar Östberg, was one of the founders of the National Romantic movement, which inspired many painters and writers in the early 20th century. This was his masterwork.

A massive square tower rises from one corner of the elegant central building, which is made of decorated brickwork, with an open-fronted portico facing the lake. The building is topped with smaller spires, domes and minarets, and the roofs are clad in a delicate green copper. An observation platform is set below the spire of the main tower under the shape of an old harbour light. Above it, gleam the Tre Kronor, the three golden crowns that symbolise the city.

Recently cleaned and polished, they capture and reflect the passing sun, especially in the early morning if you take one of the adventurous hot-air balloon journeys across the city. On this unique air voyage, which has become a popular "decade" birthday gift for Swedes, the crowns seem so close you feel you have only to lean down and touch them.

Stockholm's remarkable City Hall combines elements from Läckö Castle on the south shore of Lake Vänern, with the colonnades and grand staircase of the Blue Hall, inspired by the Doge's Palace in Venice, and the southern portico overlooking the lake, which could also be Venice.

Östberg began work in 1911 and devoted the next 12 years of his life to the City Hall. It was formally opened in 1923 and uses eight million bricks and 19 million gilded mosaic tiles, the latter mostly in the famous Golden Hall.

As you walk in, the effect is stunning. The walls are entirely clad in gilded mosaics and gleam like a Midas hoard, so bright that they seem to light up the marble floor. The window bays show events in Swedish history: the arrival of apostle Ansgar, the Battle of Brunkeberg in 1471,

and dramatic events in the reign of King Karl XII.

Twice a day the carillon on the main tower plays the battle tune that inspired the Swedes to the victory at Brunkeburg, under the nobleman Sten Sture. Brunkeburg was then a narrow gorge on a hillside, now levelled and part of modern Stockholm.

Many Swedish artists of the period took part in the interior decoration of Stadhuset, including Prince Eugen, whose large murals are displayed in the Prince's Gallery. The Oval, a reception area, is hung with the 17th-century Thureholm tapestries from Beauvais.

The gardens of the southern terrace hold a statue of the 15th-century Swedish patriot Engelbrekt, who championed the peasants in his native Dalarna and led a revolt which took his peasant army to the gates of Stockholm. Though Engelbrekt was eventually murdered, he lived on in popular memory as the first hero in the long struggle between people and nobility.

The tower is around 450 ft (105 metres) tall and there are fantastic views in every direction from the top. In the summer, the tower is open for public tours. If you can face the climb, however, you may get a surprise on the way up. But there is no need to use the stairs; there is also a lift. Also from the great tower, a procession of St. George and the Dragon emerges twice a day as the bells play the medieval tune *St Örjanslåten*.

The terrace above Lake Mälaren is full of flowers in summer and a pleasant place to stroll after a tour. Guided tours tell the story of the building and what goes on there and, when they aren't in use, you can also see the more functional rooms, such as the City Council Chamber, impressive enough to be a small parliament, with a public gallery. The long table of the session room of the Board of Administration expresses the dignity of the city, and civic notables of the past look down sternly from the walls.

The Nobel Dinner takes place in the City Hall and it may come as something of a surprise to hear that an ordinary member of the public can also hire the Golden Hall for a private function. But this is democratic Stockholm, where equality is as important as splendour.

**Left,
Stadshuset
(the City
Hall). Below,
Stadshuset's
Golden Hall.**

Källargränd opening and you come to **Storkyrkan** (the cathedral), which is both the parish church and the scene of many Royal occasions and coronations (at least until 1907, when Gustav V, the grandfather of the present king, decided against a formal coronation). This awesome Gothic cathedral is the oldest building in Gamla Stan, in part dating to the 12th century. It has high vaulted arches and sturdy pillars stripped back to their original red brick, and a magnificent organ. On a Saturday lunchtime, you can enjoy a recital, and then examine the church itself.

Storkyrkan's most famous statue is **St George and the Dragon**, the largest medieval monument in Scandinavia, a wooden sculpture carved by Bernt Notke in 1489, which somehow has retained its original colouring. Don't overlook the candelabra of various ages from the 17th century, or the plaque to the three generations of the Tessin family, who built the Royal Palace.

Outside the cathedral, overlooking Slottsbacken and the front of the Royal Palace is a statue of **Olaus Petri**, the father of the Swedish Reformation. He was at one time sentenced to death for an alleged plot against Gustav Vasa but was reprieved to become Sweden's first celebrated writer. He looks like a man whom it would be dangerous to cross.

If you feel like a rest between church and palace, cross over to the Finnish Church opposite the Palace gate. Behind it is **Bollhustäppan** (Ball Court Garden) This little courtyard has flowers, a small fountain and benches to welcome the weary sightseer and, most unexpectedly, Stockholm's smallest statue, a seated figure of a boy only a few inches high. In winter, he wears a little red, knitted hat, provided by an admirer to keep him warm.

Three generations: The present Royal Palace was built on the site of the old Tre Kronor Palace which burnt down in 1697, some say not without the help or at least a few prayers from the architect Nicodemus Tessin the Younger, who had already built a new northern wing. His father, Nicodemus the Elder, who

founded the three generations of Tessins, had been architect to the old Tre Kronor palace, and the grandson Carl Gustaf was responsible for supervising the completion of the new palace many years later.

The Palace claims 608 rooms, a cause of friendly rivalry between it and Buckingham Palace in London. Various suites are open to the public and the oldest interiors from the 1660s are in the north wing, which was not destroyed. The Palace is famous for its tapestries, both Gobelin and of Swedish design, but the most evocative room is **Oskar II's Writing Room** in the Bernadotte Apartments. This has been kept exactly as the King left it when he died in 1907; even his desk is untouched. It is a comfortable, homely room, full of 19th-century clutter and family photographs.

In the old vaults underneath the Palace are the **Crown Jewels**, including 12 royal crowns, orbs and sceptres and other pieces of jewellery. They are all immensely valuable and brilliantly lit so that they glow in the dim light of the vaults. Also below ground is the **Royal Armoury**, including the stuffed remains of the horse of Gustav II Adolf, who extended the Swedish domain as far south as Poland until his death on the battlefield of Lützen in Germany in 1632. It's easy to see from his armour what a big man he was.

At noon each day in summer, the Royal Guard marches across the bridge from Norrmalm, the modern area of Stockholm, to change the guard in the Palace yard, and two young sentries stand outside the main gate, trying to ignore attack by camera.

A noble island: To move over to **Riddarholmen**, go back past Storkyrkan and take Storkyrkobrinken down through Riddarhustorget, where you find **Riddarhuset** (the House of Nobility, once one of four parliamentary estates). It is arguably the most beautiful building in Gamla Stan, with two pavilions looking out across the water. Inside, the erstwhile power of the nobles is matched by the grandeur of the **Main Chamber**, where the nobles deliberated, watched from the ceiling by a

painting of Mother Svea, who symbolises Sweden.

In the evening and early morning, Riddarholmen is the silent island. Few live here and most of the fine buildings are Government offices. As you cross the bridge, straight ahead is **Riddarholm Church** with its latticework spire and mellow red brick. Hard to imagine that in the days of the Franciscans who built it, the walls were painted bright red. Though the church is now used only on special occasions, its interior is as noble as the name of the island because it holds almost all the graves of Swedish Royalty since Gustav II Adolf.

On a summer evening, before you turn back to the bustle of the main island, Riddarholmen is a pleasant place to stroll, past the quayside with a few pleasure boats and the graceful shape of the yacht, *Mälardrottningen*, once the luxury yacht of the American millionairess Barbara Hutton, now a waterborne hotel. There are no restaurants, cafés, or shops on this island, just slanting sun against the old buildings.

Many of Stockholm's old buildings are decorated with small statues from older times.

234

The idea of building the **Riksdag** (Parliament) on an island called Helgeandsholmen, The Holy Spirit, has a piquant charm. Do they speak with tongues on the chamber floor? The Riksdag and the old **Riksbank** (State Bank) now part of the Parliament buildings, cover almost the whole island, with the new Parliamentary extension, a copper clad, semi-circular structure attached at the second level and following the curves at one side of the old building. This has caused much argument in the city and certainly the new buildings, like a stranded spaceship, cannot be missed from any of the bridges to the west. Those in favour say the copper will soon turn to mellow green and match other roofs in the area and in its raw state it presents photographers with an interesting challenge.

Parts of the Parliament buildings are open to the public, and there is a public gallery. If you peer from the bridge at the main entrance, you will see another bridge below. Lean out far enough and you might catch a glimpse of a scurrying politician, using the walkway to get from one busy meeting to another.

Archaeological discovery: The refurbishment of the Riksdag led to a remarkable archaeological find and a new museum. When the builders began to excavate the Riksdag terrace to form an underground car park, they found layer upon layer of the past, including part of the 1530 medieval wall and the cellars of an apothecary shop. As good conservationist Swedes, the Parliamentarians immediately foreswore their claim to a car park and the new **Medieval Museum** incorporates the old wall and other treasures dug up during the excavations. It also has the town gallows.

Gamla Stan is not the place for a formal tour, rather a place for the browser, and it always reveals something you have not seen before. You could spend many happy days in and out of the criss-cross of small lanes, unexpected corners and courtyards, and along the two favourite shopping streets, **Österlånggatan** and **Västerlånggatan**, which lie just outside the

The Royal Palace Guard changes at noon each day.

line of the first city walls. This old town is alive and working and Stockholmers fight for the privilege of living in one of the tall houses that line the narrow streets, an endless parade of people, poking around the tiny shops for antiques, painting, craft jewellery, leather, glass, pottery, and other work.

Don't miss **Mårten Trotzigs gränd**, the narrowest street in Gamla Stan at the far end of Västerlånggatan. It is more a stairway than a lane, less than a metre wide, which you can clamber up to reach **Prästgatan**, a route that more than any follows the lie of the island.

There are many statues all over the old town and only a step or two from Mårten Trotzigs gränd, in **Järntorget**, is one not to miss. Evart Taube was a popular musician in the robust tradition of the Swedish troubadour, who died in 1976 much-loved and in his eighties. The statue is so alive that, at first glance, the unpretentious figure almost seems to be Taube himself, standing there ready to burst into song.

One of Gamla Stan's few museums is the **Postal Museum**, in Lilla Nygatan a couple of hundred metres from the Tunnelban station. The Postal Service has owned the gracious old building since 1720, and the collection includes the world's first stamp from 6 May 1840, as well as an early mail coach, a train sorting office, and postal boat, which all indicate the rigours of the postmen of the past in getting mail to Sweden's far-flung communities.

How Stockholm grew: Though it is not strictly part of Gamla Stan, you are so close at this southern end of the old town that it is worth detouring briefly at **Slussen**, where lake is divided from the salt water harbour by the big lock gates, for Stockholm's **City Museum**. Though Stockholm received no mention until the 13th century, the museum makes it clear that this strategic spot had been inhabited for many centuries before, and archaeologists are working against the clock to save many treasures before modern building techniques get at and destroy them.

Just as interesting are the exhibits

The Riksdag (Parliament) and its new extension.

which show the recent past and life down the recorded centuries and the early 20th-century photographic collections of the city as it was.

After the museum, it would be a pity not to make a quick trip up **Katerinahissen**, an old 19th-century lift rebuilt in 1935 that takes you to the heights of Södermalm, the next island south. At the top, you look down to one of Stockholm's outdoor markets, bright with the colour of fruit, vegetables and flowers which Swedes love, perhaps to counteract the darkness of their long winters. Here, too, you might catch a glimpse of a few Stockholm youngsters who have fallen for the craze for break-dancing and use the top platform to show off their skills.

Those footsore from discovering the hidden treasures of Gamla Stan should not forget that the old town also has a greater concentration of restaurants, jazz pubs, and cafés than anywhere else in the city. Many are in the same cellars where the merchants of old stored the exotic goods that came by sea. Today,

the restaurants also have food from many lands and, as you walk down the stone steps to a basement restaurant or sit at one of the many courtyard tables, history is still strongly in evidence.

Stockholm's playground: From Gamla Stan, it is just 10 minutes by boat across the harbour to the island of **Djurgården** but the two are worlds apart. Once a Royal deer park, parts of Djurgården are still in their natural state, with paths and woods where you may spot an old hunting lodge or pavilion through the trees. There are birds, both everyday and rare, and small creatures such as hares and the occasional deer. One good way to get around is to hire a bike at the bridge which forms the road entrance.

The advantage of the boat is that the 10-minute journey provides another angle on the city. To the right are the wharves where the big ferries leave for the Baltic, and to the left is **Kastellholmen** now a military base, topped by the Swedish flag on the fortress that gives it its name.

Behind this small island lies Skepp-

Strawberry time in a Stockholm street market.

sholmen. The sleek schooner moored off the island is the 100-year-old *af Chapman*, probably the world's most exotic youth hostel. Also on the island is one of Sweden's most controversial museums, the **Museum of Modern Art**, full of art that sounds and moves, plus modern masters such as Picasso, Dali, and Matisse.

Night music: Further away than Skeppsholmen is the waterfront of Blaisieholmen, where the big sumptuous building is one of Scandinavia's most famous hotels, the **Grand**. A little nearer is the **National Museum**, Sweden's national collection of art, with most of the great masters from 1500 to 1900. Rembrandt is particularly well represented. In summer the National Museum holds music concerts in the evening, a lovely setting for music.

As the ferry slides into the Djurgården quay, there is no mistaking that this as an island devoted to enjoyment. On the right past the quayside is **Grönalund**, an amusement park with its roots in the 18th century. Its thrill rides and ghost trains are strictly up to date and, in 1988, Grönalund acquired what they claim to be the most breathtaking roller coaster in the world. When it reaches the summit for its first terrifying plunge, you are in no doubt that they are right. The only thing to do is to open your mouth and scream.

Towards the centre of Djurgården, where the island rises in steps to a hill top, is **Skansen**, the oldest open-air museum in the world. In 1891, long before such things became fashionable, Artur Hazelius, who believed in practical education, decided to preserve the then familiar Swedish way of life, fast disappearing under a wave of Industrial Revolution that came late but fast to Scandinavia. He began to collect traditional buildings from different areas and today there are some 150, including an 18th-century church which is still in use for regular services and a popular place for weddings.

Many of the houses and workshops are grouped together to form the town quarter along a steep cobbled street.

Left, sailing ship "af Chapman", now a Stockholm youth hostel. **Below**, old merry-go-round at Grönalund.

They include authentic workshops where tradesmen once practised their craft. During the summer, many of the buildings revive their traditional use, when Skansen employs craftworkers to carry on the old skills. In the shoe-maker's house, where shoes have been made for more than 100 years, they still stitch and cut, and the glass-blowing workshop and the pottery demonstrate and sell their products. In the village shop, you can buy the old handmade sweets that few stores stock today. Two more not to miss are the tempting smells of the bakery, where Stockholmers queue up for their Sunday bread or the tasty, spicy, soft biscuits called *bullar*, and the horn and comb-maker, the last of his trade in the city, a gentle old man who delights in explaining his skills.

Skansen is not just a museum of life past; it also tries to give a picture of the Swedish countryside and wildlife to-day, so that you get a clearer view of an elk than you can hope for from a car, as the creature slips carefully back into the forest at dusk or dawn. This area, which is largely too informal and the sur-roundings too natural to be called a zoo, also holds a few more exotic beasts. Some are species once native but now extinct in Sweden, others such as mon-keys and elephants are there to please children, and there is also "Lill-Skansen," where children are allowed to handle and stroke small creatures.

Djurgården has music of many kinds, everything from chamber music in the old Skogaholm Manor at the heart of the island and nightly entertainment on the Great Stage in Grönalund, to rock con-certs in the open air and folk-dancing and special celebrations for Midsum-mer and other traditional festivals. Against the green of the hill, the tradi-tional costumes look as though they belong. If Skansen is a museum, it is a living museum. But though it was once a Royal Hunting Park, and still belongs to the Crown, hunting today is the pre-rogative of visitors who seek treasure in the island's museums and art galleries, for Djurgården is much more than just an outdoor playground.

Pop group "Treat" on the Great Stage at Grøönalund.

Bridal crowns: If you choose bus instead of boat and enter the island over the bridge from Strandvägen, the first museum you come to is the ornate building that houses the **Nordiska Museum**, which depicts Nordic life from the 16th century. It has peasant costumes, a special collection of bridal gowns and the traditional silver and gold crowns worn by Swedish brides, Lappland culture, folk art, and more, all planned to show how Swedes live and lived. A queue outside usually means a special exhibition, such as a parade of dress down the ages, popular on a winter Sunday afternoon.

Further on is the **Museum of Natural History** with animals, plants, fossils and minerals, a collection from the moon and special exhibits to show an aspect of current research, plus a popular Whale Hall. Not far from one entrance to Skansen is the **Biological Museum**, the first of its kind in the world, where Nordic animals are depicted against dioramas to create an illusion of their natural habitat. All these dioramas

were reproduced from works of one of Sweden's most distinguished nature painters, Bengt Liljefors.

The **Thiel Gallery** was designed by a popular architect of the time to house the collection of the banker Ernst Thiel. This is a marvellous range of pictures which include the Norwegian Edvard Munch, and Sweden's Anders Zorn, Carl Larsson, Gustav Fjaestad and Bengt Liljefors, who were all close friends and part of the National Romantic movement which spanned the late 19th and early 20th centuries. The gallery even has some pictures by the playwright August Strindberg, whose talent was multi-faceted.

In the early decades of the century, Thiel's gallery became a meeting place for the artists he had encouraged and befriended, poets, and writers. When Thiel went bankrupt in the 1920s, the city bought the gallery.

The second—and many say the most beautiful—gallery in the city is **Waldemarsudde**, the home of Prince Eugen, the "painter prince", brother to the late King Gustav V. He painted large, impressive landscapes. When the Prince died in 1947, he bequeathed his lovely home and garden as well as his collection, which includes many by Prince Eugen himself, to the nation. This gem of a gallery, looking south over Saltsjön, is not to be missed, not just for the pictures but for the charm of the house itself.

The third, the **Liljevalchs**, not far from the quay, is devoted largely to contemporary work and the Spring Exhibition is a must for aspiring artists.

Marine treasure: Almost impossible to miss is the huge, oddly shaped building that houses the *Wasa* **warship** which, in 1990, moves to a permanent museum on a wharf a few hundred metres north of its present home. The warship was built in the 1620s for the Thirty Years War, on the orders of Sweden's warrior king, Gustav II Adolf, in honour of the founder of his dynasty, Gustav Vasa. She was a magnificent ship, gold leaf on her poop and bow, her guns bronze, and decorated by 700 sculptures and carvings. In 1628, she set off from Stock-

Continuing the old ways in Skansen's village.

240

holm harbour on her maiden voyage, watched by King, court and people. With her gun ports open for the Royal salute, she was 1,300 tons of too, too solid oak. A sudden gust caught her, water flooded in through the gun ports, the ship heeled over and sank, drowning most of those on board.

There she lay until 1956, when a Swedish marine archaeologist, Anders Franzén, found her and spent the next years planning her recovery. In 1961, the hulk of the great ship broke the surface again, and the long process of restoration began. More than 24,000 objects have been salvaged from the sea-bed since: skeletons, sails, cannon, clothing, tools, coins, butter, rum and many everyday utensils. The marine archaeologists also found thousands of missing fragments large and small of the vessel herself, which were numbered and their positions recorded. Over the past 25 years, working inside her protective shell, the *Wasa* museum restorers have patiently pieced the ship together like a giant three-dimensional jigsaw, and now *Wasa* has regained her early splendour.

The fact that the *Vasa* sank so swiftly without fire or explosion meant that most objects were recovered and this valuable collection reveals a lot about the life of a 17th-century ship. To most people, these simple utensils that speak of everyday life are as fascinating as the structure and statuary—a sailor's kist (chest) which contains his pipe, his shoe-making kit and all the other necessities of a long voyage, as well as the admiral's cabin where 12 officers slept in no great comfort.

The *Wasa* project is part of Sweden's **National Maritime Museum** (Sjöhistoriska Museet) which has two other interesting vessels moored at piers not far from the *Wasa*. The *Sankt Erik* (1915) was Sweden's first large icebreaker and transformed winter trading in and out of the Baltic, The other is one of Sweden's last lightships, the *Finngrundet*, from 1903.

The main Maritime Museum itself, on Djurgårdsbrunnsvägen, on the other

Music for Bellmansdagen (Bellman's Day).

side of the narrow neck of water that separates Djurgården from the mainland, is not far from the road bridge. But, before you go there, detour to the **Museum of National Antiquities**, on Narvavägen, the wide road opposite the Djurgården Bridge. This museum is dedicated to Sweden's first and best known sailors, the Vikings. It is very realistic with a real Viking house, and shows not just the simple household implements which the Vikings used each day but the gold and silver treasures they made or brought back from far-off lands.

For the Maritime Museum, return to the bridge and with your back to Djurgården, turn right and continue past the Nobel Park and the English Church. The museum covers shipbuilding and merchant shipping as well as naval history. You can also follow the design stages in the building of a ship two centuries ago by one of Sweden's most famous naval architects, F.H. af Chapman, whose name is commemorated in the present-day schooner that houses the youth hostel.

At the end of an afternoon on a Royal island, with the sight of Viking gold, a Royal warship and a princely painter, nothing can bring you back to earth faster than the Maritime Museum's prosaic and long-dead lice lying in the crew's quarters of the merchant vessel *Hoppet*. They speak eloquently of the rough life that seamen endured as late as the turn of the century.

Strolling and shopping: It's anyone's guess what John Tobias Sergel might have thought of the huge illuminated obelisk, modern fountain and square that bears his name, and of the modern city around it. He was a neo-classical sculptor, famed in Rome, who returned to the cultured court of Gustav III. Sergel sculpted many statues for Gustav, including one of the king himself and another, *Oxenstierna and History*, to commemorate the early statesman Axel Oxenstierna.

The heart of this modern business and commercial area is not large but it sits somewhat uneasily with the rest. From **Sergelstorget** it is hard to miss the five

towering oblong office blocks on Sveavägen, which dominate the street and cast shadows over the other buildings. In fact, they are visible from every part of the city.

In the 1960s, Stockholm City Council, like so many others, succumbed heavily to the temptation to knock things down and build concrete and glass high-rise buildings, which are concentrated on Norrmalm's business area and around Central Station, where most of the big hotels stand today.

The destruction of many fine old buildings continued until it threatened **Kungsträdgården** (the King's Garden) with a famous statue of Karl XII on its southern side. At this point the Stockholmers had had enough. Normally placid and biddable, they mustered at the King's Garden, climbed the trees that were in danger of the axe, and swore that if the trees went so did the people. The City Fathers retreated and Kungsträdgården survives to soften the edges of the new buildings and harmonise with the older buildings that are

Decoration on the 17th-century warship Wasa.

left. This is the place to stroll or sit beside the fountains on a summer day and enjoy a coffee at its outdoor café. In winter, part of Kungsträdgården is flooded with water and becomes a popular ice rink, and the restaurant moves indoors.

On the modern side of Kungsträdgården, facing Hamngatan, is **Sverigehuset** (Sweden House) which has Stockholm's main tourist information centre on the ground floor. The centre can advise and book tours and other entertainment, sells the Stockholm card (Stockholmskortet) which provides free travel and entrance to many museums, and is the place to go for help. It has a small shop, and is the starting point for some city bus tours.

Also in Hamngatan in an early 20th-century private palace is one of Stockholm's most unusual museums, the **Hallwyl Museum**, a magpie collection of one person, Countess von Hallwyl, from her ornate piano, to china, beautiful furniture and personal knick-knacks.

Sergel mollified: Though Stockholm's modern area is not elegant, it is not large and Sergel might have been pleased that in summer people sit at the feet of his monument on the steps that lead to the lower level of his square and that many eager artists hold impromptu exhibitions of their work there. The lower level has become a meeting place where many congregate, some to talk, some to scan the protest posters and exhibitions against the injustices of the world, put up by refugee groups who have found a haven in Sweden.

The immigrant traders themselves have done much to bring variety and colour to city life. Part of the lower square is covered, with wide underground passageways leading off it to other streets in the modern city and here they spread out their wares on blankets. From bright hair-bands and sparkly, illuminated yo-yo's to jewellery or whatever else is the current fad, they are sold with all the gusto of a distant bazaar. In the background, you may hear the unexpected rhythms of South Amer-

Sergelstorget at the heart of modern Stockholm.

ica from one of the refugee groups, or the well-known tones of the old lady who has become a Stockholm landmark. Each afternoon, she sings hymns to the accompaniment of her harmonium. Whether she has converted many nobody knows, but she is one of the sounds of Stockholm.

On one side of Sergelstorget is **Kulturhuset**, a modern cultural centre, which was home to the Riksdag (parliament) during the building of the new wing of the Parliament building. Now it is a meeting place, talking shop and venue for lectures and entertainment for many Stockholmers.

From the lower level of the square, you can walk along one of the underground walkways (all well signed) to the lower entrance of **Gallerian**, a huge covered shopping arcade that stretches from Hamngatan right through to Jakobsgatan, just behind Gustav Adolfstorget and the Opera House. The covered arcade of Gallerian and the walkways from Sergelstorget to many of Stockholm's best stores are a boon

for winter shopping. Some of the major stores have frontages in Gallerian itself, others on the walkways.

At the far end of Gallerian is a little-known Stockholm treasure, the oldest auction room in the world, **Auktionsverket**, which has been in business since 1674. Everything from china to Chagall and large furniture to Larsson is crammed into the storerooms. Many items are small enough to carry, and make unusual Stockholm mementoes. To buy is easy: you just leave a bid in advance for the Wednesday and Saturday auctions, or you can take part in the big auction room yourself, no Swedish required.

Even if you do not care to bid, browsing among the showrooms sheds interesting light on Swedish homes, the way Swedes live, and what they keep or discard. The auction rooms are open six days a week and, if you stayed there long enough, eventually you would meet everyone in Stockholm.

Sweden's Harrods is **NK (Nordiska Kompaniet)** on Hamngatan (just oppo-

Students' can-can near Gärdet during Stockholm University's carnival.

site Sweden House) whose rooftop illuminated sign, constantly turning, is visible from far and wide in the city. NK sells everything from shoes to sports equipment, men and women's clothing to glass, pottery and silver, jewellery and perfume; its services range from optician to post office and travel agency, and you can get your sightseeing shoes soled and heeled when you come to collect the high-speed prints of your latest roll of film.

Find a bargain: Shopping in Sweden is rarely cheap but it is always good value. For a bargain, the words to look out for are *Rea*, which means sale, and *Extrapris*, which does not mean extra, but special low price.

Åhlens City, nicknamed "Ålle" (pronounced Olle) by Stockholmers, is on the corner of Sergelstorget and Drottningatan. It has a similar range and quality to NK and its supermarket food department is a sightseeing tour in itself. The third of this trio of stores is PUB, further along Drottningatan at Hötorget. PUB is lower-priced but the quality is excellent, something that you can take for granted in Swedish shops.

Drottninggatan (Queen's Street), an old street which leads directly through the Riksdagshuset and over the bridge from the Royal Palace, is one of Stockholm's main pedestrian ways, with multi-coloured flags strung between the buildings. In summer, it is full of casual crowds strolling in tee-shirts and shorts or sitting at one of the cafés that grow out on to the paving stones. Walking along its narrow length under the bright streamers is like making your way through a carnival.

National playwright: One small museum not to miss at Drottninggatan 85 is the **Blue Tower**, the top-storey flat where Sweden's greatest playwright, August Strindberg, spent his last years, and where in 1908 he wrote his last epic play, *The Great Highway*. Strindberg's taste in room furnishing followed his ideas for stage sets and the rooms are full of bright green, yellow and red. In contrast, the writer who so savagely satirised society's ills protected himself

South America musicians add colour and sound to central Stockholm.

THE WORLD'S LONGEST ART GALLERY

It's hard to understand what inspired the early Swedish engineering designers to cover the walls of Stockholm's underground railway with paintings at a time when every other country was lining its undergrounds with shiny, cream tiles. But it has made Stockholm's underground, Tunnelbanen, into much more than a mere transport system. Down the escalators is a whole unexpected world of caverns full of colour, texture, and shape.

Right from the start of building in the late 1940s, the designers decided to decorate all the stations and their foresight has given Stockholm the world's longest art gallery. Booking halls, ceilings, platforms and the walls behind the tracks offer an endless variety of styles and colours—all for the price of a ticket. Half of the 99 stations have paintings, sculptures, mosaics or engravings, and along the track walls are troglodyte vistas of green gardens, woods and flowers, water lilies, and geometric designs. More than 70 artists have contributed various forms of art.

T-Centralen, the hub of the network and, a station with many entrances, walking tunnels and escalators, became home to the first embellishments, and it still has more than anywhere else. In 1957, the first three were Egon Möller-Nielsen's constructed terrazzo sofas on the upper platform, and the track walls were decorated with white clinkers and figures in ceramic material, with glass prisms in varying colours and patterns, by three more artists. A year later, Tom Möller's tile decoration, *Goat*, appeared in Hammerbyhöjden (line 19).

Stockholmers argue about which is the best line for paintings, but the route out to Akalla (line 11) is a strong contender. The train leaves from T-Centralen's lower platform and to go down the second escalator is to enter a deep mysterious cave. The platform and tracks have been tunnelled out of natural stone, left in its rough-hewn form, and covered with huge blue leaf fronds on a white and blue background. The lighting emphasises the cave effect.

As you pass the various stations, also look at Västra Skogen with a 60-ft (18-metre) human profile in terrazzo, tile patterns, and cobblestones. But the high spot on this line must be Solna Centrum, which deserves a special stop. It has green hills and forests behind the rail tracks, silhouetted against red. The scene shows a man playing an accordion, and you can pick out a petrol station, an elk, an old-time aeroplane with a long trail behind it, a rural lorry clambering slowly up a hill road and many other intriguing elements. The longer you look, the more you find. This environmental theme was completed in 1975 by Karl-Olov Björk and Anders Åberg, and titled *Sweden in the 70s*.

On the other arm of this line (10), is Tensta, one of the larger immigrant communities with some 30 different nationalities represented. The paintings show a *Tribute to the Immigrants*. But many think the most interesting station on this line is Kungsträdgården, which has two very beautiful entrances. Other more unusual exhibits are the *Green Bird* sculpture at Rådsved, 23 ft (seven metres) above the platform (line 19), the scientific, engineering, and mathematical symbols of Tekniska Högskolan (the Technical High School) (lines 15 and 24), and—especially intriguing for children—the fantasy beetles in glass cases at Gärdet (lines 13 and 14). The theme *Women's Lib, The Peace, and Environment Movement* at Östermalmstorget (line 13, 14, 15, 24) shows how early the Swedes were interested in equality for women.

To the keen psychologist, these decorations might reveal more about Swedish society than the Swedes realise. In the early days, the titles were confident plain descriptions and the decorations sometimes functional. In the 1970s, they tended to themes of social consciousness, while the 1980s displayed a pictorial reality. *No use going to meet trouble half-way* is a photo-montage 315 ft (96 metres) long, picturing events in 20th-century Sweden by Larseric Vänerläf at Karlaplan (lines 13 and 14). At Vällingby (lines 17 and 18) Casimir Djuric has turned the platform pillars into giant trees.

What will Tunnelbanen and the decorations say next about Sweden in the 1990s?

against sunlight with Venetian blinds and heavy curtains. Even at the end of his life, Strindberg was astonishingly prolific, and he produced some 20 books in his four years in the Blue Tower. His study is as he left it. The wreath beside a photograph of his daughter Anne-Marie was presented to Strindberg on the first anniversary of the theatre he founded, the Intimate Theatre.

It's always interesting to work out what other people pay for food and **Hötorget** (and also **Östermalmstorget** in the next district east) has a huge food market. It has become a tourist attraction in its own right as well as the place Swedes shop for food. Here you can find Swedish delicacies such as elk steak and reindeer and the many varieties of Scandinavian cured herring.

Swedish design is world-renowned not just in beautiful objects but also in designer clothes for men and women. Wherever you go, either in the city centre or in Gamla Stan, you will never be far from shops selling crystal, china,

pottery and fur and the labels of well-known designers such as Gunilla Portén and Rhodi Heintz, on elegant, clean-cut clothes in many boutiques. In addition to Gamla Stan's antique shops, you might like to take Tunnelbanen south to **Slussen** station (five to 10 minutes) on Södermalm, once the great working class area of the city and a popular place for artists to live and work. The steep slope of Hornsgatan has a cluster of galleries and, if you start at the Galleri Origo, they will tell you about the past and present of Söder and suggest where and what you might buy.

Out of town: Several of the new satellite suburbs such as Kista, Täby, Vällingby, and Skärholmen have good shopping centres, and the one place not to be missed is the Skärholmen's Saturday and Sunday fleamarket in the basement of the Skärholmen Centre. It's as crowded as London's Portobello Road and the bargains are endless.

Also at Skärholmen is the headquarters of one of the world's biggest home-furnishing chains, IKEA. This is so

Left, part of wall painting at Solna Centrum underground station. **Below**, the modern suburb of Hallunda.

popular with visitors that on weekdays buses run from Sweden House to the shopping centre and back. Nor is there any need to carry the large wardrobe that caught your fancy back home on the plane with you: the company has 75 outlets worldwide and all you need is a catalogue.

What you do take home can benefit from Sweden's tax-free shopping scheme. The shops supply special receipts which you present at the airport or harbour and around 15 percent of the value-added tax is returned in a simple, quick process. Many shops will also send goods direct and, if you want to take a small gift to a Swede while you are in Stockholm, even the most ordinary supermarket will wrap it up specially with shiny paper and decoration to turn it into a very special present.

Islands by the thousand: It's a rare city that has 25,000 islands on its doorstep and 60 miles (100 km) of lake at its heart, but this is Stockholm's good fortune. Until the building of Tunnelbanen, boat was often the only way of getting around these great expanses of water, and boats are still part of Stockholm life.

To keep contact within the archipelago, Stockholm County Council's own shipping company, Waxholmbolaget, subsidises boat transport to all the inhabited islands, a valuable service for visitors who want to explore, as well as to the islanders themselves. The largest private company, Strömma Kanalbolaget, specialises mostly in Lake Mälaren, and there are various other touring vessels that ply lake and sea.

Between them, they provide a variety of craft from beautiful old coal-fired steamers to modern ferries, and excursions vary from brief introductory tours to day-long excursions and evening cruises with dinner, where they greet you with music and you dance your way gently through the islands.

Mälaren stretches for more than 60 miles (100 km) to the west, a lake of narrow straits, vast sweeping bays, with beaches and rocky shores. You sail out past the modern buildings on Norrmä-

"Humour" by K. Bejemark, a fun statue in Hamngatan.

larstrand but once the boat passes under the high arch of Västerbron, the shores change. On the left is the island of **Långholmen** and to the right a surprise. Right in the heart of this capital city is a bathing beach.

Smedsudden is only one of 15 similar beaches where people laze or swim, while the smooth rocks at the water's edge of many parts of the lake are strewn with lightly-clad sun-worshippers, taking advantage of the short, brilliant summer not far from their own front doors. At the weekend and in the evenings, the lake is dotted white with the sails of small boats.

Royal island: The most popular place to visit is **Drottningholm**, on **Lovön**, with its 17th-century Royal Palace, now the main home of the Royal Family who moved from Gamla Stan to provide their young family with a garden. In this they have certainly succeeded. Drottningholm, a smaller version of Versailles, looks out on to formal gardens of fountains, statues, flower beds, box hedges, and small dark trees, point-

ing upwards like green standing stones. The Palace was built by the energetic Tessin family headed by Nicodemus the Elder, and the gardens laid out by Nicodemus the Younger.

Although the Royal Family live there, much of the Palace is open and the 17th, 18th, and 19th-century interiors are magnificent. In the parkland is the Swedish version of Grand Trianon, the exotic pagoda roofs and ornamental balconies of the **Chinese Palace**. At the end of the 18th century, the courtiers of King Gustav III sunned themselves in the gardens of the Chinese Palace and played at rural life. The silk worms introduced to **Kanton**, a small village built next to the Chinese Palace, fared less well. The worms were no match for the frozen depths of a Swedish winter, thwarting the court's attempts to produce cheap silk.

But the island's greatest treasure is the 18th-century **Drottningholm Court Theatre**, opened in 1766 for Queen Louisa Ulrika, mother of Gustav III. Gustav's two great loves were the

The Stockholm archipelago provides endless sea and beach.

theatre and French culture—he wrote the language better than he wrote Swedish—and it is said that he would have much preferred to be an actor or playwright than king. But he was also a patriot, determined to turn Sweden's French theatre tradition into Swedish. He ejected the French actors from Drottningholm and replaced them with Swedes, and continued his aim of encouraging a Golden Age of the native arts.

Despite his enthusiasm for culture, Gustav's benevolent despotism was not popular with his unruly nobility. His assassination in 1792 at a masked ball inspired Verdi's *Un Ballo in Maschera*, a memorial Gustav himself might have approved of. On his death, the Court Theatre fell into disuse. Not until the 1920s was the building used again, after Professor Agne Beijer discovered it, complete and undamaged, just waiting for restoration. That unlikely chance makes it the oldest theatre in the world which still uses its original backdrops and stage machinery.

A guided tour alone of this beautiful little theatre, with the names of the different court officials still clear on their theatre seats, takes you back two centuries, but to attend a performance on a warm summer evening is magic from an earlier age. Not far from the theatre is a restaurant for an early supper, and you can easily return to Central Stockholm over the bridge by bus.

Island road: It is just as easy to reach Drottningholm by car or bus. Drottningholmsvägen starts at Fridhelmsplan on Kungsholmen (reached from Stadshuset via Hant Verkargatan). It leads straight out to the main Mälaren islands.

The first island is **Kärsön**, which in the 13th century was part of a rich religious order, Klara Cloister, through **Lovön** and Drottningholm, and then on to **Svartsjölandet** with its Castle and the Hillehög runestone carving. From there, the next island is **Ekerö**, an important trading centre in the fifth and sixth centuries; archaeologists are now excavating it. At the north end of the

Drottningholm Palace from Lake Mälaren.

island is Munsö Church, a "fortified church" used by the villagers in times of strife because it was usually the strongest building and the safest place to be.

Trade and church: Further west is **Björkö**, the site of Sweden's oldest city, **Birka**, though many others have laid claim to that title. In its heyday between A.D. 800 and 975, Birka was the trading centre for the 40,000 inhabitants of the rich Mälaren area, and the meeting point for traders from Russia and Arabia as well as from Central and Western Europe, at a time when the lake was still navigable from the Baltic.

This was also where Christianity came to Sweden, when Ansgar the Saxon missionary landed in the early part of the ninth century. Much of what is known about Birka's earliest days come from Ansgar's biography, *Vita Ansgarii*.

The **Ansgar chapel**, built in the l930s, commemorates the missionary. It is a simple red sandstone building with three sculptures by Carl Eldh, including one of Frideborg who is said to

be the first Birka woman to be baptised, and on the whitewashed walls by the altar several paintings by Olle Hjortzberg. The church is used regularly by different denominations and Ansgar's monument stands at the top of the hill which holds the remains of a fort. From the top you catch a glimpse of the **Adelö church** on the island opposite, a Royal estate in the days of Birka.

Almost nothing is left of Birka above ground, but many archaeological digs have revealed the past at sites which include the old town, and the "sacrificial stones". Sadly for Ansgar, the sheer numbers of pagan graves show that he was largely unsuccessful in converting the island, and Sweden had to wait a further 200 years for Christianity to take hold.

A guide meets the boat at Björkö which can only be reached by water and this gentle green island also has many excellent bathing beaches.

If you choose not to go ashore at Björkö, the boat carries on to **Strängnäs**, a pretty little town with a

The formal gardens at Drottningholm Palace.

cathedral, which is a good place to shop. There are also tours to other towns and castles on the lakeside. **Mariefred** is an idyllic small 18th-century town, with the mighty fortress of **Gripsholm Castle**. **Skokloster Castle** is a magnificent baroque castle and **Sigtuna** is one of Sweden's oldest cities, as well as the ancient capital of **Uppsala**, and its historic university. In some cases, you can chose to return by train.

Baltic gateway: To the east, the islands of the archipelago seem endless, almost as though every Stockholm family could have an isle of its own. A sense of freedom and distance begins the moment you start to skim through the skerries in a small boat or look down from the deck of a steamer.

Although now it is as easy to get there by bus, in summer take the boat to the island suburb of **Lidingö**, and **Millesgården**, the summer home of the sculptor, Carl Milles and his wife, the Austrian painter Olga Granner. Here, summer after summer, Milles patiently reproduced the statues that had made

him more famous in his adopted country of America than in Sweden, though you can see a fine specimen in front of the Concert Hall at Hötorget. The hallmark of Milles' work is his ability to make his figures seem almost to evade gravity. They soar and fly, and step lightly over water, emphasised by their position on terraces carved from the steep cliffs of the island which was once a peaceful small community, closely involved in Stockholm's artistic and intellectual life. Today, it is part of the city and looks directly across the water to wharfs and buildings but the view is still spectacular.

From here, the boat continues through the winding skerries to **Vaxholm**, to the northeast. The urban area of Vaxholm is very much the trading centre for the 60 or so islands in this group, with rail and train links to the mainland as well as the more leisurely boat, and car ferries to nearby islands. It is all part of an elaborate transport network that somehow manages to keep a remarkable number of islands in contact

Vaxholm Fortress in the Stockholm Archipelago.

with the city of Stockholm itself.

Tough sailors: Before the 1926 road connection to the city, Vaxholm depended on the local "oarswomen", a tough breed, and rowing still has a status all its own on the island. You can also sail, canoe and wind-surf, or swim from several good bathing beaches. Fishing for your own Baltic herring from the town's quayside is a popular early summer occupation but you could just sample them at lunch in the hotel near the harbour, or on one of the special Herring Picnics at **Vaxholm Fort**.

Vaxholm still has many traces of the mid-18th century, when the wealthier Stockholmers began to turn it into an ideal summer resort and built elegantly decorated wooden summer homes. The island already had a 16th-century fortress built under the supervision of King Gustav Vasa "in order that the archipelago and approaches to Stockholm may in no way be occupied by enemies and essential supplies thus hindered." It is now a museum. A walk round the town reveals the old **Saven Inn**, now offices,

And the parrot came too!

the **customs house**, whose inspector was once the most important man in town, the **battery** on the ramparts, and the **Homestead Museum** in a century-old fishing cottage.

The journey out to Vaxholm takes not much over an hour and is a pleasant introduction to the archipelago. Though these Waxholmbolaget boats are primarily designed to serve the islands, many have special day trips which allow you to stop off, spend a day on an island and wait for the steamer's return.

The islands divide roughly into three areas which run parallel to the mainland: first, the big inner islands, then a belt of smaller skerries and, far out to sea, the isolated outer isles surrounded by pale, clear shallows. Each one is different, some wooded, some with heather, some scorched bare by the sea winds, and others steeped in silence and solitude.

Two wheels: The bigger islands are ideal for cycling and you can arrange a special excursion to **Ljusterö**, an hour or so out from Vaxholm. Waiting for

you there are cycle, picnic box, a list of suggested routes and a map. In the evening, when you're aching in places you never knew you possessed, the steamer *SS Storskär* returns for the journey to Stockholm, a beautiful trip in the long Scandinavian evening, winding in and out of the islands.

A similar cycling trip to **Utö** in the southern part of the archipelago, reveals a hotel, restaurant, bakery, camping and bathing and, though central Sweden was the traditional home of the iron and copper industry in Sweden, Utö claims the oldest iron mine in Sweden, with a museum.

Many islands are rich in wildlife— elk and deer, otters, mink, fox, badger and the occasional lynx. Others are a haven for birds and birdwatchers, with the rare white-tailed eagle, gulls, ducks, many wading birds such as turnstones, and oyster-catchers, with seabirds perching on the yellow lichen-covered rocks, and swans by the battalion.

The further you go in the seaward skerries, the more peaceful and unchanged the islands become. In spring and summer many are beautiful with cowslips and wild pansies and orchids, and the scarlet of poppies.

Changing weather: These outer islands are not always easy to reach and the weather can be fickle, but they repay any difficulty in getting there. Three of the most beautiful are accessible from Stockholm.

Gällnö lies in the middle of the archipelago. It has a year-round population of farmers and you will find youth hostels and camping sites, which stipulate a maximum stay of two days, though it may be possible to stay longer. Waxholmbolaget boats serve Gällnö.

Svartlöga is also on the scheduled route, via Blidö towards the northern end of the archipelago, and you can combine it with a visit to nearby **Rödlöga**. Svartlöga has the only deciduous trees in the archipelago, and a small general store, open in summer, and there is excellent bathing near the quay.

Bullerö, just south of Sandhamn, is one of the remotest islands in the archipelago, part of a nature reserve that takes in some 900 islands, islets and skerries. An exhibition in an old studio on the island gives information about island culture and nature and you reach it by taxiboat from the inner island of Stävsnäs, or direct from Stockholm.

In all this remoteness, the bigger island of **Sandhamn** is a surprise, ideal for a short stay or a day excursion, which leaves at 9 a.m. For, though Sandhamn is on the outer edge of the archipelago, the village is a lively place with a restaurant and museum and a large harbour stuffed with the masts of visiting boats. It is the headquarters of the Royal Stockholm Yacht Club.

Despite the influx, which swells the island's winter population of around 100 by several thousand, on this island you feel you have really left the land behind. Sandhamn is part of the Baltic, and the island helps to explain what it is that from early times made the Swedes a maritime race, and fires their present-day ambitions for a boat…and a star to steer her by.

Below, many islands of the archipelago are rich in wildlife. Right, winter in the Stockholm Archipelago.

AROUND STOCKHOLM

Three districts—Uppland, Södermanland and Västmanland—surround Stockholm. Together they stretch from the ragged Baltic coastline of bays, inlets and islets to the thousands of lakes and streams glinting in the green forests of the interior. In the centre are Lake Mälaren's waterways linking the districts and the capital with ribbons of water and dozens of white, chugging lake steamers. Along the banks rise castles, manors and palaces from 500 years of Swedish history and architecture.

This is the heart of Sweden today, a synopsis of the country's past, its natural wonders and its cultural riches. Its wealth stems from the area's mineral deposits that provided the iron for the Eiffel Tower and the copper for the roofs of Versailles. Sweden's excellent road system and fine-mesh network of ferries and cruise ships, make the riches of the region easily accessible.

Uppland culture: Head north from Stockholm into the plain of Uppland and, where the sea meets the forest, you find **Sigtuna**, Sweden's oldest town. In the 11th century this was the commercial centre for the Svea and Vandal tribes. Merchant ships from as far away as Asia dropped anchor here. Monasteries and abbeys competed with one another in building the most glorious churches in town.

Today, Sigtuna is a sleepy little village on the edge of the sea, with crooked lanes and quaint, wooden houses and a miniature town hall. The ruins of the medieval monasteries provide a cultural focus, as do the summer evening concerts at the gazebo on the green.

Skokloster, a bit farther up the road, is what a castle is supposed to be—imposing, imperious, towered and abundantly endowed. This is the family seat of the Wrangles, great baroque lords who ruled over most of northern Europe. Their descendants live comfortably in "the old castle" and this majestic pile is open to the public. The collection of weapons, paintings, anthropologia, textiles and books from the early 1600s are among the best to be found.

Less than an hour's drive north of Stockholm on the E4, lies **Uppsala**, Sweden's ancient capital, last bastion of heathenism and seat of one of Europe's greatest universities. At first glance, Uppsala appears to be the typical university town, a jumble of charming, eccentric old buildings strewn along the Furu River and populated by a rag-tag of students.

But appearances can be deceiving. This is the birthplace of Ingmar Bergman and the setting for his film *Fanny and Alexander*. Visit the town on the last day of April for a rousting *Sista April*, with the students decked in evening dress and white "student caps"—the size, shape and tassle of which tells all about the wearer.

An early morning speech by the King from the balcony of the university library starts the day's fun with a stampede down university hill by the ele-

gantly-dressed student body. The herd head directly for the beer barrels set up in the halls of the 16th and 17th-century palaces called *nationer* (student unions).

The town is also an Episcopal See with the largest **Gothic cathedral** in Scandinavia. Its vaults, from 1435, house the shrine of Saint Erik, a king and the patron of Sweden, as well as the graves of other early monarchs, bishops, generals and a philosopher or two. Emanual Swedenborg lies here in an enormous red granite sarcophagus containing two skulls. One is his own, recently reunited with its body following an auction of anthropological relics in London. The other skull belongs to an executed sailor who did stand-in duty for Swedenborg's cranium during its centuries-long museum work. The cathedral treasury is remarkable for its textiles which include cloth-of-gold ecclesiastical robes and medieval verdure tapestries.

Just across the road is the **Gustavianum**, an ancient, onion-domed edifice

housing a 17th-century anatomical theatre built for the Renaissance genius Olof Rudbeck. Across the town's lush parks and greens rises **Uppsala Castle**, a typically squat, dominating brick fortress from the days of the Vasa Dynasty. Its magnificent halls were the venue of the abidication of imperious Queen Kristina who preferred exile in Rome to "ruling a country of barbarians." She may have been right about that. The University's dazzling collection of ancient manuscripts, such as the sixth-century *Codex Argenteus* (Silver Bible), are booty plucked from war-ravaged Prague by her father's troops.

Father of Botany: Another university genius from Uppsala was professor Carl von Linnaeus (1707-1778), the father of our system of botanical classification. His residence in the heart of town is now a museum adjoining his own botanical gardens with 1,600 different exotic plants set out to Linnaeus' plan. Slightly southeast of town in Linnaeus's last home, **Hammarby Farm**, a charming 18th-century cross between manor and

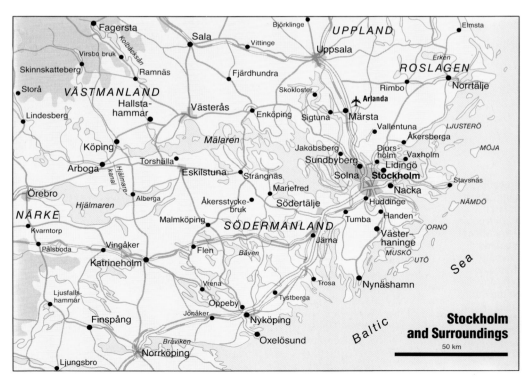

cottage. Family heirlooms and carefully-tended flower beds give Hammarby a homey, lived-in appeal.

A few minutes north of the town lies **Old Uppsala** (Gamle Uppsala) the fifth-century bastion of the Yngling dynasty. The three huge grave mounds of kings Aun, Egil and Adils (who are described in the opening passages of *Beowulf*) dominate the evocative grave fields surrounding Gamle Uppsala's parish church. This strange brick construction replaced Scandinavia's last heathen temple—"a wooden house of sin, spouting dragon heads from its many eaves and held together athwart with chains of massive gold to keep bound the evil of fork-bearded Thor and one-eyed Odin and dreadful Frej whose idols reigned within."

By boat: But why drive when the ferry from Stockholm's city hall steams all the way to Uppsala? Steamers stop at all places mentioned.

A bit farther afield lies **Örbyhus Castle**, looking every bit the ancient fortress. Another King Erik (XIV) was purportedly poisoned with pea soup while held here in house-arrest by his power-hungry brother. Poor Erik's Renaissance suite is preserved, but the rest of the castle has been rebuilt many times since the 1590s and is now a splendid baroque palace. In the grounds are a "Turkish" orangerie and stables and a spreading English park.

At **Älvkarleby**, the Dalälven tumbles into the Baltic over stunningly beautiful cliffs renowned as early as the 12th century for excellent salmon fishing. Despite a latter-day power station, the salmon still run thick here. There's an angling museum and a State game-fish research centre and a hatchery.

Furuvik has the region's largest amusement park, with a circus, ghosts' castle and other attractions. Gardens offer sites for picnics, a cafeteria and camping facilities. Just outside the county boundary is **Gävle**, this corner of Uppland's main centre for entertainment and shopping. The old town is a knot of twisting lanes with wooden gingerbread houses from the past two

The old church at Gamle Uppsala.

centuries. The Swedish Railway Museum has collected here some remarkable vintage steam locomotives and narrow-gauge rolling stock.

Out on the edge of the Baltic is **Bönan**, a fishing village famous for its *böckling* (smoked Baltic herring). You will smell it smoking before you see town. Try the village's excellent (and only) restaurant with its Baltic panorama and kaleidoscopic *smörgåsbord*. There is a pilot's museum and camping site on the beach.

Take the road marked 272 from **Gävle** or **Sandviken** and head for **Oslättfors Bruk**. The village church stands with its feet in the water and the gingerbread houses are surrounded by the deep green of Gästrikland's forests. Nature trails abound.

At **Norrtälje** you can buy herring and salmon in the marketplace or visit the **Humour Museum**. The **Roslags Museum** gives a good idea of life gone by in this island world. Try the nearby Wallinska Farm for more heritage.

On a spit of land sticking even farther into the Baltic is **Grisslehamm**, the nearest point to Finland's Åland Islands. Boats can be hired here and fresh-smoked whitefish is the speciality in the fishermen's huts.

Neighbouring **Osthammar** and **Öregrund** are summer retreats. Much of their 18th-century architecture is preserved. Visit the Gammelhus open-air heritage museum and narrow Tullports Street or simply stretch out on a warm, wave washed stone.

Iron prosperity: Sweden grew rich in the 17th and 18th centuries on its iron ore. Scots and Belgian Walloons emigrated to this area of Sweden to found thriving forges, smelting ovens and dynasties. Their estates, actually small foundry villages (called *bruk*) are found here where forest, swift streams and the Baltic supplied the right conditions for smelting metal.

Forsmark's manor house dating from the 1570s and its many outbuildings no longer produce cannons and ploughshares. The site is now a nuclear power station set among forested is-

Skokloster, family seat of the Wrangles family.

lands. But the inn still serves specialities from the heyday of the iron masters.

Nearby **Österbybruk** is the oldest iron foundry in Uppland, dating from 1443. The original Walloon forge (the last of its kind) is preserved and open to the public. The manor house gardens and stables are interesting as is the exhibition of Bruno Liljefors' impressionistic hunt scenes in the main house.

Wealthy **Lövstabruk** was Sweden's largest iron producer in the 1600s. The foundry street is immaculately kept and gives a resounding idea of the hierarchy of *bruk* society. The villagers—that is, the shopkeepers, foundrymen, various mongers and the priest—resided in small, uniform bungalows, while directly across the street stretched the iron master's French *parterres* and, in the distance, his manor house. Tours are conducted here by the residing family's art historians.

The gently shelving bay at **Rullsand** offers Uppland's best sandy beaches. Windsurfing is good near the mouth of the **Dalälven**.

South to Sodermanland: Natives of Norrköping, on the E4 south of Stockholm, call their city the "Paris of the North", alluding to its tree-lined avenues, outdoor café society, trams and elegant architecture. The "**Norrköping à la Carte**" is the city discount card that gets you in everywhere, including **Kolmården Zoo**. This is Scandinavia's wild safari, natural habitat and amusement park supreme.

Nearby flows the Göta Canal with its attractive cruise boats. A bit to the north is **Reijmyre Glassworks**, the second oldest glass furnace in the country. Visitors are welcome to watch the glassblowers at work. The "seconds" shop is nothing less than sensational.

A bit farther along route 55 is **Julita Manor** on the shores of Lake Mälar. The public is welcome in the Manor's imposing salons and typically Swedish halls or in the stable's cafeteria.

Next stop are **Malmköping's** vintage vehicles at the **Tramway Museum**, **Military Vehicle Museum** and the **Machine Museum**, with real steamrol-

Living near the water, Gräsö, Uppland.

lers, traction engines and road maintenance vehicles. Outside the town lies the **Moors at Malmahed**, with its military museum.

The road continues to criss-cross Lake Mälaren's bays and inlets on the way to **Strängnäs**, a charming small town dominated by a magnificent Gothic cathedral. The church's altar screens are in themselves worth a detour. Next to the church at **Boglösa**, on the opposite banks of the lake, are hundreds of **rock carvings** dating from the Bronze Age. The church museum will explain the symbols and the mythology.

Medieval mythology can be seen on the ceilings of **Härkeberga Church**, where Albertus Pictor, an ambulating vault painter in the 1400s recorded the lives and hopes of the parishioners. Next stop is Sweden's longest vintage railway, the **Lännakatten**, linking Länna with Uppsala.

At the western end of Lake Hjälmaren lies bustling **Örebro**, capital of Västmanland and mountainous Bergslagen. This was where Swedish steel was born. The forests gave fuel, the rushing rivers powered the trip hammers and the lakes provided cheap transport forthe swords, cannons and cast-iron building materials produced by family-run forges. **Lilla Nora**, a picturesque village of wooden houses, perfectly preserves the feel of the old days in its shops and tea houses.

Old Stråssa Mine is now open to visitors who are taken below earth in the original mining carts. At Pershyttan and Löa, metallurgy is still practised in the old manner. The Manor at **Siggebo-hyttan** gives a taste of the opulent life of the iron-masters in Victorian days.

Victorian fun, in all its former glory, is waiting in **Grythyttan Inn**, a venerable (dating from the 1640s) dispenser of delectable victuals. Under the baleful painted eyes of Catherine the Great and Queen Kristina, the inn's guests are encouraged to hold dance *soirées*, polka to brass quintets and tell ghost stories in the wine caverns. Grythyttan is Bergslagen in essence.

Start at the west end of Lake Mälaren

SS Mariefred on Lake Mälaren, often the easiest way to get around.

at splendid, baroque **Strömholm Castle** and Equestrian Centre. This former royal residence is open for visitors as is its riding and training centre—the best in the country. The carriage museum, shop and Stenköket restaurant adjoin the castle and nearby are the **Kolbäck River and Strömholm Canal** water sports areas.

On the next peninsula rises **Tidö Castle**, the 1625 home of Axel Oxenstierna, a regent of Sweden and feared warrior. The present owners have converted part of their home into a toy museum with 35,000 exhibits. Tidö also has a fascinating door collection. The wooded grounds offer a deer park with plenty of deer, and an inn.

On a picturesque inlet of the lake is **Västerås**, a 1,000-year old settlement boasting a cathedral from the 13th century (don't miss the **tomb of King Erik XIV**), a fortress of the same vintage and, at **Anundshög**, Sweden's largest burial mounds and ship tumuli dating from the Iron Age and Viking times. The harbour here is one of the lake region's largest for pleasure craft, ferries run to the capital and to Elba—an island retreat.

Camping sites: Engsö Castle might date from the 13th century but it has up-to-date facilities for hiking, swimming, camping, canoeing and fishing. The locals smoke perch and pike which can be eaten in the castle.

Campers can try **Härjarö Reserve**, on yet another spit of land jutting into the lake. On the opposite shore lies idyllic **Mariefred** and **Gripsholm Castle**. This is a lazy, summer lake town, with enough outdoor cafés and restaurants to suit all tastes from hamburgers to Dover soles.

The impressive pile of the castle protects the royal portrait collections and a marvellous theatre from the late 1700s. Best of all is the architecture of this fortress, begun in the 1370s and continually up-dated. Around the edge of the moat is a collection of rune stones—flat rocks carved in the deepest Dark Ages with serpents, ships and magic inscriptions in the runic alphabet.

Veteran car rally at Mariefred.

DALARNA—THE FOLKLORE COUNTY

There's nothing very Swedish about the landscape of **Dalarna** when you approach it from the south. The train which started life as an express in Stockholm trundles lazily through fertile green farmlands which could easily be England and bear no resemblance to the soulless forests of Småland or the endless tundra which starts only a few hundred miles to the north.

But first impressions can be misleading. Not far away from southern Dalarna you start getting into forest zones again and, indeed, two-thirds of the province is afforested. At the northern extremity of Dalarna is the deceptively gentle start of the mountain range which marches north, gaining height all the time until it culminates in the snow-topped peaks of the Kebnekajse range in Lappland.

So Dalarna is really a transition zone between the softer landscapes of southern Sweden and the more dramatic but harsher landscapes of the north. It is even divided within itself between the more densely-populated area south and east of Lake Siljan (dense by Swedish standards, that is) and the relatively uninhabited zones to the north and west of the lake.

Dalarna is sometimes called "The Heart of Sweden", which is not accurate in the pedantic geographical sense (that distinction goes to Medelpad, 100 miles or so further north), but it is probably more typically Swedish than any other part of the country.

Folklore and festivals: The advertising copywriters have dubbed Dalarna "The Folklore District"—an accurate description because the old folk traditions remain an important part of everyday life and are not just recycled for the benefit of the tourists. Many of the locals still dress in their traditional regional costumes for important festivals like Midsummer, and the *spelmansstämmor*—folk-music festivals dominated by the fiddle—are popular events in the summer.

But the first impressions of Dalarna as a rural area are wholly misleading. The provincial capital, **Falun**, has been a centre of industry for probably 1,000 years, and the **Bergslagen** area in the south has been a noted centre for mining for several hundred years.

The Bergslagen district covers not just Dalarna but also parts of **Värmland** and **Västmanland** and is worth some exploration by anyone interested in industrial archaeology. The more promising sites can be tracked down from the map when you see suffixes like *gruva* or *berg*, which indicate where iron ore was mined, or *hytta*, indicating where the ore was processed.

Near Ludvika is **Grängesberg**, where a large iron-ore mining complex—still worked today—and the railway serving it were financed by capital from the City of London in the 19th century. Steam enthusiasts will not want to miss the **Railway Museum** with its vintage locomotives which used to handle the iron-ore trains. In **Ludvika** itself, where iron-ore mining

LAKE SILJAN

Legend has it that Siljan, the huge lake in the centre of Dalarna, was formed when a giant meteorite crashed to earth 360 million years ago. Why one out of some 6,000 lakes in Dalarna should have been singled out for the meteoric treatment isn't quite clear, but at all events it was a bull's-eye shot: Siljan is right in the centre of the province and is something of a symbol for the local folklore traditions.

Some of Sweden's most typical Midsummer celebrations are held at the many small villages round the lake, notably at Rättvik, where the long "church-boats" bring hundreds of villagers to church for the annual service, dressed in their traditional local costumes. Rättvik's church, right by the lake-shore, is a magnificent building and is huge in relation to the comparatively small size of the village. Parts of it date from the 13th century, but the most attractive features for many visitors are the folk-art paintings showing Biblical scenes in a Dalarna setting, with Old Testament prophets dressed in long frock-coats and tall hats.

Further along the north shore of Siljan, as you approach Mora, is the small village of Nusnäs, headquarters for the production of the traditional brightly-painted Dalarna wood-carved horses

which became almost a Swedish national symbol after they were shown at the New York World Exhibition in 1939. The Dalarna horse is a traditional local craft but they have been in "mass" production in Nusnäs only since 1928. You can watch the horses being made and painted and, naturally, buy one to take home.

Mora is a pleasant small lakeside town which even has its own airport. It is best known as the home of the Swedish artist Anders Zorn, who was a close friend of another Dalarna artist, Carl Larsson. But Zorn's paintings are rather harsher than those of Larsson, whose works usually reflect family life. Mora has a museum devoted to Zorn's work and you can also visit his house and studio. It's not difficult to deduce that he was a chain-smoker when you see the hundreds of burn-marks all over the studio floor.

Heading down the west side of the lake, it is worth making a detour to the island of Sollerön, which is claimed to have the sunniest and warmest climate in the Siljan region. The island is one of the places where the Siljan church-boats (direct descendants of the Viking longships) are still constructed. Sollerön also has some remarkable Viking graves, an elegant 18th-century church and an excellent handicrafts centre.

Nearby, back on the "mainland", is an excellent mountain-top viewpoint, Gesundaberget, which has a spectacular view of the lake. On the slopes of Gesundaberget is a relatively new tourist attraction, Santaworld, aimed at the children and presumably built to rival a similar establishment in Finland. The kids can meet Santa and place their orders for Christmas as well as seeing his animals—including the rare musk-ox—and the workshops where all the toys are made.

Further down the west side of the lake is the strategically-sited peninsula of Siljansnäs, which has a well laid-out self-catering village and a tourist hotel with plenty of sporting facilities. There are also two old villages, Alvik and Almo, with some beautifully-preserved wooden buildings, some dating back to the 17th century.

Leksand, at the southern tip of Siljan, is a bustling little community with a population of about 4,500 and the centre for many cultural attractions in summer, including a traditional mystery play, *Himlaspelet*, which is performed every year in an open-air theatre. Leksand also has one of Dalarna's oldest museums as well as a new cultural centre, which together provide a good interpretation of the local folk culture.

One of the best-known resorts on Siljan is the village of Tällberg, some seven miles (11 km) from Leksand. Its population of about 500 is more than doubled in the holiday season by the visitors who fill its 750-plus hotel beds.

Tällberg is a typical Dalarna village, complete with its maypole and its many timber buildings. It is sited on a slope which rises up gently from Siljan, and a quiet stroll down to the lakeside at sunset is as good a way to round off the day as you'll find anywhere in Sweden.

started in the 16th century, there is a well-preserved mine-owner's manor-house with a **mining museum** whose exhibits include a large water-wheel which has become the town's symbol.

Making money: On the approach to Dalarna from the southeast, the first major town is **Avesta**, another centre with a long industrial tradition dating back to the 14th century. It was once the home of the Swedish Mint and there is a **Mint Museum** containing what is claimed to be the world's largest copper coin, weighing 43 lb (20 kg) and dating back to 1644.

Hedemora claims to be the oldest town in Dalarna, with a charter dating to 1459 and its privileges as a market town go back even earlier than that, while parts of the church are 13th century. The locals have devised **Husby-ringen**, a 35-mile "museum trail" which you can take by car through the area northeast of the town to see a number of industrial archaeology sites.

Continuing northwest, **Säter** is claimed to be one of the seven best-preserved wooden towns in Sweden. But compared with Hedemora it is quite an upstart, with a town charter going back to 1642.

Falun is something special when it comes to industrial history. It is the headquarters of Stora, the fairly new corporate name for Stora Kopparberg (The Great Copper Mountain), the oldest company in the world with a history going back at least to 1288. Falun's main claim to fame for the past 300 years has been a huge hole in the ground which was formed in 1687 when the whole copper mine caved in. No one was killed, as it happened, because it was Midsummer and all the miners were carousing, but production never returned to previous levels.

In fact, Stora Kopparberg wanted to close down the mine in the 1880s, but gold was discovered in the workings and is still mined today, along with lead, zinc and the original copper-ore. An interesting by-product is the red ochre which forms the basis for the distinctive paint which is used on buildings not just in Dalarna but over much of the rest of Sweden as well. Anyone visiting Falun should certainly don a miner's helmet and boots and take one of the guided tours down into the old mine workings.

Just outside Falun is **Sundborn**, a picturesque small village which was the home of a much-loved Swedish artist, Carl Larsson, in the early part of this century. The house, by the side of a small lake, has been authentically pre-served and is open for conducted tours—by one of the artist's descen-dants if you are lucky. Larsson's paint-ings reflect his happy family life and were strongly influenced by the local Dalarna folk-art traditions.

Longest ski race: Another route to the Norwegian border passes through **Sälen**, the starting point for a 53-mile cross-country skiing race to Mora, the *Vasaloppet*, held in March each year to commemorate King Gustav Vasa's flight from his enemies in the 16th century. Each year the race attracts more than 10,000 competitors, who in the past have included the present King, Carl XVI Gustav.

Left, Mid-summer symbols at Lake Siljan.

Dalarna

THE SWEDISH KLONDIKE

The jewel in the crown of Swedish mining history is **Falun**, the great copper centre close on 1,000 years old. Its 17-th century heyday coincided with Sweden's period as a great power. The intrepid traveller and botanist Linnaeus described the mine—Falu Gruva—as "Sweden's greatest wonder, but as terrible as hell." At its peak, it produced two-thirds of the world's copper.

The great pit is open to the public. It is 325 ft (99 metres) deep and 1,300 ft (396 metres) wide. Its present shape is the result of a massive cave-in in 1687 when galleries and chambers collapsed to a depth of 1,000 ft (304 metres). The mine was closed to the public in 1914 but reopened a few years ago.

Visitors have to put on Wellington boots, waterproof capes and safety helmets before they set off in the lift for the 180-ft (55-metre) descent into the mine. There, a tunnel or drift leads to the oldest part of the workings, the Creutz shaft. This was opened in 1662 and is 680 ft (207 metres) deep. All the shafts, drifts, and chambers have names, such as the Christmas Gift, discovered at Christmas, or the General Peace, named after the shortlived peace treaty between Britain and France in 1801.

There must have been little peace in that early mine when men scraped out copper with inadequate picks, frail ropes, and flickering torches against the black of that great cavern. As you walk round its galleries and shafts, dim and eerie even with electric light, the overwhelming feeling is one of awe for the achievements of those long ago miners.

Copper Plus: Next to the Great Pit is the old 1882 wire rolling mill and the Stora Kopparberg museum which has an outstanding collection of exhibits of the industrial past. Mining is the dominant but not the only industry which comes under the term "industrial archaeology" in Sweden: it also embraces shipbuilding, railways, textile and forestry, but people like mining best.

A continuing tradition, metalworking today.

The heart of Sweden's mining country was a broad swathe across the centre of Sweden, from east to west, and this is where you will find the majority of the country's industrial archaeological treasures. The catalyst for all this was the 17th-century discovery of minerals and the combination of water power and timber (for charcoal) which led to furious activity. Once it had peaked, mining slowly dimished, although the manufacture of steel and other metals continued, largely with the use of imported ores and powered by hydro-electricity. Today, large-scale mining is restricted to the far north.

Copper was not the only treasure in the ground around Falun. At **Korså Bruk**, 21 miles (34 km) to the east is a Lancashire forge, with its water wheels and hammers, now an industrial monument. The Swedes prized iron ore out of the ground at Vintjärn and you can follow the **Malmensväg**, the long route taken by the iron to the blast furnace at **Ågs Bruk**. After that, the iron moved over the Järnetsväg (Iron Way) to the forges at Korså.

The biggest mining centre was in Bergslagen which lies to the south of Falun. Here, mining flourished for over 600 years as a major industry and at **Långban**, more than 300 different minerals have been discovered—the most abundant source in the world. Långban has a preserved mining village with mine shafts, a blast furnace (built in 1855) and a mineral museum.

Silver too: There are remains of old mines throughout this area—at Mörkhult, Gåsgruvan, Högbbergsfället, Aggruavan and the old silver mines at **Hornkullen**, as well as numerous well-preserved blast furnaces, some quite small and more like pottery kilns. Look for them at Storbrohyttan, Brattfors, Motjärnshyttan, Torsbäcken and Saxån. Among the preserved smelting houses is a good example at **Loåhyttan**, and **Surahammar** has a foundry museum with implements and models.

Right at the heart of this area, Kopparberg has a mining museum and, at the preserved mine at **Strass Gruva**, visitors can go 639 ft (195 metres) underground.

Around **Nora**, now a quiet little lakeside town, there is more evidence of the tremendous activity that must have taken place in this Swedish Klondike. At **Pershyttan**, men produced iron as early as the 14th century, and at one of the best-preserved blast furnaces here you can get a good sense of how these early industries must have been. At **Siggebohyttan**, north of Nora, master miner's homesteads tell something about life at home.The iron masters were the new aristocracy of the times and built themselves impressive manor houses. Many of these have survived and some, like **Hennickehammar** and **Saxå Herrgård**, are now attractive country hotels.

Further west, in Värmland, **Munkfors**, now the home of one of Sweden's major steelworks, has preserved the old plant—**Gamal Bruket**—with workshops, office, and manor house. In the grounds of Ransäter's museum complex is a water-driven tilt hammer.

In Gästrikland, to the east, are many traces of the county's mining background. The best centres are **Gysinge**, **Tjärnäs** and **Vidbyhyttan**, which has a smelting house from the days of Sweden's great king, Gustav Vasa.

Giant waterwheel: The **Edske** blast furnace has particular significance as it was the first to use the Bessemer process to make steel. Between Fagersta and Avesta, at **Norberg**, is the famous Polhemshjulet, a huge waterwheel 49 ft (15 metres) in diameter.

Further north, you come to the interesting ironworks museum at **Iggesund** where most of the old works remain: blast furnaces, Bessermer converter, hammer forge and part of the old rolling mill. In the same area is the **Moviken** blast furnace and the 18th-century **Strömbacka** hammer forge.

Not many countries have preserved as many of the places that laid the foundations of their prosperity. In tracing Sweden's industrial archaeology, you are following a direct line which led to what today is one of the most successful industrial countries in the world.

THE CENTRAL HEARTLANDS

Five counties stretch across central Sweden. In the east are Gästrikland, Hälsingland and Medelpad, which share the long coastline from Furuvik and Sörfjärden, known as Jungfrukusten (the Virgin Coast). Further inland come Härjedalen and Jämtland, which stretch west to the Norwegian border, the land lakes, conifer and birch forests. Härjedalen has the beginning of the great northern mountain ranges and the further north you go, the more dramatic the scenery.

The small county of Gästrikland has one major town, **Gävle**, in the southeast corner of this whole region. Though the history of this coastal town goes back over 500 years, on the surface this busy commercial centre is unexceptional. But don't let this note of discouragement overshadow Gävle's attractions. It has a castle, built by Johan II, a town hall built by Gustav III, and a sizeable county museum, **Länsmuseet**, which requires four floors to display its 16,000 varied exhibits. Gävle was one of Sweden's great shipping towns and the most treasured exhibit is the **Björke** boat, built in A.D. 100, and among the most notable finds in Northern Europe.

Railway collection: There is also the Silvanum, a forestry museum, and the Railway Museum which occupies a spacious site on the outskirts of the town. The collection embraces 29 gleaming locomotives, around 30 coaches and wagons (including the 1874 coach of King Oscar II), plus a multitude of smaller exhibits from tickets to beautiful scale models. It is a paradise for railway enthusiasts.

The **Gamla Gefle** area has preserved, wooden houses with an artists' quarter. Beside the river Gävle is the **Stadsträdgården** and **Boulogneskogen** which together form one of the largest municipal parks in Sweden. A park of a different kind is **Furuviksparken**, on the coast six miles (10 km) south of the town, which combines extensive zoo-

logical gardens and a variety of attractions for children. Today, all this makes Gävle the main centre for shopping, sport and entertainment for people from a wide area around the town, who flock in for sporting events, theatre, and art exhibitions. It is also a place for a good night out.

Gästrikland is at the eastern end of the swathe of land which gave Sweden its early mining and smelting industries, and moving only a few miles inland to **Sandviken** you are in an area which saw the development of the Swedish steel industry. Sandviken grew up with the development of the Bessemer process in the 1860s and Sandviken steels are well known today. **Jädraås**, some 50 miles (80 km) to the north is the starting point for a museum railway with steam trains running for some five and a half miles (9 km) to Tallås. This is typical of the many little railways used to haul minerals or timber, and it has the coach used by the much-travelled King Oscar II, when he went hunting bear in Dalarna.

Herring delicacies: Only a few miles north of Gävle and also on the coast, **Bönan** is famous for its golden-brown smoked herring, cured over spruce wood. **Engeltofta** is a good restaurant to try it in summer when you can catch the boat over from Gävle on a Wednesday evening. In fact, grilled herring and potatoes with dill butter are favourites all along the Virgin Coast, which also has small fishing villages and working harbours, where catching the Baltic herring is still an important industry. In particular **Skärså**, north of Söderhamn retains much of its original fishing village environment.

The main highway north (the E4) skirts two coastal towns in Hälsingland, **Söderhamn** and **Hudiksvall**. Söderhamn, set between two hills, was founded in 1620 as an armoury for the Swedish army, and the museum is situated in part of what was the gun and rifle factory. Although a commercial centre, the town has an impressive town hall, plus a church to match, a pleasant riverside park and boat trips around the archipelago. On top of the hill on the eastern side of the town is **Oskarsberg**, a look-out tower built in 1895, which— for reasons not immediately apparent— was paid for by the enthusiastic members of the choral society.

Timber barons: Next to Gävle, **Hudiksvall** is the second oldest town in Norrland and celebrated its 400th anniversary in 1982. Around 100 years ago, when the timber industry was at its peak, the town had a reputation for high living, a place of punsch (a Swedish liqueur) plush, and timber barons. Today, it has no buildings built by unusual benefactors but it has a theatre of distinction which was opened in 1882. It also has a group of the best preserved 19th-century wooden buildings in Sweden, the **Fiskarstan** (fisherman's town) while **Strömmingsundet**'s wooden wharves and warehouses also merit a glance.

South of Hudiksvall, at **Iggesund**, is an impressive ironworks museum, which was operating as late as 1953. Its blast furnaces and the Bessemer steel-

All-day dancing at the Hälsinge Hambo is hard on the feet.

The Central Heartlands

100 km

NORWAY

1019 ▲ Hotagsfj.

Sösjöfjällen ▲ 1246

JÄMTLAND

Kallsjön

Strömsund

Junsele

Örnsköldsvik

Storlien

Järpen

Hammerdal

Lunddörrsfj. ▲ 1796 ▲ 1504 Helagsfjällen ▲ Oviksfj. 1371

Storsjön

Östersund

Sollefteå

Bispgården

Kramfors

Härnösand

Funäsdalen

Ånge

MEDEL-PAD

Hede

HÄRJEDALEN

1204 ▲ Storvättes-hågna

Sveg

Ljusnan

Ljusdal

Sundsvall

Gulf

Hudiksvall

Särna

HÄLSINGLAND

Iggesund

of

1040 ▲ Fulufjället

Edsbyn

Arbrå

Söderhamn

DALARNA

Bollnäs

Bothnia

Höljes

Transtrand

Mora

Jädraås

Siljan

Torsby

Malung

Vansbro

Falun

Gävle

Sandviken

GRÄSÖ

Borlänge

Säter

Ekshärad

Ludvika

Dalälven

Östhammar

BERGSLAGEN

Avesta

Gysinge

works are still to be seen.

The interior of the county has the best scenery, particularly the valley of the river **Ljusnan** (Ljusnandalen) which is laced with lakes along its entire length.

West of **Ljusdal**, where the Ljusnan meets the Hennan river, the forests begin. The life of the early charcoal burners who lived in these forests was not easy but at Albert Viksten's cabin village at **Lassekrog**, you can find out what it is like to spend a night in a charcoal burner's cabin and bake your own "charcoal bread" over the fire.

Thousands of dancers: South of Ljusdal, and halfway between the river's source and the sea is **Järvsö**, a small town in farming and forestry country and a minor holiday and winter sports centre. Once a year, this peaceful routine is broken by an unforgettable festival: the *Hälsingehambo*, a competitive event which involves around 3,000 folk dancers.

At dawn on a July morning, groups of competitors in traditional costumes begin to dance. To the tune **Hågalåten**, they dance all the way up the Ljusnan valley, north from Bolllnäs and Arbrå, to a grand finale in Järvsö, in front of the Stenegård manor house.

Today, the "Hambo" is a joyous event but its origins are much more macabre, with something of the Pied Piper of Hamlin about them. Legend has it that a sinister fiddler seduced the dancing couples, who did not realise that he was the Devil. Lured by the music, they danced to their own perdidition at the top of the Hårgaberget. By the time the night ended, only their skulls remained, whirling around to form a visible ring in the solid rock.

Bollnäs, which is situated further south, has a tradition of sweet-making. In 1919, in a little cottage at Hå, southeast of the town, Olof Käller invented a special peppermint sweet. Today, the factory uses the most modern techniques to produce these popular sweets but, during the summer, you can still watch them being boiled, rolled, and stretched out in the old way at Hå, and the general store has the whole

Traditional hay-making still goes on in Central Sweden.

range piled high from floor to ceiling.

At Järvsö, **Stenegård's** second function is as a handicrafts centre, where the craftworkers include glass-blowers, silversmiths, blacksmiths, woodworkers and potters. On an island on the river between the house and village is the parish church. When it was built in 1832, it was the largest country church in Sweden, seating 2,400, which may say something about the piety of the country people of that era. Later, this was reduced to 1,400. The pulpit comes from an earlier church and the parsonage, which dates back to 1731 and was in use until 1879, is now a museum.

Järvsö has several local mountains including Gluggberget 1,689 ft (515 metres). The latter has a viewing platform at the summit, while Öjeberget 1,314 ft (370 metres) has the advantage that you can drive to the top.

Fiddlers' rally: To absorb this region you need to drive first along the minor road from Järvsö to **Delsbo**, which attracts an enormous number of folk fiddlers for the annual *Delsbostämman*, and then on the secondary road through Friggesund and Hassela and back to the coast. Surrounded by dark forests, this is Dellenbygden, rural Sweden at its best, and includes the Dellen lakes area, with boat trips and canoe trails, and walking trails leading along the ridges and over open pastures.

The most northerly coastal town of this central area is Sundsvall in Medelpad, which has only a small area of coastline. Mainly industrial, **Sundsvall** still enjoys a fine location, partly on the mainland and partly on the island of Alnö, connected by bridge. It has a 13th-century church and an open-air museum (**Hembygdsgård**) with some 20 old buildings. South of the town at **Galtsröm** is another restored ironworks, complete with blast furnace, work's office, chapel and forestry museum. Drive west on the E75, which starts at Sundsvall, and you will come to **Torpshammar**, which is claimed to be the very centre of Sweden.

Together the counties of Medelpad, Härjedalen and Jämtland are as big as

Folk fiddlers' rallies, like the annual Delsbo-stämman at Delsbo, attract hundreds of musicians.

Denmark. Though they cover an area of 19,300 square miles (50,000 sq. km), the population is only 135,000. As 55,000 live in **Östersund**, the principal town of Jämtland, this means that people are few and far between outside the main towns. To the east and southeast are extensive forests with low hills, rivers and lakes, and the higher mountains rise up to 5,900 ft (1,800 metres) beginning in Härjedalen and spreading north and west.

This heartland has four main rivers, the Ångermanälven, Indalsälven, Ljungan and Ljusnan, all well stocked with fish, especially trout and grayling, and 4,000 lakes and watercourses make these counties a fishing Utopia. Perch, pike and whitefish are the most common in the forested regions, but many tarns have been stocked with salmon and trout in recent years. Most fishing waters are open to the general public though you may need a permit, bought cheaply nearby or at the tourist offices. The vast tracts of near uninhabited territory are also home to wildlife such as bear, wolverine, lynx and the ubiquitous elk.

When tourism was in its infancy, Härjedalen was one of the first Swedish counties to attract skiers, who still return to pit their skills against its varied terrain, and come back in the summer for mountain-walking. The scenery is impressive and, north of **Funäsdalen**, not far from the Norwegian border, the county boasts Sweden's highest road over the—to English speakers—oddly-named Flatruet Plateau, which goes up to around 3,000 ft (nearly 1,000 metres). Also not far from the Norwegian border is the **Rogen** area, a remnant of the Ice Age with scratched and furrowed boulders, like water set in stone.

For a driver, mile after mile of forest road stretching ahead can be mesmeric and the art is not to fall asleep. But roads are not plentiful, apart from a few minor ones, just the cross of the north-south route, Highway 81, and east-west, Highway 84, which meet at **Sweg**, a small town, but the county's largest at around 4,000 people. **Vemdalen**, fur-

The endless railway lines stretch as far north as Kiruna.

ther northwest, has an eight-sided wooden church with a separate onion-domed bell tower. Beyond the village the road climbs steeply between two mountains—the Vemdalsfjällen—before crossing the county boundary.

Lake, river and mountain: Jämtland is by far the biggest county in central Sweden, a huge territory of lake, river and mountain. Its heart is **Lake Storsjön**, the fifth largest stretch of inland water in the country. North of Storsjön, on the north bank of Lake Alsensjön at Glösa are **Hällristningar**, primitive rock carvings.

At the centre of this network of water is the largest town **Östersund**, connected by a bridge to the beautiful island of **Frösön**, which has been inhabited since prehistoric times. According to legend, it was dedicated to Fröj, the god of fertility, a place of pagan sacrifice, and the most northerly spot where a rune stone has been found.

Today, its oldest religious building is of another faith, Christianity. In part it dates back to the 12th century, with a nave and porch added in 1610, the altar in 1708 and the pulpit in 1781. The separate bell tower is 18th-century, though one of the bells is 400 years older.

From the island you can see long, magnificent views over endless lakes and waterways, and endless stretches towards Norway and the mountains of the west. Five minutes' walk from the church is **Stocketitt** which combines a local museum and a good viewpoint.

The island was home to the noted Swedish composer and critic Wilhelm Peterson-Berger (1867-1942). This prolific composer produced a total of five operas, five symphonies and a violin concerto, as well as choral works, chamber music, piano pieces, and songs. His most popular major work, the opera *Arnljot*, is performed every summer on the island.

Frösön also has a 52-acre (21 hectare) zoo with 600 animals and a challenging golf course, kept in impeccable condition, even though it spends several months a year covered in snow.

All over Sweden you come across open-air museums which may be merely a handful of local buildings re-erected on one site, perhaps with a café, some indoor exhibits or traditional craft demonstration. In a different league is **Jämtli** at Östersund, one of the oldest and biggest open-air museums in the country. Its 60 buildings cover around a square mile and it was established as early as 1912.

In summer, local people perform bygone tasks using traditional implements and equipment and visitors can also have a go. The buildings are 18th and 19th century and include a *shieling* (summer farm) a baker's cottage, a smithy, and an old inn. The food in the café is first class.

Saucers, tail and horns: Lake Storsjön is reputed to have its own monster, a Swedish version of the world-famous Scottish "Nessie", the serpent-like creature supposed to inhabit the depths of Loch Ness. Lake Storsjön's monster is reputed to vary in length from 12ft (3.6 metres) to 90 ft (27 metres) and to have eyes like saucers, large ears, a tail

The northern lynx, now a well protected species.

and horns. Among its 40,000 exhibits, Östersund's county museum has traps with hooks and cables which were owned by a company set up in 1894 to find the monster. After failing to catch anything, the comany went into liquidation and donated the implements to the museum. Present-day monster seekers can take a cruise on the lake in the 1875 steamer *Thomee*.

In western Jämtland, the peaks rise up to nearly 6,000 ft (about 1,800 metres) above sea level. It is a spendid area for trekking in summer and skiing in winter. Centuries ago, melting ice left many strange and unusual formations such as the deep canyon between the Drommen and Falkfångarfjället mountains (the nearest road ends at Högelkardalen). An equally impressive Ice Age landscape is near Vallbo, at the end of a minor road from Undesåker.

The E75 is the main highway west from Östersund to the Norwegian frontier. It is an age old route which was once used by pilgrims on their trek to the grave of St Olaf at Trondheim. It was also the scene of frequent fighting between Norway and Sweden, marked today by a few monuments and the remains of some fortifications.

In 1718, the Swedes suffered a major defeat along this route. When Sweden's great warrior king Karl XII made his last fatal attack against the southern Norwegian fort of Frederiksten in the south, he ordered his general Carl Gustav Armfelt to attack Trondheim from the north. It was a tragic failure. The king was killed at Frederiksten by an unknown bullet and, in the northern retreat, over 3,000 men froze to death in a desperate attempt to withdraw into the safety of Sweden in bitter weather. You will find memorial stones to this disaster at Handöl, Ånn, Duved and Bustvalen.

Later in the 18th century, the area was the scene of frantic activity after the finding of copper—a boom period that lasted around 100 years.

Climbing the easy way: Halfway between Östersund and the border is **Åre**, a popular winter sports resort. A funicular railway goes from the town centre part way up the local mountain Åreskutan, which reaches 4,658 ft (1,420 metres). From that halfway point, a cable car goes almost to the summit, which can then be reached without difficulty. Lakes and mountains on every side make a superb view.

Western Jämtland is also rich in waterfalls, such as Ristafallet near Hålland or Storfallet, northwest of Höglekardalen and Tännforsen, west of Åre. Northwards, the county is a patchwork of forests and lakes. Monotonous? Yes, to a degree, it is. But you need to be there at ground level to absorb the immensity of the region. If one birch looks like any other one of the thousands, there are compensations: the sight of the brilliant blue lakes, their waters gently rippled by the breeze, the dark and mysterious outlines of the distant mountains, the space, and the silence.

In an area where towns, even villages, are few and far between and in general disappointing, you soon come to appreciate that when it comes to creating an impression nature wins hands down.

A hard day, hunting elk.

LAPPLAND

"The vast Swedish *Norrland* is rarely visited by travellers, the points of interest being few, the distances great and the communications imperfect." This dismissive statement appeared in *Baedeker's Guide to Norway and Sweden*, published in 1892.

Today, it would be hard to write anything further from the truth. In the great search for natural landscapes and the open air, Lappland, Sweden's largest and most northerly county, becomes more and more popular each year. To some, this could be a two-edged "benefit" because of the danger of too many people in a fragile environment, but the Swedes are among the most aware of the need for conservation.

Distances may still be great but modern communications are easy, with a rail link to the far north and good quality roads. As for "the points of interest being few," what about the magnificent scenery? Lappland's uplands, lakes, mountains and hillsides are among the finest in Europe and remarkable enough to put any human attraction in the shade.

The best way to absorb the immensity of Lappland is to take the inland road—Highway 88—from south to north. In that way, this scenic extravaganza will build up like a highly polished piece of drama into a climactic grand finale.

Dorotea is named after Queen Vilhelmina-Dorotea, consort of King Gustav IV Adolf, and its best claim to fame is the Dorotea Hotel which is renowned for its cuisine. **Vilhelmina** (which also gets its name from the same Queen) lies on the Ångermanälven river and is of greater interest. Off the main road, on a hillside is its well-preserved church village with an imposing church at one end. The wooden houses now provide accommodation for tourists.

A secondary road heads west at Vilhelmina, alongside the Malogomaj lake, and gives access to some splendid fell country, notably Kittelfjäll and Klimfjäll. This is a largely uninhabited

area with mile upon mile of untouched mountain scenery where the peaks rise up to 4,500 ft (1,375 metres) above sea level. Eventually this road crosses the Norwegian frontier at Skalmodalen and links up with the E6 near Mosjøen. The E6 runs up the Norwegian west coast and the east-west roads in Sweden all feed into it, allowing the itinerant tourist to criss-cross from one country to the other with few formalities.

Storuman is a more important road junction, where Highway 88 is bisected by the E79, commonly known as the Blue Highway because it follows a succession of lakes and the river Umeälven. It starts on the Swedish east coast at **Holmsund**, on the Gulf of Bothnia, and passes **Lycksele**—where there is an extensive zoo which concentrates on animals from the Nordic fauna including bear, elk, musk-ox, wolves and reindeer. From Storuman the road continues through Tärnaby where it joins the E6 at Mo-i-Rana.

At **Slagnäs** there is a secondary road through glorious, peaceful lakeside scenery to **Arjeplog** and this is an enjoyable alternative to the main road (Highway 95). Arjeplog is one of Lappland's most interesting little towns and it is almost surrounded by the waters of **Lakes Uddjaure**, and **Hornavon** which at 725ft (221 metres) is the deepest lake in Sweden.

The Lapps' doctor: The main attraction at Arjeplog is the silver museum. Housed in the old school, a typical beige-coloured wooden building, it provides a fascinating insight into the region's history and, above all, the Lapps. It owes its existence to **Einar Wallqvist**—"the doctor of the Lapplanders"—a most remarkable man who came to the town in 1922.

Besides his medical work Dr Wallqvist began to collect all kinds of cultural objects as a hobby. Later he decided to establish a museum in the old schoolhouse and today it has the finest collection of Lappish silver in existence plus a host of artefacts relating to the life and times of the settlers and the Lapps. He wrote 20 books, lectured widely,

Peceding pages: the summit of Kebnekajse; herding reindeer; sunset at the gateway to Lappland.

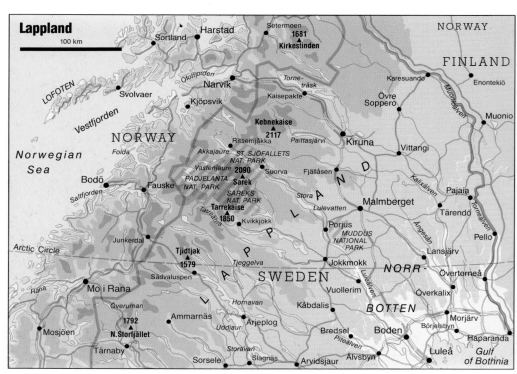

Lappland
100 km

NORWAY
FINLAND

Sortland
Harstad
Setermoen
1681
Kirkestinden

LOFOTEN
Ofotfjorden
Narvik
Torne träsk
Karesuando
Enontekiö

Svolvaer
Kjöpsvik
Kaisepakte
Övre Soppero
Muonio

Vestfjorden
Kebnekaise
2117
Ritsemjåkka
Paittasjärvi
Kiruna
Vittangi

NORWAY
Akkajaure
ST. SJÖFALLETS NAT. PARK
Folda

Norwegian Sea
Vastenjaure 2090
PADJELANTA NAT. PARK
Sarek
SAREKS NAT. PARK
Suorva
Fjällåsen
Kalixälven
Pajala

Bodö
Fauske
Tarrekaise
Tarreätno
1850
Kvikkjokk
Stora
Lulevatten
Malmberget
Tärendö
Pello

Saltfjorden
Porjus
MUDDUS NATIONAL PARK
Tornälven

Arctic Circle
Junkerdal
Tjidtjak
1579
Tjeggelva
Jokkmokk
Lansjärv

Rana
Sädvaluspen
SWEDEN
NORR-
Övertorneå

Mo i Rana
Överuman
Hornavan
Vuollerim
Luleälven
BOTTEN
Överkalix
Morjärv

1792
Ammarnäs
Uddjaur
Arjeplog
Kåbdalis
Boden
Börjelsbyn
Haparanda

Mosjöen
N.Storfjället
Storavan
Bredsel
Piteälven
Älvsbyn
Luleå
Gulf of Bothnia

Tärnaby
Sorsele
Slagnäs
Arvidsjaur

was a gifted linguist and had a sparkling wit. He continued as the museum's curator until his death in 1986. **Arjeplog's local church**, which is 17th century and quite impressive, was founded by Queen Kristina.

Beware reindeer: Drivers in Lappland would do well to keep a watchful eye on the reindeer. All reindeer belong to the Lapps and an injured or dead animal has to be paid for in compensation. This is not always easy because reindeer, it has to be said, are not very bright and have little road sense. In summer, when only the older animals will wander near roads, the worst hazards are in the mountains. Another word of caution in dealing with these northern people: never forget that reindeer are currency to the Lapps. It is not "done" to ask a Lapp how many reindeer he owns, because it is like asking him how much he earns a year.

Arjeplog is roughly halfway along highway 95, which is the historic **Silver Road** stretching from **Skellefteå** on the Gulf of Bothnia to **Bodø** on the Norwegian west coast. In the 17th century there were silver mines around **Nasafjäll** and the ore was transported, first by reindeer sleigh and then by boat, to the Swedish east coast. Not until 1972 did it become an asphalt-surfaced highway throughout its length, to open up an area of outstanding beauty.

West of Arjeplog and to the south of road 95 is the isolated community of **Laisvall**, most of whom work in one of the biggest lead mines in Europe. It extends below Lake Storlaison and is open to visitors, but not to children under 15 years of age.

One of the finest viewpoints in this entire area is from the top of **Galtisbuouda** which is 2,624ft (800 metres) above sea level. It is six miles (9.6 km) from Arjeplog and there is a good road to just below the summit, where a rough track continues to the very top. The outlook is magnificent with a network of lakes and range upon range of mountains stretching to infinity and creating a magical atmosphere.

Lapp village: The wide main street of

Helicopter pick-up at the end of a day's walking.

DOGSLEDGING IN LAPPLAND

Swedes are a tough breed. They love to be out in all that unspoiled countryside, enjoying it to the full, even in the depths of winter, and one winter activity that is enjoying increasing popularity is dog-sledging. People with an adventurous spirit—not just from Sweden, but from elsewhere in Europe—are answering the call of the wild and heading far north of the Arctic Circle to Lappland, arriving in the iron-ore town of Kiruna by train or plane to join husky teams at outposts like Jukkasjärvi and Abisko.

A sled team usually consists of between five and a dozen dogs, most of them Siberian or Alaskan huskies. The dogs enjoy the work: indeed, showing a sled to a husky is like showing any other dog a lead and calling "Walkies".

Once a dog is clipped in, it becomes extremely impatient to get going, and as more dogs join the line a greater strain is put on the anchor that stops the sled being dragged off into the wilderness. That frustration leads to a deafening crescendo of yelping and yapping until, at last, the driver releases the anchor and they're off like a flash.

Standing up at the back of a sled, the driver has to be well wrapped up against temperatures that could be down around minus 20°C or less. At that kind of temperature instant icicles form in the nose.

Reindeer skin is the traditional protection against the cold in Lappland, but these days modern fabrics are fairly widespread. Thermal underwear is a must, then a pile-fibre all-in-one suit topped by a windproof jacket and overtrousers should keep out draughts,. A couple of pairs of socks and thickly lined boots, a couple of pairs of gloves and a balaclava and hood should take care of the extremities. Tinted goggles are also necessary to protect the eyes from cold and snow-glare. Doctors also advise against washing or showering before going out in such low temperatures, as the skin's natural oils give extra protection against the cold. Face creams should be oil-based rather than water-based.

It's an amazing area, Sweden's northern wilderness, and a dog sled is a fascinating way of exploring it. There are high mountains, frozen rivers and lakes, and deep, beautiful valleys, sometimes sheltering Same settlements.

Wildlife, though, is minimal in winter. The reindeer and elk move south in search of food and the bears are in hibernation. This leaves Arctic foxes and grouse, which in their white winter outfits are difficult to see, and the vicious wolverines. The latter do most of their prowling at night, so all you're likely to see are their tracks in the morning snow.

Most expeditions travel between 15 and 30 miles (25 and 50 km) a day, though the dogs can cover far greater distances if they're allowed to. In one of the highlights of Lappland's dogsledging season, the Nordic Marathon, dozens of teams compete in a 150-mile (250-km) circular race from Abisko around Kebnekaise, Sweden's highest mountain. The fastest teams complete the course in about 16 hours, and that includes an eight-hour compulsory rest-stop.

It requires a fair degree of concentration to drive the dogs, to make sure the line doesn't become slack. If the sled starts to catch the dogs, they ease off, then quickly become entangled in one another's lines and that can lead to a fight. A watchful eye ensures that peace is maintained in the ranks.

To help keep that line taut, the sled has a rudimentary footbrake, a kind of metal grid with spikes, which the driver steps on and presses hard into the snow. It won't actually stop 12 eager dogs, but it will slow them down.

Stopping them is next to impossible. To do that, the driver slows them as much as possible with the footbrake and then crouches down precariously to ram the anchor, a large steel hook attached to the sled by a length of rope, into the ground. If he mistimes it or loses his balance, an unskilled driver could be lying out flat in the snow watching his team disappearing into the distance.

At night, while the team drivers generally stay in the well-equipped mountain stations built in many of the remote parts of Sweden, the huskies sleep outside. A bowl of food high in protein, fat and carbohydrates, keeps them happy; then they burrow into the snow and curl up for the night. Huskies, like Swedes, are a tough breed.

Arvidsjaur has something of the atmosphere of a frontier town which, to some degree, it is. Once a trading post, it is now a junction of both roads and railways and has grown and expanded within the last 100 years. The major historic attraction is the Lapp village with nearly 80 buildings, including both the **Kåtor**, the tent-shaped wooden huts, and the **Härbron**, the distinctive wooden store houses.

Although not permanently inhabited the village is still used from time to time by the Same people—the correct name for the Lapps—and is the oldest surviving example in Sweden, dating from the late 1700s.

In summer Arvidsjaur is a tourist centre with all the essential adjuncts: hotels, cabins, camping site, swimming pool, putting green, tennis courts and sports ground, In winter, when it is intensely cold, it is taken over by Europe's automotive industry which uses the area to test the ability of its products to perform satisfactorily in sub-zero temperatures.

The Swedish Army has a year-round presence in Arvidsjaur, where there are barracks, and a major base on the town's outskirts. The camp has modern chalets, which double as holiday homes for visitors in summer and rooms for Swedish conscripts in winter.

Ninety-seven miles (156 km) north of Arvidsjaur is the Arctic Circle, marked by a multi-lingual sign by the side of the road. At a nearby café you can buy a suitably inscribed certificate to prove you have crossed the line. Only a short distance further north is **Jokkmokk** which is the principal town in the *kommun* or district of the same name. Jokkmokk Kommun is the biggest in Sweden covering an area of about 7,500 square miles (19,474 square km), equal to the whole of Wales, or Connecticut and Delaware put together. The population, on the other hand, is a meagre 7,000 and about half of them live in Jokkmokk itself.

The word Jokkmokk was the name of a group of Lapps and it means "a bend in the stream". It is the only place where

Left, morning salute from a husky. **Below**, husky team in action.

you will see nomadic Lapps in summer, but the big event is the market which takes place every February. This attracts thousands of people not so much to buy or sell but to experience the unique atmosphere. If you need accommodation at the time of the fair you have to book at least a year in advance and it is no time for camping out with the temperature often dropping to –35° C. Other smaller fairs take place in various parts of this country.

In summer, the main street has numerous shops and stalls, which sell Lapp handicrafts. For a more studied examination of Lapp culture, there is a well-arranged and extensive museum devoted to the Same people.

The next stretch of Highway 88 goes through a sparsely populated area to **Porjus**. It lies at the southern end of Lake Lulevatten and is a major centre for the generation of hydro-electric power. The original switchgear building is a monumental edifice and today Porjus is the headquarters for the state-owned power stations which are on the upper part of the Store Lule river.

From Porjus a very minor road follows Lake Lulevatten for 3.7 miles (six km) to **Stora Sjöfallet** which is the largest waterfall in Sweden. This should not be confused with Storforsen, north of Älvsbyn, which claims to be the largest unrestricted waterfall in Europe.

To the east of Porjus and road 88 is a wild, untouched area which is the Muddus National Park and the home of bear, lynx and wolverine. It is open to the public but no visitors are allowed in the park during the breeding season between mid-March and the end of July.

A relatively short drive brings the bulk of the **Dundret Mountain** in sight, beyond which is **Gällivare**, one of the two major centres of population in northern Lappland. High on the side of Dundret is an extensive holiday centre, with a superb view as well as a hotel, self-catering facilities, restaurants, night club, indoor pool and caravan park. Like all of northern Lappland, in summer it also has rapacious, hungry mosquitoes with an appetite for foreign blood. Do not forget the insect repellant.

Midnight sun: Mosquitoes aside, the bustling Dundret Centre ("The Holiday Camp of Arctic Sweden") is something of a culture shock after the peace and solitude of the area. But it gives you the chance to ride, walk, windsurf, fish, play golf, white water raft, or even pan for gold. Although the track is rough in parts, you can also drive right to the top of the mountain. At an altitude of 2,690 ft (820 metres) the views are marvellous and, from 2 June to 12 July, this is the place to see the Midnight Sun.

Gällivare owes its growth to the discovery of iron ore and now has a population of 22,000. The main mining area is in its twin town of Malmberget, where most of the mineworkers live. Here too, you find the contrast of a suburban small town at odds with the grandeur of the countryside all around it.

Gällivare is the end of the *Inlandsbanen*, a railway line which has faithfully followed road 88, give or take a few miles, all the way from Östersund. The line was completed in 1937 and **Ice fishing.**

took all of 30 years to build. At one time its future was in doubt, but the line was saved by a decision to turn it into a tourist route. Today, with new diesel trains, it has regained its youth as a useful alternative way into the far north.

Gällivare has a **mining museum**, an interesting church (1740), a park with some preserved buildings and a Lapp camp which appears to exist purely for the tourists. The town is also the jumping off point for treks into the vast region to the west which includes the **Padjelanta** and **St. Sjöfallets National Parks**. Only a few minor roads penetrate into this enormous area and it is very much for those who want to trek.

Beyond Gällivare, road 88 joins up with highway 98 and together they go north to **Svappavaara**, a mining centre which had declined and is no longer of importance. Here the 88 goes off to the north-east to **Karesuando**, just short of the Finnish frontier. Many of the place names in northern Lappland owe more to Finnish than to Swedish. In **Kiruna**, for example, a fifth of the population are Finnish immigrants.

Church of the north: Karesuando has two main distinctions. It is home to the most northerly church in Sweden, 155 miles (250 km) inside the Arctic Circle and also has the dubious honour of producing the coldest average winter temperatures in the country. All around the village is Sweden's only tundra scenery and about 2.5 miles (4 km) to the south is **Kaarevaara Mountain**. Though the summit is no higher than 1,696 ft (517 metres) from the top you can see Sweden, Finland and Norway. Better still, you can drive up there.

Distances in the far north between towns and settlements and places of interest are often great. Shared driving is a great advantage, particularly when the road runs mile after mile through an unchanging landscape. This happens beyond Svappavaara, where road 98 swings northwest through uninspiring scenery to **Kiruna**. With 27,000 inhabitants, this is the biggest centre of population in Lappland. Like Gällivare it grew and developed through the discovery and extraction of iron ore. Mining

on a large scale began in 1900 and, though it has declined since, it is still the main industry, and the Kirunavaara (mine) is the world's largest underground mine. In summer, you can tour it by bus.

Kiruna is at the south of Lake Luossajärvi and dominated by the iron ore mountain which brought it into being. Although most mining is now underground, there is also a huge opencast site. The mine led to the opening in 1903 of the town's railway line, to take iron ore either to the port of Luleå on the gulf of Bothnia to the east, or across the Norwegian border to the ice-free port of Narvik on the Norwegian west coast. In 1903, this was an outstanding feat of engineering and, until 1984 when Kiruna and Narvik were joined by road, the rail line was the only cross-border link in this remote area.

With the decline in mining Kiruna has switched its emphasis to tourism and scientific research. The **Kiruna Geophysical Institute**, among other things investigates the phenomena of

Summer camping in Lappland.

the Northern Lights while on the banks of the Vittangi river is **Esrange**—not something out of Disneyworld, but a rocket testing station. Esrange sends research rockets and balloons into different layers of inner space, while beside the **Tarfalasjö** lake, the scientists research the Ice Age. **Abisko** has a natural sciences research station.

Apart from a visit to the mine, try not to miss the **Samegård** which provides a glimpse of the life and history of the Lapps and the **Tramway Museum** (**Museispårvägen**). A secondary road just outside Kiruna takes you to the village of **Jukkasjärvi**, a centre for winter and summer excursions. In winter the dog sledging is truly arctic, in a snow-covered wilderness. In summer Jukkasjärvi provides the stomach-churning thrill of white water rafting through the rapids in an inflatable boat. You can choose from day and week-long trips using the Torne, Kalik and Kaitum rivers. The village also has a modest but interesting **wooden church** and a **small open air museum**.

Tourism received its biggest boost in 1984 with the opening of road 98 from Kiruna via the Norwegian frontier to Narvik. This is the Nordkalottvägen, an outstanding piece of road building which penetrates for 105 miles (170 km) through one of Europe's last wilderness areas. It starts undramatically but by the time you have **Lake Torne Träsk** on the right with distant mountains, and even more impressive mountains rising up to 6,500 ft (2,000 metres) on the left, the journey changes from interesting to spectacular. The clarity of the air sharply etches the outlines of the mountains some snow-capped even in mid-summer against the sky, while the lake is a brilliant blue.

The mountains to the southwest of the highway can only be reached on foot or by pony and it is in this hinterland that **Kebnekaise**, Sweden's highest peak at 6,945 ft (2,117 metres) reigns supreme.

Abisko is a popular base from which to set out along the **Kungsleden**, a trail which, for almost a century, has enabled even inexperienced walkers to see something of the most mountainous region of Sweden. Abisko, Björkliden and **Riksgränsen** (the last place before the frontier) all have hotels and no doubt there will be further developments along the highway. But the huge area without roads should remain safe from commercial predators for some time to come.

This area presents wonderful opportunities for the angler and an inexpensive permit lets you fish in 3,000 lakes. Apart from walking and fishing there are trips on **Lake Torne Träsk** and **sightseeing flights** by seaplane or helicopter. From Riksgränsen the highway crosses the frontier and descends to meet the E6 at the edge of the Rombak fjord, and on to the coast at Narvik, a town which was made famous during World War II.

Despite these engineering feats, the abiding impression of Lappland must be that however clever are human achievements they are all upstaged by nature. This awe-inspiring combination of rivers, lakes and mountains cannot fail to leave its mark on the visitor.

Best of both worlds: left, summer skiing; and right, ice cave in the far north.

HEADING FOR THE FAR NORTHEAST

The Gulf of Bothnia, the stretch of water that separates Sweden from its eastern neighbour, Finland, forms the common bond between the three counties of the northeast, Ångermanland, Västerbotten, and Norrbotten, which share its seaboard. For the most part, the coastline is low-lying and ranges from polished rock to sand and shingle beaches, and from wide bays to small coves and inlets.

All the major towns are on the coast, a harking back to the days when the sea was the easy way to travel, compared with the dense forests and rolling hills further inland. Most of these coastal towns grew up as trading settlements and today, particularly in the west, there are still few people and towns in the endless square miles of forest.

The coast is fringed with islands which at times form an almost continuous archipelago. Only a handful are inhabited and, even on those, few of the descendants of the early fishermen who established these small settlements now seek a livelihood from the sea. The boats are still there but today their owners are holidaymakers, who have turned the islands into a playground to indulge the Swedish passion for sailing and the sea. Only the occasional small, simple chapel, which you come across on the islands, speaks of the past.

Inland, lakes provide tranquil blue oases in the dense forests, while river valleys cut swathes through the trees. The greatest charm of the area is its rich wildlife, with bear, lynx, elk and beaver in abundance.

Starting in the south of this great stretch of empty land, the main coastal town of Ångermanland is **Härnösand**, not all that far north of Sundsvall in Medelpad. In 1585, King Johan III not so much granted, but forced a charter on the old trading and seafaring centre. The King was looking for duties and taxes, and threatened the inhabitants with deportation to Russia if they did not agree to create a permanent trading centre. That threat was enough to turn Härnösand into a successful commercial town.

Sea city: The town is part island, part mainland, with the major section on Härnö Island, four miles by six miles (seven km by 10 km). In the 17th and 18th centuries, it blossomed into the cultural and administrative centre of northern Sweden.

Although it is now a commercial and industrial town, its splendid location makes it attractive. The fine town hall, with its classic lines and impressive pillared entrance was completed in 1791, and the equally handsome cathedral, built between 1843 and 1846, is in the same style. It replaces an earlier building which in 1721 was burnt by marauding Russians during a turbulent time in Sweden's history when Russia was never far away. There are some well-preserved 18th-century wooden houses in **Östanbäcken** but the rest of the town is of modern design.

Overlooking the town and harbour is the **Murberget**, which holds the second

largest open-air and historical museum in Sweden (Stockholm's Skansen is the first). The view from the top of Vårdkasen makes the climb worthwhile, and you can get there even more easily by car.

Härnösand stands at the entrance of the Ångermanälven river estuary which cuts through a wide gorge with hilly ground on either side. Just a bit further north at **Sandö**, the E4 highway crosses the river by a spectacular bridge 3,360 ft (1,024 metres) long and 131 ft (40 metres) high, completed in 1964.

Also on the river is **Kramfors**, the home of the musician Frans Berwald, one of Sweden's best-known composers, and Kalle Grönstedt, a musician who made the town the country's centre for accordionists.

Near **Ytterlännäs**, also on Highway 90, look out for a 13th-century church, regarded as an antiquarian wonder. The 16th-century golden Madonna is by Haake Gulleson; the ornate vaults and walls were decorated by an unknown farmer-painter in the 1480s.

Best-kept secret: Between Härnösand and **Docksta** to the north, the coast changes dramatically to form the **High Coast** (Höga Kusten) where the low-lying shoreline gives way to one with a much higher profile. This beautiful area with its impressive coastal landscape is Sweden's best-kept secret, which does not seem to be widely known or appreciated even by Swedes and few foreigners ever reach it.

The heart of the High Coast is the **Nordingrå** peninsula, where the bedrock is an intense red *rapakivi* granite. The word is Finnish and means "rotten stone", because of the way it weathers easily into gravel and shingle. To get to the High Coast, leave the E4 north of Härnösand and take the short ferry crossing over the estuary to Nydal. Further north, you reach the peninsula by leaving the same road at either **Lockestrand** or **Sundbron**. Offshore are several attractive islands, such as **Mjälltön** which achieves the record for the highest Swedish island at 774 ft (236 metres) high.

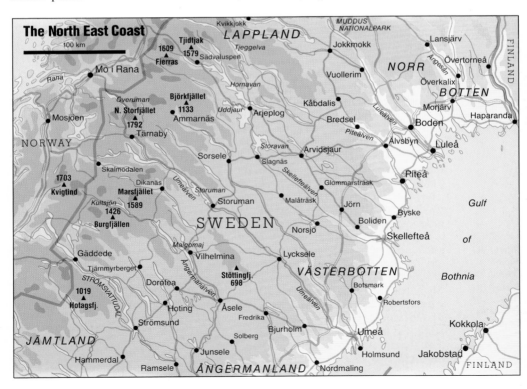

The peninsula has a whole variety of scenic treasures—the wide sweep of **Omne bay**, the villages of Måviken, Norrfällsviken and the view from the church over Vagsfjärden. **Bonhamn** is a tiny little place tucked away among the rocks, where Arne's Sjöbad (Arne's Boathouse) justifies its popularity as a rendezvous for meals of salmon or fresh grilled herrings and mashed potatoes. Equally popular is the Café Mannaminne near **Haggvik** run by Anders Åbey, which provides sustenance, including home-baked delicacies, handicrafts and musical evenings.

The Höga Kusten walk, a 16-mile (25-km) footpath through the peninsula, starts at **Fjördbotten**. There are bathing places at Storsand, Norrfällsviken and Hörsång and Noraström.

On the inland side of the E4 is another surprise, the looming outline of the **Skuleberget**, some 960 ft (290 metres) above sea level. Particularly from the north, it rises suddenly just before Docksta, and the easy way up is by chair lift to the top.

Behind Skuleberget is the **Skuleskogen National Park**, noted for its birds and mammals which include the rare white-backed woodpecker, grouse, Siberian jay, and waxwing, as well as a whole range of mammals—moose, deer, lynx, fox, badger and marten, ermine, blue hare and squirrel.

Örnsköldsvik, commonly called Övik, is the nearest town to the High Coast and is twice the size of Härnösand, with 60,000 inhabitants. The town itself is industrial but there are some good views from the Vansberget (you can drive up) and it has a beautiful archipelago. In bygone years, many of the local people were fisher-farmers, combining the two jobs to make ends meet—the counterparts of the west coasters.

There are two attractive islands, **Ulvön Södra** and **Ulvön Norra**. Södra has one of the oldest fishermen's chapels in Sweden, which dates back to 1622. It has well-preserved paintings on the walls and ceiling. Another attractive island is Trysund, a favourite with the

The road north, Sandsbron at Kramfors.

sailing fraternity because of its lagoon-like bay.

Royal beginnings: Umeå on the Umeälven River and at the junction of the E4 and E79 roads may be larger than Övik but, thanks to its layout and location, is undoubtedly more attractive. Like so many towns in Sweden, it was founded by King Gustav II Adolf, in 1622. After a devastating fire in 1888—a commonplace event in a country where virtually all the buildings were made of wood—the town planted avenues of birches as protective firebreaks and these have created a gracious appearance which goes well with its riverside location. Umeå is the principal town of Västerbotten and has a population of 75,000.

It was not always peaceful. Between 1808 and 1809, at the time when Sweden lost its 800-year-old rule over Finland, the Russians crossed the winter ice from Finland and attacked the town, which resulted in bitter fighting.

The town's main attraction is **Gammlia**, yet another open-air mu-seum, but distinguished by the fact that it was established as early as the 1920s. Apart from a variety of old buildings, it includes the country museum of Lapp culture.

An alternative to the main road along the coast from Umeå to the next place north, **Skellefteå**, an industrial centre, is to take the secondary road (number 364) inland, more interesting and very quiet. There are no dramatic panoramas, just a succession of pleasant rural views, always with the backdrop of green forests. You pass the Bygde-träsket lake and reach a smaller lake at **Burträsk** which has an imposing village church and a very small open-air museum—"every community should have one" might well be the Swedish motto. Never mind: this museum serves good coffee and waffles.

By now, you will have become so used to northern Sweden's quiet rural landscape that to turn off and go inland into **Piteå** is something of a culture shock. It lies just north of the Västerbotten-Norrbotten county boundary on a

Evening camp on a canoe hike.

peninsula that dates back to the 17th century, and has a few narrow lanes and wooden houses to recall the past. So far so good, but now it has developed into an industrial centre with timber, paper and pulp industries and—more surprisingly—a popular holiday resort.

This big holiday centre, **Pilhomens Havsbad**, is a mass of self-catering cabins, camping sites, all kinds of entertainment with a candy floss atmosphere. It has more than two miles (four km) of beach and is full of noise and people. The Norwegians love it, and migrate there in great flocks from the austere calm of their northern fjords.

Biggest waterfall: From Piteå, the road leads north-west and follows the course of the Piteälven river through Älvsbyn and on to **Bredsel**, and **Storforsen**. This magnificent waterfall is said to be Europe's highest unfettered waterfall with a 265-ft (81-metre) drop.

Back to the coast and it is not long to **Luleå**, the most northerly major town in Sweden. Today, it stands at the mouth of the Luleälven, surrounded on three sides by water and fringed with islands. In olden times, the town was some six miles (10 km) further inland. It had been given its own charter by King Gustav II Adolf in 1621 but, in 1649, the King decreed that trade had grown too large for that first small harbour and the town must move.

Though the townspeople were reluctant to leave their homes, the King insisted and, at last, issued a decree forcing them to go. But he could not force the new town to develop quickly and in 1742, when the intrepid Linnaeus passed through Luleå on his Lappland journey, he dismissed it as "a pretty village".

The early shipyards closed when the first steamship appeared; then the discovery of iron ore in Lappland and the opening of the railways gave the town a chance to develop. The first steelworks were built in the 1940s, followed by a massive but stillborn project for a new steelworks on 618 acres (250 hectares) of reclaimed land. It was due for completion in 1980 but, by then, over-pro-

When the wind blows, the answer is a snow hole.

duction of steel elsewhere made the new works a non-starter.

Though it has been dogged by a certain amount of misfortune, Luleå is today a pleasant town. Its museum, the **Norrbotten Museum** in Hermelin Park, provides a well-rounded picture of the twin strands of the county with the inclusion of a major collection of Lapp artefacts.

One happy legacy of the King's decision to move Luleå is that it left the old church town, **Gammelstad**, on its original site. It survives today as the only protected church town or *Kyrkbyn* in Sweden. The 15th-century church at its centre has walls of red and grey granite. The altarpiece, carved in wood, and gilded, was made in Antwerp, and the chancel frescoes date from the 1480s. The truimphal crucifix is a remarkable example of medieval art, while the sandstone baptismal font is even older than the church itself. The ornate pulpit in baroque style was the work of a village joiner, Nils Fluur.

Surrounded by 500 cottages in a unique period townscape, the church is more than a museum. It is still used today on important religious occasions. Close to the original harbour is an open-air museum with farm buildings, cottages, stables, a log cabin, a croft and a fisherman's dwelling. It also includes one of the typical haysheds which are a feature of the farming landscape in Norrbotten. Once a necessity, hundreds survive today as relics from the past.

Invasion fears: Inland from Luleå and on the Luleälven river is a town once called the "Gibraltar of the North". **Boden** has been a military town for many years and, at the end of the 19th century was referred to as "one of the strongest fortresses of Europe—that is to say in the whole world." The reason for the great fortress was the loss of Finland to the Russians in 1809, which left Sweden fearful of an attempted invasion by its eastern neighbour.

Today, Boden remains the largest garrison town in Sweden and is the home of six regiments. The **Garrison Museum** (Garnisonsmuseet) has much

Heading north on the old Royal way, Kungsleden.

to reveal about Sweden's military history over the last 400 years, and it has a collection of weapons, uniforms and other militaria.

Even now, Sweden has remained sensitive about military issues and a major slice of eastern Norrbotten is a defence area. This means restrictions on foreigners entering and staying in the designated area, and there are multilingual signs on all the roads which cross its threshold.

Sweden's easternmost town is **Haparanda**, which lies on the western side of the Torneälven, and is another result of Sweden's losing the 1808-9 War. Along with Finland went the important Finnish town, Tornio. To compensate for that loss, the Swedes built Haparanda opposite Tornio on the Torneälven river which forms the border between the two countries for many miles. On the Swedish side it also skirts a largely uninhabited region of Norbotten and Lappland. All these northern counties, collectively called Norrland have a distinctive northern terrain and,

whether it be on mountain, lake or river, they offer endless outdoor pastimes.

Water sports: The Torneälven and the other northern rivers provide splendid canoeing and white water rafting, and fishing for mountain char (röding), trout, grayling, pike, perch, and whitefish. All along this northern curve of the Gulf of Bothnia is archipelago, river, island and wonderful scenery. Between Haparanda and Luleå lies **Kalix**, which has a medieval church from the 15th century and in death the graveyard unites Russian and Swedish soldiers from the two warring sides. Much earlier Viking graves lie nearby at Sangis.

This is also Lapp country and further inland than Kalix on the same Kalixälven is **Överkalix**, a typical Lappland township. There are fine views here from the top of the local moutain, the **Brännaberget**, and if you time it well, you have the chance to see the glories of the Midnight Sun that draws many people to the north and gives the mountain its other name—the Mountain of the Midnight Sun.

Golf at midnight, under the midnight sun. Following pages; students from Uppsala in University boat race.

TRAVEL TIPS

GETTING THERE

BY AIR

The number of direct trans-Atlantic flights to Sweden is increasing steadily, so avoiding the need to change planes in Copenhagen, Scandinavia's main hub airport. SAS Scandinavian Airlines and Pan American both operate daily non-stop services between New York and Stockholm during the summer and TWA also operates several times weekly.

SAS and other European airlines link Stockholm with all the major Continental gateways, usually with non-stop flights. From the UK, SAS and British Airways operate from London (Heathrow or Gatwick) to Stockholm, Gothenburg and Malmö, while BA also has a Manchester-Stockholm service routed via Copenhagen. A new contender is a Swedish carrier, Baltic Airlines, which operates between Southend and Malmö. In June 1989 the British airline Air Europe started a daily service from Gatwick to Stockholm with fares which undercut the "establishment" airlines. There are also low-cost charter flights from the UK to Stockholm which again undercut scheduled fares.

BY SEA

The main year-round North Sea link is operated from the UK by Scandinavian Seaways (the posh new name for DFDS Seaways) from Harwich to Gothenburg, and there is also a seasonal service to Gothenburg from Newcastle upon Tyne.

The journey takes about 24 hours and there are two or three sailings a week. These services are ideal for anyone planning a motoring holiday in Sweden because they obviate the long overland drive across Europe. There are innumerable ferry links between Denmark and Sweden, so there are no logistical problems in planning a motoring holiday combining the two countries.

BY RAIL

It's quite an expedition to travel from the UK to Sweden by rail. The conventional way is to take the Sealink ferry from Harwich to Hook of Holland and then hop on the North-West Express to Copenhagen, where there is a connecting train to Stockholm. The London-Stockholm journey takes about 30 hours and the fare is not particularly competitive with cheap flights, unless you happen to be taking advantage of one of the discount schemes for young travellers.

BY ROAD

Ideal for travellers who really are on a tight budget and feel up to a 47-hour journey from London to Stockholm. This "express" service, operated by the Swedish company GDG Continentbus, is routed from London to Dover with a ferry crossing to Zeebrugge, followed by the long journey through the Netherlands and Germany to the ferry port of Travemünde and another crossing to Trelleborg in southern Sweden. This epic trip is rounded off by the 10-hour journey from Malmö to Stockholm.

TRAVEL ESSENTIALS

VISAS & PASSPORTS

Immigration never seems to be a hassle in Sweden, and if you're arriving from one of the other Scandinavian countries your passport probably won't be checked at all. A valid passport entitles you to a stay of up to three months and visas are not normally required. The only problems arise if you are planning to seek work in Sweden, in which case you should obtain a work permit from the Swedish Embassy before you travel.

MONEY MATTERS

The Swedish krona (plural "kronor") is usually abbreviated to "kr" in shops (or "Skr" to distinguish it from the Norwegian or Danish krone). It is also sometimes referred to by the international banking abbreviation "SEK". The krona is split into 100 öre and coins are issued to the value of 10 or 50 öre and the easily-confused 1 krona and 5 kronor. Bank-notes are printed in values of 10, 50, 100, 500, 1,000 and 10,000 kronor.

You can take up to 6,000 Skr in or out of Sweden and there is no limit on the amount of foreign currency which can be imported. Travellers' cheques can be exchanged at banks all over Sweden without difficulty. A foreign exchange service is also provided by about 500 Post Offices with the "PK Exchange" sign. Exchange rates at the time of going to press (end 1989) were £1=10.80 Skr and US$1=6.41 Skr.

Uniform Eurocheques are accepted in banks, restaurants and shops all over Swe-

den. The cheques must be written in Swedish currency and are guaranteed up to a limit of 1,400 Skr.

All the leading credit cards—Visa, MasterCard/Access, American Express and Diners' Club—are accepted by most hotels, restaurants and shops throughout Sweden.

HEALTH

One advantage of Sweden being a Nordic country is that it is not prone to some of those nasties which require a never-ending round of inoculations when one is planning a visit to the tropics. Standards of hygiene are among the highest in the world and the water is perfectly safe to drink from the tap, so food poisoning or related problems are highly unlikely.

But anyone visiting the far north of Sweden in high summer needs to take precautions against the vicious mosquitoes which inhabit those latitudes. Even the strongest insect repellents are not entirely proof against their incursions and, if possible, it's advisable to head north in the autumn.

Sweden has a reciprocal medical agreement with the UK and other countries under which visitors are entitled to treatment under the same conditions as the Swedes. Sweden does not operate a general-practitioner system; you simply visit the nearest hospital clinic, taking your passport with you, and ask to see a doctor. You can go to either the *Akutmottagning* at a normal hospital or to a *Vårdcentral* in more remote areas.The fee for a hospital visit is 60 Skr and if you need any medicine the doctor will give you a prescription which you take to a chemist (*Apotek*) for dispensing. There is no charge if you have to stay in hospital.

WHAT TO WEAR

Sweden's weather is just as unpredictable as it is in other parts of northern Europe, so it's best to plan for any eventuality. With luck, you'll encounter hot sunny days during the summer—even in the Arctic North—when shorts and T-shirts are the order of the day. Or it could be one of those summers when the sun never appears from one week to the next and you'll need to wrap up in sweaters and rainwear. Winters can be very cold, but it is a "dry" cold which is not at all uncomfortable, although you need to take a heavy coat and some warm headgear, not to mention a modest selection of thermal underwear. For winter visits bring some sturdy and unsmart footwear in case you have to plough your way through slushy streets.

CUSTOMS

As with immigration, Swedish Customs formalities are usually painless and foreign visitors rarely have to suffer the indignity of having their baggage opened. But it's naturally sensible to stick to the rules and observe the duty-free limits.

Visitors from other European countries aged 15 or over can take into Sweden, duty free, 200 cigarettes or 100 cigarillos or 50 cigars or 9oz (250g) of tobacco and 200 cigarette papers. Visitors aged 20 and over can take in 1 litre of spirits, 1 litre of wine (or 2 litres if no spirits are taken in) and 2 litres of beer. Travellers from non-European countries can take in, duty free, 400 cigarettes or 200 cigarillos or 100 cigars or about 1 lb (500g) of tobacco and 200 cigarette papers. Their allowance for alcoholic drinks is the same as that for European residents.

Anyone planning to bring in provisions for a self-catering holiday should be careful of the Customs restrictions. For example, no fresh, smoked or frozen meat may be imported and even the faithful potato may not be taken into Sweden. Tinned meat can be taken in, however. Presents up to a value of 600 Skr may be imported, but the value of any food taken in is included in that limit.

GETTING ACQUAINTED

GOVERNMENT & ECONOMY

Sweden is a constitutional monarchy with a Parliamentary form of government and a one-chamber legislature. The Prime Minister is appointed by a majority of the Swedish Parliament and he heads a Cabinet with about a dozen ministries.

The country is divided into 24 counties, or provinces, each headed by a Governor appointed by the Cabinet. Regionally-elected county councils are responsible for medical care and regional planning, and the lowest tier of local government is exercised by the 284 municipalities, whose responsibilities include planning, social welfare and local education.

With its rich natural resources in terms of ore deposits, forests and hydro-electric power, Sweden has always been a highly industrialised country and companies like Volvo, Saab and Electrolux are now worldwide household names. The old mining region of Bergslagen in central Sweden is still the home of the country's iron and steel industry, while in more recent years a thriving electrical and electronics industry has become established, notably in Stockholm and Västerås.

Farming is still important, particularly in the southern region of Skåne, although only about five percent of Sweden's work force are involved in agriculture and less than 10 percent of the country's area is farmland. Forestry and the related pulp and paper industries remain important, particularly along the shores of the Gulf of Bothnia and Lake Vänern—a throwback to the days when timber was rafted down the rivers.

Sweden. A great escape
whichever way you look at it.

There's a land that's a million miles from the madding crowd. Where the only running around you'll do is along Europe's quietest roads. There's a land where you can't help but see the wood for the trees. (Not to mention the lakes, the rivers, the forests and mountains.) There's a land that's served by frequent ferries and flights from Britain. Sweden. It's a great escape. Whichever way you look at it. For full details just cut out the coupon.

SWEDEN

Name _____ Address _____ Postcode _____ SN2

Please send me your 1989 Brochure of self-catering, touring, hotel and city break holidays in Sweden. Swedish National Tourist Office, PO Box 35, Abingdon, Oxon OX14 4SF. Telephone: 0235 353535.

We offer more connections from the UK to Sweden than any other airline

SAS

GEOGRAPHY & POPULATION

Sweden is a long thin country stretching almost 1,000 miles (1,600 km) from north to south and just over 300 miles (480 km) from west to east at its widest point, reaching a latitude of almost 69° North at its northernmost point, well beyond the Arctic Circle.

It is in a geologically stable land mass and is not prone to earthquakes, but the landscape has been influenced by the most recent Ice Age, which created its archipelagos and smoothed the rocks along the coastline. There are still glaciers in the far north in the region of Sweden's highest mountain, Kebnekaise, the summit of a range which runs along the border between Sweden and Norway. But the country's landscape is characterised mainly by forests which form the basis of one of the country's traditional industries.

The population of Sweden is about 8.4 million, of whom 1.4 million live in the Stockholm area, 700,000 in Gothenburg and 460,000 in Malmö.

TIME ZONES

Sweden is in the Central European Time zone, which is one hour ahead of Greenwich Mean Time and six hours ahead of Eastern Standard Time. Clocks are put forward by one hour between the end of March and the end of September.

CLIMATE

Considering its position on much the same latitude as Alaska, Sweden has a remarkably favourable climate, thanks in part to the influence of the Gulf Stream. The weather in summer is similar to that in Britain—and just as unpredictable—although in a good year some remarkably high temperatures can be recorded up in the Arctic regions because of the constant sunlight.

Indeed, the area round Piteå on the Gulf of Bothnia is sometimes known as the Northern Riviera because of its agreeable climate and warm sea. But in the north of the country autumn and winter arrive early and spring does not arrive till late in May, in contrast to southernmost Skåne, where the weather sometimes starts to improve in February. Winter temperatures can be cold throughout the country; even in Stockholm, daily maximum temperatures are likely to remain below freezing throughout January and February.

CULTURE & CUSTOMS

Swedes are meticulously polite to foreign visitors. As a guest, regardless of sex, you will always be invited to enter a room or a lift before your escort. But there are few social traps for the unwary apart from the rituals involved in eating and drinking (see the chapter on "*skåling*" customs and related traditions on Page 144).

Tipping is no great hassle; in hotels and restaurants, for instance, a service charge is usually included in the bill and a further tip is not expected. Taxi-drivers expect a tip of about 10 percent (to save the agonies of mental arithmetic just ask the driver to add the service charge and you won't normally be ripped off). Hairdressers should also be given about 10 percent, while cloakroom attendants receive about 7 Skr per coat.

ELECTRICITY

The supply in Sweden is 220 volts AC. You may need an adaptor for the standard two-pin round continental plugs used in Sweden if you are taking hairdriers or other electrical appliances.

BUSINESS HOURS

Most shops open between 9 a.m. and 6 p.m. on weekdays and until between 1 p.m. and 4 p.m. on Saturdays. In some larger towns, department stores remain open until 8 p.m. or 10 p.m. and some are even open on Sundays. Shops generally close early on the day before a public holiday. Banks are open Monday to Friday between 9.30 a.m. and 3 p.m. In some larger cities certain banks stay open till 6 p.m. All banks are closed on Saturdays. If you're in Stockholm and in desperate need of money out of hours the bank at Stockholm's Arlanda Airport is open daily between 7 a.m. and 10 p.m. Similarly in Gothenburg there is a bank at the city's Landvetter Airport, open daily from 8 a.m. to 8 p.m.

HOLIDAYS

No sooner have the Swedes got the Christmas and the New Year celebrations out of the way than they down tools again on 6 January to mark Epiphany. Then it's back to work till the usual Easter break, followed by a Labour Day holiday on 1 May and the movable feasts of Ascension Day and Whit Monday. Midsummer's Day is celebrated on about 24 June each year, and then there is another break till early November (All Saints' Day) and Christmas. Actually, the whole of July seems to be a public holiday in Sweden because it's virtually impossible to transact any business during that month.

RELIGIOUS SERVICES

The Swedish State Church is in the Lutheran tradition, and there are churches throughout the country. Stockholm, not surprisingly, has the widest range of places of worship. Protestant services in English are held at Immanuel Church, there is a Greek Orthodox church and several synagogues and three Islamic mosques.

COMMUNICATIONS

MEDIA

English-language newspapers are widely available at kiosks in the larger cities, usually on the day of publication. For a free read, the House of Culture (Kulturhuset) in Stockholm at Sergels Torg has a good selection of English-language newspapers and magazines, as does the City Library in Gothenburg on the main square, Götaplatsen. Radio Sweden has frequent 30-minute programmes in English with news and information about Sweden which can be picked up in most of the country on medium wave 1179 KHz (254m) and also in the Stockholm area on FM 89.6 MHz. Your hotel will often have details of the broadcast schedule. English-language books are widely available. An excellent shop in Stockholm is Hedengrens Bokhandel, Kungsgatan 4.

POSTAL SERVICES

Post Offices are generally open from 9 a.m. to 6 p.m. on weekdays, 10 a.m. to 1 p.m. on Saturdays, although some branches may be closed on Saturdays during July.

At the time of going to press, postage for letters within Europe cost 3.10 Skr and postcards 2.50 Skr. Airmail letters to the USA and Canada weighing less than 20 grams cost 3.60 Skr; airmail postcards, 3.10 Skr. Stamps and aerogrammes are on sale at post offices and also at most bookstalls and at stationers' shops.

TELEPHONE SERVICES

If you have an uncontrollable urge to phone home, don't head for the Post Office as you might do elsewhere in Europe. In Sweden the Post Offices do not have telephone facilities, but there are plenty of payphones and special Telegraph Offices marked "Tele" or "Telebutik" from which you can make calls. Calls within Europe cost about 7 Skr per minute. Follow the normal rule of thumb and avoid phoning from your hotel room; as elsewhere, hotels add on their own frequently exorbitant mark-up.

EMERGENCIES

SECURITY & CRIME

Sweden is a generally a law-abiding country, the sort of place where it's safe to walk around without any worries about being mugged. The assassination of Prime Minister Olof Palme in a Stockholm street in 1986 was, sadly, the exception that proved the rule.

Drug trafficking is regarded as a serious offence which can attract heavy prison sentences, so don't be tempted.

Dial 90 000 anywhere in Sweden if you require emergency assistance from the police, fire brigade or ambulance etc. You don't need to insert any money if you dial 90 000 from a pay phone.

Chemists' shops are generally open on a rota basis outside normal hours in larger towns and cities. All-night pharmacies are available in Stockholm (C W Scheele, Klarabergsgatan 64), in Gothenburg (Vasen, Götgatan 12) and in Malmö (Gripen, Bergsgatan 48).

If you need urgent dental treatment, dentists' surgeries are indicated by the sign "Tandläkare"; in Stockholm there is an emergency dental care service at Regeringsgatan 20 (tel. 08-20 06 17) which is open daily between 8 a.m. and 6 p.m.

GETTING AROUND

FROM THE AIRPORT

All three of Sweden's major international airports—Stockholm (Arlanda), Gothenburg (Landvetter) and Malmö (Sturup)—have excellent bus links to the city. From Arlanda there are frequent services from both the international and domestic terminals to the City Terminal at Klarabergsgatan above the Central Station. In both Gothenburg and Malmö coaches operate from the airport to the city's Central Station. For all three cities, fares are in the range 30-35 Skr.

Taxi fares into town from all three airports are expensive, but SAS Scandinavian Airlines operates a limousine service which is useful if your ultimate destination is not the main railway station. Typical fares per person from airport to city centre are 185 Skr in Stockholm, 105 Skr in Gothenburg and 180 Skr in Malmö, and three passengers going to the same address travel for the price of two.

DOMESTIC TRAVEL

Air travel: In a country which covers such vast distances, air travel is part of everyday life. All major cities and towns are linked by an efficient network of services operated by SAS Scandinavian Airlines and its associated domestic airline, Linjeflyg, and Stockholm alone has services to more than 30 points within Sweden. Low-price fares are available on selected domestic flights throughout the year, and there are low-cost standby fares for young people under 25 and special fares for senior citizens. Some of the best cheap fare offers are available during the summer peak season from the end of June till the beginning of August when few business executives are travelling.

Rail: Swedish State Railways (SJ) operates an efficient network, mostly electrified, covering the whole of the country. The route from Trelleborg in the south to Riksgränsen in the far north is actually reckoned to be the longest continuous stretch of electrified line in the world. Swedish trains operate at a high frequency, particularly on the main trunk route linking Stockholm with Gothenburg, on which there is an hourly service. It's always advisable to reserve your seat (at a cost of 15 Skr) and on some trains, marked with an "R" or "IC" in the timetable, reservations are compulsory. Most trains have a restaurant car or buffet.

SJ has recently changed its fare structure, under which everyone used to travel at a discount except on Fridays and Sundays. Now the full fares apply on every day of the week, although on some trains—described as "Red" departures—you can travel at half-price. The tickets are valid for 36 hours, so if you miss your planned train, you can still qualify for the discount provided that you use a designated "Red" service. Stopovers are not allowed if you use the discount fare.

Long-distance rail trips in Sweden are particularly good value because there is a flat-rate maximum fare for all journeys of 560 miles (about 900 km) or more.

A go-as-you-please ticket is available between early June and late August on the "Inlandsbanan" (Inland Railway) which runs for more than 800 miles (1,300 km) down the spine of Sweden from Gällivare, north of the Arctic Circle, to Kristinehamn in the south. A special card gives unrestricted travel over the line for 14 or 21 days. Cost in 1988 was 390 Skr for 14 days and 440 Skr for 21 days, and the card also gives discounts on overnight accommodation.

WATER TRANSPORT

Ferries: For a country which is always boasting about its 96,000 lakes (who had the task of counting them in the first place?) and countless rivers and canals, water transport plays a surprisingly small part in the public transport scene. The main ferry links serve the Baltic island of Gotland, with services from Nynäshamn, Västervik and Oskarshamn. There are also innumerable commuter services in the Stockholm archipelago operated by the famous white boats of the Waxholm Steamship Company. During the summer you can buy a season ticket— "Båtluffarkortet"—which gives you unlimited travel on the Waxholm boats for 16 days.

PUBLIC TRANSPORT

Bus: There is an efficient network of express bus services linking all major towns and cities operated mainly by GDG Continentbus and Swedish State Railways (SJ). There are also weekend-only services on a number of key routes, while in the north of the country post buses are a useful way of getting around. The local bus network in Stockholm is claimed to be the world's largest and is run by the Stockholm Transit Authority, which also operates the underground (see below) and local main line rail services. Public transport in Gothenburg is distinguished by its efficient and ecologically sound tram system.

Underground: Stockholm is justifiably proud of its underground railway, known as "T-banan" (the "T" stands for "tunnel" and all stations are identified by the "T" sign). The T-banan is spotlessly clean, and the newest line with its mural paintings is claimed to be the world's largest living art exhibition. The system has almost 100 stations and covers more than 60 route-miles.

PRIVATE TRANSPORT

Car: Sweden's roads are mercifully uncrowded, with toll-free motorways covering more than 700 miles plus some 50,000 miles of trunk road, not to mention thousands of miles of often picturesque byroads. Speed limits outside built-up areas are 68, 56 or 43 miles (110, 90 or 70 km) an hour, depending on road width and traffic density. In built-up areas the limit is 31 miles per hour (50 km an hour), or 19 miles per hour (30 km an hour) around school areas.

You always have to give way to traffic approaching from the right unless road signs indicate otherwise and you must give way to traffic already on a roundabout. The driver and all passengers must use seat belts. Dipped headlights are obligatory when driving, both by day and by night.

You are not required to call the police if you have an accident, but drivers must give their name and address to the other parties involved and may not leave the scene until this is done. Drivers who do not stop after an accident may be liable to a fine or even imprisonment.

If you have a breakdown, contact either the police or the "Larmtjänst" organisation which is run by the Swedish insurance companies and operates a 24-hour service. Its telephone numbers are listed in Swedish telephone directories. The emergency number 90 000 should be used only in the case of accidents or injury.

Sweden's drink-drive laws are strictly enforced and heavy fines are imposed on motorists found to be under the influence of alcohol or other stimulants. You can be prosecuted even if you have drunk no more than the equivalent of two cans of beer.

Car hire: All the major companies have the usual desks at Stockholm (Arlanda), Gothenburg (Landvetter) or Malmö (Sturup) airports. Town offices are located as follows:

STOCKHOLM

Avis, Sveavägen 61 Tel. 08-34 99 10
Hertz, Mäster Samuelsgatan 67 Tel. 08-24 07 20
Interrent, Hotel Sheraton, Tegelbacken 6 Tel. 08-21 06 50
Gothenburg
Avis, Central Station Tel. 031-17 04 10
Budget, Odinsgatan 8 Tel. 031-80 09 70
Europcar, Odinsgatan 19 Tel. 031-80 53 95
Hertz, Engelbrektsgatan 73 Tel. 031-81 07 90

Interrent, P-Huset, Nordstan Tel. 031-80 26 00

MALMÖ

Avis, Stortorget 9 Tel. 040-778 30
Budget, Baltzarsgatan 14 Tel. 040-775 75
Europcar, Djäknegatan 2 Tel. 040-716 40
Hertz, Skeppsbron 3 Tel. 040-749 55
Interrent, Mäster Nilsgatan 22 Tel. 040-38 02 40

Taxi: The Swedish taxi service is usually efficient, but relies more on the telephone than the traditional London method of waving an umbrella. In the larger cities, a miraculous computer system spews out instructions to the driver to indicate where his or her next fare is to be picked up. Fares are on the steep side with a minimum charge of about 15 Skr, and the meter starts running as soon as the driver is directed to pick you up. There is also an extra charge of about 30 Skr if you order a taxi in advance, which seems an unfair reward for helping the taxi company organise its commitments well in advance.

Bicycles: Cycling holidays are popular in Sweden and bikes can be hired easily in most places; just inquire at the local Tourist Office. Average hire cost is about 50 Skr per day or 200 Skr for a week. The Swedish Touring Club (STF), Box 25, S-101 20 Stockholm (tel. 08-790 31 00) has information about cycling packages which include overnight accommodation, meals and cycle hire. Cykelfrämjandet, Box 3070, 103 61 Stockholm, (tel. 08-10 10 86), publishes an English-language guide to cycling holidays.

ON FOOT

All three of Sweden's largest cities are compact enough to be able to do a lot of sightseeing on foot, and all are pedestrian-friendly to the extent of having traffic lights which motorists actually observe. Conversely, Swedish pedestrians are so disciplined that they respect red lights even when there is not a single car in sight.

In the countryside serious walkers will find plenty of long-distance paths, including the *Kungsleden* (King's Trail) which traverses the high peaks of Lappland. The Swedish Touring Club (see above for address) maintains a network of cabins where long-distance walkers can find overnight accommodation. It also operates Sweden's youth hostels.

HITCHHIKING

It is officially discouraged, and in any case finding a lift can be a problem during the holiday season, when every Swedish car seems to be groaning under a payload of children, camping gear and surf-boards.

WHERE TO STAY

HOTELS

Swedish hotels are of a uniformly high standard, although not surprisingly they tend to be on the expensive side. Over the past few years, hoteliers seem to have been increasing their rates at an annual rate of 10 percent, well above the country's level of inflation. But, particularly in the larger towns and cities, hotel rates actually come down in high summer because the expense-account business travellers on whom they depend for their profits are on holiday themselves. Unusually, the big international hotel chains like Hilton or Sheraton have made little impact on Sweden. Instead, the accommodation scene is dominated by Scandinavian chains like SARA, Scandic or RESO. Like most chain hotels, they tend to lack character, but they are usually run very efficiently and it is difficult to fault their service.

Away from the big cities, there are plenty of privately-owned hotels which offer the individuality lacking in the properties run by the chains. Many of them are located in scenic rural settings and are converted manor-houses or mine-owners' mansions. About 100 of these private establishments throughout the country belong to the Sweden Hotels consortium, which runs a central booking service in Stockholm.

All the hotel groups run special discount schemes during the summer peak, including the SARA Bonus Pass, the Scandic Hotel Cheque, the RESO Passepartout Card, the Sweden Hotels Pass and the Best Western Scandinavia Hotel Cheque.

In addition, the three major cities—Stockholm, Gothenburg and Malmö—all offer special packages at weekends year-round and daily during the summer which offer much-reduced hotel accommodation plus a card which gives free travel on public transport and free admission to visitor attractions.

MOTELS

As a highly motorised country, Sweden has a large number of motels, most of them constructed quite recently. They are ideal for family touring holidays because they are easy to reach and are usually located on the outskirts of towns or in agreeable countryside areas. Many have family rooms with four beds at very reasonable rates.

BUDGET ACCOMMODATION

The bed-and-breakfast system is not so widespread in Sweden as elsewhere. But if you're looking for inexpensive accommodation, look out for the "Rum" sign. It means "room" and that's all you get (no breakfast thrown in). It's always worth inquiring at local tourist offices if any "rum" accommodation is available. Prices are extremely reasonable—only about 160 Skr per person per night in Stockholm, for instance.

CAMPGROUNDS

Camping is highly popular among the Swedes and there are about 750 officially-approved sites, many in picturesque locations by a lake or by the sea. Most sites are open from early June to the end of August, but some are also open with more limited facilities outside the peak season. A typical price for one night for a family plus tent or caravan is about 50 Skr, which is claimed to be one of the cheapest rates in Europe.

SELF-CATERING

Many Swedish families have their own country chalet, or "stuga", where they retreat for their holidays, but there are also plenty of chalets available to rent, all of a very high standard. Cooking utensils and blankets are usually provided and visitors have to supply only their own sheets and towels. There are about 250 chalet villages with extra amenities like a restaurant or swimming pool, as well as activities like tennis or badminton. The villages are fine for families, but probably not quite right if you want to get away from it all.

YOUTH HOSTELS

Sweden has about 280 youth hostels, or "vandrarhem", generally far removed from the spartan image which hostels often enjoy. They range from mansion houses and medieval castles to renovated sailing ships like the 100-year-old "*af Chapman*" moored in Stockholm harbour but there are many modern purpose-built hostels as well.

Most have two- and four-bedded rooms or family rooms and self-catering facilities, while meals or light refreshments are provided in some hostels. The hostels are run by the Swedish Touring Club (STF), but if you are a member of an affiliated Youth Hostels Association you qualify for a cheaper rate. Normal members' price for youth-hostel accommodation varies between about 40 and 55 Skr per night (60-90 Skr for non-members). You must provide your own sheet sleeping bag. All hostels are open during the summer and some for the whole year.

ACCOMMODATION INFORMATION

SARA Hotels, Svärdvägen 23, S-182 84 Danderyd/Stockholm Tel. 08-753 73 50
RESO Hotels, S-113 92 Stockholm Tel. 08-23 57 00
Scandic Hotels, Box 6197, S-102 33 Stockholm Tel. 08-34 55 50
Sweden Hotels, Kammakargatan 48, S-111 60 Stockholm Tel. 08-20 43 11
Best Western Hotels, Saltmätargatan 5, S-113 59 Stockholm Tel. 08-30 04 20
Swedish Touring Club (STF), (Youth hostels, mountain cabins) Box 25, S-101 20 Stockholm Tel. 08-790 32 00.

An invaluable free guide for anyone planning a visit to Sweden is the Swedish Tourist Board's *Hotels in Sweden*, an annual guide published by the Swedish Tourist Board. It lists all the main hotels in each town or city with full details of the amenities each offers and an indication of prices. There is also a rundown (in English) on all the main discount schemes offered by the main hotel groups.

It would need a whole book to give a comprehensive listing of hotels for a country the size of Sweden, so the list that follows is necessarily a personal selection of places to stay in the three main cities, Stockholm, Gothenburg and Malmö. Prices quoted were valid at the time of going to press but, alas, are likely to continue the inflationary trend of recent years. The rates are based on a normal midweek stay for two people sharing a double room (usually including breakfast), but may be significantly lower at weekends and probably in midweek as well during the summer peak season.

STOCKHOLM

Clas på Hörnet, Surbrunnsgatan 20, S-113 48 Stockholm Tel. 08-16 51 30. You need to book early because it has only 10 rooms. It has only fairly recently been converted into a hotel, reverting to its 18th century role as an inn. A little way outside the city centre. 995 Skr.

Karelia, Birger Jarlsgatan 35, S-111 83 Stockholm Tel. 08-24 76 60. A listed building in fairly central location on a main shopping street. Restaurant specialises in Russian cuisine. 103 rooms. 900 Skr.

Kristineberg, Hjalmar Söderbergs väg 10, Box 25052, S-100 23 Stockholm Tel. 08-13 03 00. Comfortable and recently modernised hotel, a little way out of the city centre but only 10 minutes by underground. 98 rooms. 690 Skr.

Mälardrottningen, Riddarholmen, S-111 28 Stockholm Tel. 08-24 36 00. Stockholm's most unusual hotel—a luxury yacht once owned by Barbara Hutton and now permanently moored in the Old Town. Excellent but fairly expensive restaurant. Its new name means "Queen of Lake Mälaren". 59 rooms (correction, cabins). 825 Skr.

Mornington, Nybrogatan 53, S-111 40 Stockholm Tel. 08-663 12 40. A comfortable hotel in a fairly quiet street, but close to all the city-centre attractions, with impeccable service from the apparently all-female staff. 141 rooms. 870 Skr.

Reisen, Skeppsbron 12-14, S-111 30 Stockholm Tel. 08-22 32 60. A popular 19th-century hotel now run by the SARA group, located right on the waterfront in the Old Town. Its piano bar is a favourite if somewhat smoky late-night rendezvous. 113 rooms. 1,100 Skr.

SAS Strand, Nybrokajen 9, S-103 27 Stockholm Tel. 08-22 29 00. Probably out of the price bracket for the average tourist, but has to be included in any listing because of its waterside location and its turn-of-the-century atmosphere. It was taken over by the SAS airline group in 1986. 137 rooms. 1,650 Skr.

GOTHENBURG

Eggers, Drottningtorget, Box 323, S-401 25 Göteborg Tel. 031-17 15 70. One of the classic 19th-century railway hotels, located opposite the Central Station. Rooms are individually furnished and have been renovated recently. 77 rooms. 895 Skr.

Europa, Köpmansgatan 38, S-401 24 Göteborg Tel. 031-80 12 80. Also bang opposite the Central Station and adjoining the airport bus stop and the huge Nordstan shopping centre. Run by the SARA group. 480 rooms. 1,095 Skr.

Liseberg Heden, Sten Sturegatan, S-411 38 Göteborg Tel. 031-20 02 80. Fairly central location, not far from the city's best-known tourist attraction, the Liseberg amusement park. 160 rooms. 710 Skr.

MALMÖ

Garden, Baltzarsgatan 20, Box 4075, S-203 11 Malmö Tel. 040-10 40 00. A comfortable and quiet hotel in a central location near the main shopping and entertainment area. 173 rooms. 890 Skr.

Noble House, Gustav Adolfstorg 47, S-211 39 Malmö Tel. 040-10 15 00. Fairly new and centrally-located hotel. 128 rooms. 925 Skr.

Plaza, S. Förstadsgatan 30, S-211 44 Malmö Tel. 040-771 00. Unpretentious hotel with fairly central location. 52 rooms. 690 Skr.

FOOD DIGEST

WHAT TO EAT

Not so long ago you didn't have an enormous variety of cuisine to choose from on a visit to Sweden. In short, you could enjoy any style of cooking as long as it was Swedish. But the past few years have changed all that and, certainly in the major cities, you can now sample food based on French, Italian, Greek or any other gastronomic tradition you care to think of. Even in remote towns far away from the bright lights you'll find Chinese restaurants which have, admittedly, adjusted their menus to suit Swedish palates.

Stockholm, for instance, now has more than 700 restaurants covering more than 30 national cuisines, and the *Guide Michelin* has singled out more than 20 Stockholm establishments, giving five of them a star rating.

Gothenburg, too, is a good centre for dining, with particular reference to seafood, and Malmö claims to have more restaurants per head than any other Swedish city. Perhaps because of its maritime traditions, it also has a highly cosmopolitan selection of restaurants. Some of the highlights of Swedish gastronomy—notably the smörgåsbord—are described in the chapter on "Food and Drink", so suffice it to say that you will not return home hungry. Restaurant prices may seem on the high side at times, but portions are generous and you will certainly get value for money. It is worth re-emphasising that Swedish hotel breakfasts are usually of generous proportions so you'll save money during the day by stocking up first thing in the morning.

WHERE TO EAT

Top-class restaurants catering mainly for a business clientele can be expensive, but for the traveller on a budget there is no shortage of places where you can find an inexpensive meal. Even some of the swisher hotels in the main cities have a special lunchtime menu at a fraction of their evening prices.

Look out anywhere for the *dagens rätt* (dish of the day), a business lunch costing only about 40 Skr for a main course, salad, soft drink and coffee. Fast-food outlets are, inevitably, to be found everywhere and you'll see familiar names like Wimpy and McDonald's as well as Clock, an indigenous chain. Typical price for a Big Mac with french fries is about 28 Skr. Pizzerias are also popular and good value for money.

The Swedes generally eat fairly early. Restaurants start serving lunch at about 11 a.m. and some small hotels, particularly in country areas, serve the evening meal at around 6 p.m. But at motels and in the cities you can eat much later, and in the cities you can often find good-class cafés which are open after midnight for a late snack.

A useful tip if you're looking for good value is to look in Swedish newspapers next to the entertainments section, where restaurants with "special offers" or fixed-price menus often advertise.

As mentioned in the "Food and Drink" chapter, the ubiquitous *korvkiosk* is the nearest equivalent to the British "chippy", selling fast-food delicacies like grilled chicken, sausages and hamburgers.

As with our choice of hotels, the list of restaurants in the three main cities which follows can be no more than a limited personal choice, and anyway part of the fun of visiting a new country is to make your own gastronomic discoveries. The information booklets issued by each local tourist office usually give a full listing of restaurants and an indication of price.The symbols which follow each entry give a rough indication of prices, based on the typical cost of a three-course evening meal per head, excluding wine. * = less than 100 Skr; ** = 100-250 Skr; *** = more than 250 Skr.

Annorlunda, Malmskillnadsgatan 50 Tel. 08-21 95 69. Caters mainly for vegetarians, but some fish and meat dishes too. **

Birger Bar, Birger Jarlsgatan 5 Tel. 08-20 72 10. Not a pub, but a fairly new and inexpensive Italian restaurant. *

Centralens Restaurang, Central Railway Station, Vasagatan Tel. 08-20 20 49. A rather superior station buffet which opens early for breakfast. Good for a quick meal. **

Eriks, Strandvägen 17 Tel. 08-60 60 60. Floating restaurant on a converted barge near the city centre. Excellent—and expensive—seafood. ***

La Brochette, Storgatan 27 Tel. 08-62 20 00. Highly popular French restaurant with grilled meat on skewers the speciality, as the name implies. ***

La Grenouille, Grev Turegatan 16 Tel. 08-20 10 00. Three restaurants in one, with varying price levels. The most expensive features the eponymous frogs' legs. ** or ***

Operakällaren, Operan (Royal Opera House) Tel. 08-11 11 25. Arguably Stockholm's best-known restaurant and worth visiting for the décor alone. Its Christmas smörgåsbord was nominated by Jan Morris in London's *Times* as "The Best Meal in the World". ***

Sarajevo, Lilla Nygatan 11 Tel. 08-20 41 01. Long-established Yugoslavian restaurant famed for its generous portions. **

Stekhuset Falstaff, Tegeluddsvägen 90 Tel. 08-63 48 40. Good-value steak house, where you can watch your own steak being grilled. **

Vau de Ville, Hamngatan 17 Tel. 08-21 25 22. Two restaurants in one—a snack-bar offering lighter fare and a brasserie with a more varied menu. **

GOTHENBURG

Annorlunda, Lilla Korsgatan 2 Tel. 031-13 80 26. A vegetarian restaurant. *

Centralens Restaurang, Central Station Tel. 031-15 20 81. Newly-renovated station restaurant, plus bar with open fireplace. **

Déjà Vu, Viktoriagatan 1 Tel. 031-13 38 52. Popular with young people. Reasonable prices. *

Gamle Port, Östra Larmgatan 18 Tel. 031-11 07 02. Turn-of-the-century atmosphere, with pub on the ground floor. **

Johanna, Södra Hamngatan 47 Tel. 031-11 22 50. Probably Gothenburg's most exclusive restaurant, with prices to match. ***

Räkan, Lorensbergsgatan 16 Tel. 031-16 98 99. Popular seafood restaurant with a gimmick. Order shrimps and they'll come in a radio-controlled "fishing boat" which you steer yourself! **

MALMÖ

Centralens Restaurang, Central Station Tel. 040-766 80. Unpretentious, but offers good salad buffet and dish of the day. *

Kockska Krogen, Stortorget Tel. 040-703 20. Well-known cellar restaurant in 16th-century town house. ***

Översten, Regementsgatan 52 Tel. 040-91 91 00. Restaurant on the 26th floor of a tower block with view across the straits to Denmark. ***

Rådhuskällaren, Stortorget Tel. 040-790 20. Another 16th-century cellar restaurant. Seafood a speciality. **

DRINKING NOTES

As mentioned in the "Food and Drink" chapter, alcohol is something of a luxury in Sweden because of the high Customs and excise duties. The best bet is probably to stick to low- or medium-strength beer (Class I or II) or the excellent "Ramlösa" mineral water, although if you're being entertained you may well be pressed to sample one of the excellent indigenous schnapps.

There is no difficulty in ordering a drink with your meal, although the stronger potions like Class III beer may not be available until noon. You can buy wine, spirits and export beer only through the State-controlled monopoly "Systembolaget", which has branches all over the country. They are generally open between 9 a.m. and 6 p.m. Monday to Friday but close early on the day before a public holiday. The minimum age for buying alcoholic beverages is 20.

THINGS TO DO

MUSEUMS & ART GALLERIES

STOCKHOLM

You could spend a month touring Stockholm's museums and galleries and you still wouldn't have time to see them all. This listing is a personal selection of "musts", but a comprehensive guide to all the main museums is given in the booklet *What To See And Do In Stockholm*, obtainable from the Tourist Centre at Sweden House.

Admission prices quoted were correct at the time of going to press but will probably have increased before the 1990 summer season. However, prices are academic if you obtain the "Key to Stockholm" card ("Stockholmskortet") which gives free admission to all the main visitor attractions plus free transport on the bus and underground network. Similar cards are available in Gothenburg and Malmö.

Opening times quoted apply to the main summer season (late June to mid-August). Check locally on times for the rest of the year.

Wasa Museum at Djurgården. Adults 8 Skr, children 5 Skr. Sweden's best-known museum, with the 17th-century man of war which capsized on her maiden voyage and was raised from the harbour in 1961. Limited opening in 1989 pending opening of new museum in spring 1990; check times locally.

Vaxholm Fortress Museum, at Vaxholm in the Stockholm archipelago. Houses old weapons, uniforms and historical documents. Adults 8 Skr, children 5 Skr. Open daily 12 noon to 4 p.m. Reached by half-hourly boat service.

Science and Technology Museum

(Tekniska Museet), Museivägen 7. Adults 10 Skr, children 5 Skr. Open 10 a.m.-4 p.m. Plenty of buttons to press for children of all ages.

Royal Palace, in the Old Town. Several museums in one, with different charges and opening times; check locally. Highlights are the State Apartments, the Treasury and the Royal Armoury.

Medieval Museum (Medeltidsmuseet), Strömparterren. Adults 15 Skr, children 5 Skr. Open daily except Monday 11 a.m.-5 p.m. Depicts the story of Stockholm's founding and development in the Middle Ages.

Nordic Museum (Nordiska Museet), Djurgården. Adults 10 Skr, children 5 Skr. Open daily 10 a.m.-4 p.m. (opens at 12 noon at weekend). A logical follow-on from the Medieval Museum, showing how Swedish people have lived since the 16th century.

National Museum, Blasieholmen. Adults 20 Skr, children free. Open daily except Monday 10 a.m.-4 p.m. Sweden's national art gallery, containing many Old Masters, including some Rembrandts.

Millesgården, Carl Milles väg 2. Adults 10 Skr, children 2 Skr. Open daily 10 a.m.-5 p.m. Collection of many of the works of the Swedish-American sculptor Carl Milles.

Toy Museum (Leksaksmuseet), Maria-torget 1. Adults 12 Skr, children 6 Skr. Open daily except Monday 10 a.m.-4 p.m. (opens 12 noon at weekends). A "must" for children, with a collection of 10,000 toys past and present.

Museum of National Antiquities (Historiska Museet), Narvavägen 13-17. Adults 20 Skr, children 15 Skr. Open daily except Monday 11 a.m.-4 p.m. Exhibits show daily life from prehistoric times to the Middle Ages.

Rosendal Palace, Djurgården. Adults 15 Skr, children 5 Skr. Open daily 12 noon to 3 p.m. A royal hideaway built in the early 19th century.

GOTHENBURG

Most Gothenburg museums are open daily from 12 noon to 4 p.m except Sunday, when the opening times are 11 a.m.-5 p.m. Admission is normally 10 Skr for adults and free for children. An exception is the Maritime Centre (see below).

Elfsborg Fortress. Built in the 17th century to guard the harbour mouth, and still bears traces of battles with the Danes. Reached by boat from Stenpiren in Gothenburg harbour.

East Indies House, Norra Hamngatan 12. 18th-century building containing three museums: Archaeological, Ethnographical and Historical.

Natural History Museum, Slottsskogen. Located in parkland, with displays of thousands of animals.

Art Gallery, Götaplatsen. Has one of the most comprehensive displays of Scandinavian art from the 19th century to the present day.

Maritime Centre, Lilla Bommen. Adults 45 Skr, children 20 Skr (Gothenburg Card not valid). Open daily 10 a.m.-6 p.m. One of the city's newest tourist attractions—a living exhibition of ships old and new, located in the harbour itself.

Röhsska Art and Crafts Museum, Vasagatan 37-39. Collections include earthenware, textiles, and Chinese and Japanese art.

MALMÖ

Malmöhus Castle, Malmöhusvägen. 10 Skr. Open 12 noon to 4 p.m. Several museums under one roof in the 16th-century castle—the City Museum, the Art Museum, the Natural History Museum and the Aquarium.

Kommendanthuset, Malmöhusvägen. Admission free. Open 12 noon-4 p.m. Near Malmöhus Castle. Exhibition of military history on ground floor, upstairs displays about modern-day Malmö.

Malmö Art Gallery (Malmö Konsthall), St Johannesgatan 7. Admission free. Open Tuesday and Thursday 11 a.m.-8 p.m.; Wednesday 11 a.m.-9 p.m.; Friday to Monday 11 a.m.-5 p.m. Claimed to be one of northern Europe's largest galleries. Guided tours on Wednesdays and Saturdays.

Carriage Museum (Vagnmuseet), Drottningtorget. Admission free. Open Monday only, 9 a.m.-4 p.m. Unusual collection of old coaches, carts and other vintage vehicles.

MUSIC & OPERA

As with the theatre, the musical scene in Sweden tends to be barren in the summer, with the commendable exception of rural areas like Dalarna, where a number of communities organise music festivals.

In Stockholm the main concert hall is "Konserthuset", the home of the Stockholm Philharmonic Orchestra, whose season runs from September to May or June. The new Berwald Concert Hall is the base for Swedish National Radio's musical activities, with regular performances by the Radio Symphony Orchestra.

Stockholm's famous Royal Opera House has performances of top-rank international standard between mid-August and June.

Gothenburg and Malmö both have top-rank concert halls; Malmö's 1,300-seat hall was opened as recently as 1985, giving its Symphony Orchestra a permanent home for the first time in 60 years.

THEATRES

Sweden has a lively theatrical life, in the major cities at least. The disadvantage for the tourist is that many theatres tend to be closed during the peak summer months, when artists take off for their own well-deserved holidays. In any event, most performances are in Swedish, so the average foreign visitor will not be unduly worried. An exception is the Regina on Drottninggatan, the only permanent English-speaking theatre in Scandinavia.

In Stockholm, the most prestigious theatre is the Royal Dramatic Theatre on Nybroplan, which has four separate auditoriums. Perhaps the most unusual theatre is the Drottningholm Court at Drottningholm Palace, founded by King Gustav III in 1766. More than 30 sets from those days are still in use today, and in the summer there are ballet and opera performances.

Current performances are listed in newspapers and in the "Stockholm This Week" booklet. There is a booth on Norrmalmstorg square where you can buy last-minute theatre seats at prices at least 25 percent below the normal box-office rates.

In Gothenburg the two main theatres are Stadsteatern and Folkteatern which, as in Stockholm, both close down in June, July and August. Present your Gothenburg Card at the box-office half-an-hour before the performance is due to start and you'll be given a discount if any last-minute seats are available.

Malmö's Stadsteater is a modern building with three separate stages. All plays are performed in Swedish, but you can often pick up an opera or musical performance. The Malmö Card gives you a 50 percent discount on the normal price if you buy your ticket at the box office after 12 noon on the day of performance.

If you're in the right place during the summer, you may be able to see one of the traditional mystery plays. At Leksand in Dalarna, there are annual performances at the end of July of "Himlaspelet" (The Road to Heaven). And in Visby, on the island of Gotland, there are annual open-air performances in the ruins of St Nicolaus Church of "Petrus de Dacia", a musical drama telling the authentic story of a Dominican monk—who was buried by the high altar—and his sublimated love for a German peasant girl.

MOVIES

Virtually all foreign films are shown with their original sound-tracks, with Swedish sub-titles, and dubbing is almost unknown. Local newspapers have full details of programmes and timings. In Stockholm, cinemas showing first-run international films include the Grand, Sveavägen 45 (tel. 08-11 24 00) and Lilla Kvarn, Biblioteksgatan 5 (tel. 08-21 14 22). For real film buffs, the place to head for in Stockholm is Filmstaden (Film City), Mäster Samuelsgatan 25 (tel. 08-22 54 20), which has 11 cinemas under one roof and is open every day between noon and midnight.

NIGHTLIFE

As in other countries, there is an active nightlife in the larger cities but nothing particularly hectic in the smaller communities. Given the high cost of drinking in Sweden, a night out on the town can be an expensive exercise. The best value is probably to be had at one of the jazz clubs favoured by the younger generation or at one of the piano-bars which offer a relaxing environment for a late-night drink for those whose decibel tolerance can't cope with discos.

An important point to note is that some night-spots have remarkably high minimum age-limits, so it's advisable for younger visitors to check first. It's even possible to find some of the posher discos imposing a minimum age of 26 for men and 24 for women.

STOCKHOLM

Café Opera, Operahuset Tel. 08-11 00 26. One of the most popular late-night spots for the younger generation. It's always crowded and you have to queue up to get in. Disco starts late at night.

Börsen, Jakobsgatan 6 Tel. 08-24 92 10. The city's largest night-club with top-rank cabaret and dancing.

Maxim, Drottninggatan 81 Tel. 08-10 30 90. Combines night-club, restaurant and piano-bar under the same roof.

King Creole, Kungsgatan 18 Tel. 08-24 47 00. Big-band dance music for the older generation during the week; noisier disco music for the youngsters at the weekend.

Fasching, Kungsgatan 63 Tel. 08-21 93 65. Stockholm's largest and probably most popular jazz club.

Karlsson, Kungsgatan 65 Tel. 08-11 92 98. Not long established, but already one of Stockholm's leading discos.

GOTHENBURG

Gamle Port, Östra Larmgatan 18 Tel. 031-11 07 02. Several bars and dance-floors, plus restaurants and pub. Highly popular spot.

Nya Club Opalen, Hotel Opalen, Engelbrektsgatan 73 Tel. 031-81 03 00. Dancing to international orchestras. Restaurant and cocktail bar.

Jazzhuset, Erik Dahlbergsgatan 3 Tel. 031-13 35 44. The best spot in town for fans of traditional or modern jazz.

MALMÖ

Kronprinsen, Mariedalsvägen 32 Tel. 040-772 40 Southern Sweden's only cabaret restaurant; dancing to live music. Booking advised; closed June to August.

Baldakinen, Generalsgatan 1 Tel. 040-749 45. Dancing to live or disco music.

SHOPPING

WHAT TO BUY

Sweden is world-famous for its elegant design and you'll find plenty of good buys in glassware, stainless steel and silver, pottery and ceramics, textiles and leather goods. Big department stores like NK, Åhléns, Tempo and Domus have branches all over the country and are particularly noted for high-quality and inexpensive kitchenware.

The best bargains in glassware are to be had in the "Glass Country" area in Småland, in the southeast of Sweden. Major glassworks like Orrefors, Kosta-Boda have large supermarkets adjoining their factories where you can pick up "seconds" for only a fraction of the normal price.

For really flawless glass products you need to shop at any of the major department shops like NK or specialist stores like the Crystal Showrooms or Nordiska Kristall-magasinet in Stockholm. These outlets are aimed particularly at the American market and the goods are often priced in dollars.

Sweden is also renowned for its high-quality porcelain and you can find bargains at the Gustavsberg factory outside Stockholm and at the Rörstrand factory in Lidköping. Many foreign visitors head for one of the "IKEA" stores, usually located on the outskirts of towns, where you can pick up elegantly-designed furniture and fittings for the home, but at budget prices. IKEA operates an export service.

Modern, fashionable clothing at inexpensive prices can be found at Hennes & Mauritz (H & M), which has branches throughout Sweden, but the best place to pick up bargains in textiles is probably Borås, not far from Gothenburg and the centre of the area known as "Tygriket" ("The Weavers' Country"). "Knallebygden" is a large shopping centre in Borås where you can pick up bargains in clothing from the leading direct-mail companies. The centre of the fur business is Tranås in the province of Småland, where you can also usually find plenty of bargain buys.

SHOPPING AREAS

Offbeat Shopping: All the major cities have unusual markets where you can discover all kinds of gastronomic goodies. Stockholm has markets at Östermalmstorg and Hötorget which are well worth a visit, while Gothenburg has its Fish Church, built in the ecclesiastical style but actually a thriving fish market. Gothenburg also has a fascinating market hall (Saluhallen) with a collection of 39 shops, mostly butchers, grocers and greengrocers. Malmö has a similar but more upmarket Saluhallen in an old building at Lilla Torg, where there are restaurants and cafés as well as delicatessens.

Stockholm also has what is claimed to be northern Europe's largest flea market at Skärholmen, 20 minutes on the underground from the city centre. It's open daily, but Saturday and Sunday are the best days to go.

All three major cities give useful hints about local shopping in their information booklets.

In the countryside, it's worth looking out for "Hemslöjd" handicraft centres where you can buy attractive locally-produced items. Women's and children's clothes are especially good buys, as well as furs and needlework. All over Sweden, in fact, you can see craftsmen at work and buy examples of their work at inexpensive prices.

SHOPPING HOURS

Most shops are open between 9 a.m. and 6 p.m. on weekdays and until between 1 p.m. and 4 p.m. on Saturdays. In larger towns, some department stores remain open until 9 p.m., and some are also open on Sundays. In country areas, shops and petrol stations generally close between 5 p.m. and 6 p.m. Shops generally close early on the day before a public holiday.

Summer can be the best time of year for shopping because that's when many stores hold their annual sales, indicated by "REA" stickers in the windows.

TAX-FREE SHOPPING

Sweden is something of a pioneer in establishing an efficient tax-free shopping system, given its relatively high level of Value Added Tax (called "Moms" in Swedish), which stands at 19 percent on all products. More than 19,000 shops throughout Sweden take part in the Sweden Tax Free Shopping Service, which enables you to reclaim a refund on the VAT which you have paid on your purchases, less a service charge. The refund is made on departure from Sweden, either at the airport or seaport, or in some cases on board ship. Some shops may offer the tax-free facility only on purchases of more than 200 Skr.

SPORTS

PARTICIPANT

Sweden is a health-conscious country and the provision of sporting facilities has always been generous, not least in the area of lawn tennis, as opponents of Borg, Edberg, Wilander etc will testify. There is a wide range of indoor and outdoor courts for public use throughout the country and tennis is not at all an exclusive sport.

Riding, too, is a sport which is by no means the prerogative of the well-to-do. Almost every town has riding stables or a riding school and more experienced riders can enjoy a pony-trekking safari in the Kebnekaise mountain range. Golf is also very popular, with almost 200 courses. The best are in the south of the country, but you can even play a round in the light of the Midnight Sun inside the Arctic Circle at Boden.

With its countless lakes and waterways, Sweden has a lot to offer to devotees of watersports like water skiing, windsurfing or canoeing. All that water means that Sweden is an important country for anglers— coarse, game or sea. To fish in fresh water you normally need a permit, but sea fishing is free.

Swedes learn to ski when they are not much more than toddlers so there are plenty of facilities for both downhill and cross-country enthusiasts. The best-known resorts are Åre, which was a close contender for the 1994 Winter Olympics, and Sälen in the province of Dalarna. Summer skiing can be enjoyed at Riksgränsen in the far north of the country.

SPECTATOR

Tennis must again come top of the list, now that Sweden is increasingly dominating the game internationally. The main tournaments are the Swedish Open at Båstad on the south-west coast in mid-July and the Stockholm Open in early November.

Horse-racing and trotting are popular spectator sports in Sweden with the best-known courses at Stockholm (Täby), Gothenburg (Åby) and Malmö (Jägersro). The Swedish Derby is held in July at Jägersro, which is also the venue for a major horse show in August. Another important annual international horse show is held at the Gothenburg Scandinavium in April.

Gothenburg is probably the most sport-conscious town in Sweden, and its Scandinavium is the venue for many major events, including tennis, ice hockey and table tennis. The city's other main arena is Ullevi Stadium, where international tournaments in football, athletics and speedway are staged regularly.

In athletics, Stockholm usually has an international meeting in early July, and the city stages one of the world's biggest marathons each year—usually in early June—with some 16,000 competitors from about 30 countries.

SPECIAL INFORMATION

DOING BUSINESS

The Swedes tend to be rather formal when it comes to business dealings. There is little small talk when you turn up for a meeting, so it's straight down to business. Lengthy business lunches are not the order of the day; you may well be taken out to lunch by your business contacts, but after an hour they'll start fidgeting and looking at their watches, and you may get only a low-alcohol beer to drink.

Formal business dress should be worn and you should always arrive for meetings punctually. Do your homework before you leave for Sweden and always have all the facts at your fingertips because the Swedes are sticklers for detail.

You are on to a winner if you can strike up personal friendships among your business contacts. It's a particularly good sign if you're invited to a client's home for dinner. A gift like a bottle of good malt whisky—prohibitively expensive in Sweden—will be very acceptable to your host, and some flowers or chocolates for your hostess (see the chapter on "skåling" customs and related social etiquette.

The only problem about business negotiations with Swedes is that they can be difficult to track down at times. Offices tend to be curiously deserted on a Friday afternoon, particularly in the summer, and the whole country seems to close down from the beginning of July to the middle of August. There is a similar mass exodus for a week or two in mid-winter, when the schools have a long half-term holiday so that the youngsters can head off for a skiing trip.

As a rule of thumb, fix meetings for the early morning (the earlier the better because

Swedish people often start thinking about lunch at around 11.30 a.m.). Late-afternoon meetings are unpopular because Swedish executives are basically home-lovers and don't like to linger in the office beyond the official closing time. Similarly, try to avoid meetings in the few days before a public holiday like Easter when executives want to clear their desks.

CHILDREN

The Swedes are good at devising attractions for the whole family, with amusement parks like Liseberg in Gothenburg and Gröna Lund Tivoli in Stockholm both "musts" for young visitors. There are also an increasing number of "Sommarland" (Summerland) developments, the largest of which is at Skara, north-east of Gothenburg. It has 50 attractions, including a water-slide, a Grand Prix race track, a mini-zoo, railway and three boating lakes. The admission fee to "Sommarland" sites normally covers all the attractions.

The best-known zoo and safari park is at Kolmården near Norrköping, which has a fine collection of lions, zebras, giraffes and other exotic species, as well as Sweden's only dolphinarium. Other noted zoos are located in Borås, Furuvik, Molstaberg and Skansen in Stockholm. A much-praised and fairly new attraction is the Grönklitt bear park near Orsa in Dalarna where the animals live in a natural forest habitat.

Not far from Orsa is Santaworld, another fairly new Swedish-style theme park where the children can discover Santa's house, workshop, animals and the Snow Queen's Palace, as well as placing their orders for Christmas.

Sweden has a number of vintage railways, some of which are still operated by steam locomotives. The longest preserved railway is the 20-mile narrow-gauge line from Uppsala to Lenna, which operates at weekends between June and August.

An unusual visitor attraction in the province of Småland is High Chaparral, an authentically-reconstructed Wild West town created by the industrialist Bengt Er-landsson, where Big Bengt himself is the sheriff and daily shoot-outs are laid on.

DISABLED

In line with its enlightened social attitudes, Sweden has always pioneered improvements to cater for the disabled traveller. Many hotels have rooms adapted for the needs both of people with mobility problems and those suffering from allergies.

A number of hotels have also invested in technical aids so that those with limited mobility can still enjoy activities like swimming or riding.

The annual guide "Hotels in Sweden" lists hotels with rooms suitable for disabled visitors, and many chalet villages have cabins with wheelchair access.

The Swedish Tourist Board in Stockholm has a special section which monitors facilities for disabled travellers and is always glad to give advice on suitable hotels or holiday activities.

LANGUAGE

Good morning	*God morgon*
Good afternoon	*God eftermiddag*
Good evening	*God kväll*
Today	*i dag*
Tomorrow	*i morgon*
Yesterday	*i går*
Hello	*Hej*
How do you do	*Goddag*
Goodbye	*Adjö*
Thank you	*Tack*
How much is this?	*Vad kostar det?*
It costs	*Det kostar*
How do I get to?	*Hur kommer jag till?*
Where is …?	*Var är …?*
Right	*Höger*
To the right	*Till höger*
Left	*Vänster*
To the left	*Till vänster*
Straight on	*Rakt fram*

Can I order please?	
	Får jag beställa?
Could I have the bill please?	
	Kan jag få notan?
Could I have the key please?	
	Kan jag få nyckeln?
What time is it?	
	Vad är klockan?
It is (the time is)	
	Den är (klockan är)
Could I have your name please?	
	Hur var namnet?
My name is	
	Jag heter
Do you have English newspapers?	
	Har du engelska tidningar?
Do you speak English?	
	Talar du engelska?
I only speak English	
	Jag talar bara engelska

Can I help you?	
	Kan jag hjälpa till?
I do not understand	
	Jag förstår inte
I do not know	
	Jag vet inte
It has disappeared	
	Den är borta

Chemist	*Apotek*
Hospital	*Sjukhus*
Doctor	*Doktor*
Police station	*Polisstation*
Parking	*Parkering, Garage*
Department store	*Varuhus*
Toilet	*Toalett*
Gentlemen	*Herrar*
Ladies	*Damer*
Vacant	*Ledig*
Engaged	*Upptagen*
Entrance	*Ingång*
Exit	*Utgång*
No entry	*Ingen ingång*
Open	*Öppen/öppet*
Closed	*Stängt*
Push	*Skjut*
Pull	*Drag*
No smoking	*Rökning förbjuden*

Breakfast	*Frukost*
Lunch	*Lunch*
Dinner	*Middag*
Eat	*Äta*
Drink	*Dricka*
Phrase book	*Frasbok*
Dictionary	*Lexikon*
Bus/coach	*Buss*
Train	*Tåg*
Aircraft	*Flygplan*

Clothes	*Kläder*
Overcoat	*Kappa, Överrock*
Jacket	*Jacka*
Suit	*Kostym*
Shoes	*Skor*
Skirt	*Kjol*
Blouse	*Blus*
Jersey	*Tröja, jumper*
Car	*Bil*
Handicraft	*Hemslöjd*
Cheers	*Skål!*
To rent	*Att hyra*
Free	*Ledigt*
Room to rent	*Rum att hyra*
Chalet	*Stuga*

Grocery store (in countryside)	
	Lanthandel
Shop	*Affär*
Food	*Mat*
To buy	*Att köpa*
Sauna	*Bastu*
Off-licence	*Systembolag*
Yes	*Ja*
No	*Nej*
Wash	*Tvätta*
Launderette	*Tvättomat*
Dry cleaning	*Kemtvätt*
Dirty	*Smutsigt*
Clean	*Ren*
Stain	*Fläck*
Money	*Pengar*

Monday	*måndag*
Tuesday	*tisdag*
Wednesday	*onsdag*
Thursday	*torsdag*
Friday	*fredag*
Saturday	*lördag*
Sunday	*söndag*

1	*en/et*	11	*elva*
2	*två*	12	*tolv*
3	*tre*	13	*tretton*
4	*fyra*	14	*fjorton*
5	*fem*	15	*femton*
6	*sex*	16	*sexton*
7	*sju*	17	*sjutton*
8	*åtta*	18	*aderton*
9	*nio*	19	*nitton*
10	*tio*	20	*tjugo*

21	*tjugoen*
22	*tjugotvå*
30	*trettio*
40	*fyrtio*
50	*femtio*
60	*sextio*
70	*sjuttio*
80	*åttio*
90	*nittio*
100	*hundra*
200	*tvåhundra*
1000	*tusen*

USEFUL ADDRESSES

Swedish Tourist Board (Sveriges Turis-tråd), Box 7473, S-103 92 Stockholm, Sweden
Foreign offices of the Swedish Tourist Board:
Swedish National Tourist Office, 3 Cork Street, London W1X 1HA, United Kingdom
Swedish Tourist Board, 655 Third Avenue, 18th Floor, New York, NY 10017, USA
Sveriges Turistbyrå, Fr. Nansens Plass 8, N-0160 Oslo 1, Norway
Sveriges Turistbureau, Vester Farimagade 1, DK-1606 Copenhagen V, Denmark
Sveriges Turistbyrå, Georgsgatan 11, SF-00120 Helsinki 12, Finland
Schwedische Touristik-Information, Glockengiesserwall 2-4, D-2000 Hamburg, Federal Republic of Germany
Schwedische Touristik-Information, Postfach 390, Wiesenstrasse 9, CH-8034 Zurich, Switzerland
Office du Tourisme Suédois, 146-150 Avenue des Champs Elysées, F-75008 Paris, France
Zweeds Nationaal Verkeersburo, Saxen Weimarlaan 52, NL-1075 CE Amsterdam, Netherlands
Scandinavian Tourist Board, Sanno Grand Building, Room 401, 14-2 Nagata-cho 2-chome, Chiyoda-ku, Tokyo 100, Japan

TOURIST INFORMATION

Sweden has a country-wide network of tourist information offices, or "Turistbyrå", in more than 350 cities and towns throughout the country, which can be identified by the international "I" sign. These offices usually run a hotel booking service—

"Rumsförmedling" or "Hotellcentral"—and have information about local sightseeing and sporting activities. Some offices are open only during the summer months. A list of tourist information offices is published by the Swedish National Tourist Office.

The country's busiest tourist information office is in Stockholm at Sverigehuset (Sweden House) at the corner of Hamngatan and Kungsträdgården (tel. 08-789 20 00). It is run by the Stockholm Information Service (SIS) and has its own "Excursion Shop" where you can book sightseeing tours on the spot. There are also tourist offices at the Central Station, in the Kaknäs TV tower and, during the summer, at the City Hall and the Värta ferry terminal. SIS publishes an excellent guide, *What To See And Do In And Around Stockholm*, and it's also worth getting hold of *Stockholm This Week*, which lists all the current cultural attractions as well as giving some useful travel tips and telephone numbers.

In Gothenburg the main tourist office is in the city centre at Basargatan 10 (tel. 031-10 07 40). There is also an office in the Nordstan shopping centre near the main railway station (tel. 031-15 07 05).

Malmö's tourist office is at Hamngatan 1 (tel. 040-34 12 70), near the city centre and only a few minutes from the Central Station.

EMBASSIES

All in Stockholm. UK— Skarpögatan 6-8 (tel. 08-667 01 40); US—Strandvägen 101 (tel. 08-783 53 00); Canada—Tegelbacken 4 (tel. 08-23 79 20).

Art/Photo Credits

Aarni, Teddy/Tiofoto	54
Abrahamsson, Tore/Tiofoto	298/299
Andersson, Hans/Tiofoto	86
Allsport Picture Agency	116
Arbetarrörelsens Arkiv och Bibliotek	52, 56, 60, 82
Chmura, Frantisek/Tiofoto	71, 130
Dahlström, Lars/Tiofoto	74/75, 310/311
Gibbs, Brian/Topham	282
Hammarskiold, Hans/Tiofoto	42, 46, 48
Hasselblad	145, 158/159
Henriksson, Janerik/Topham	68
Historical Museum	28, 29, 30, 31, 32, 33
Holmström A./Topham	55
Jansson, Leif R./Topham	62, 128, 132, 144, 150, 230, 252
Johansson, Kenneth/Hasselblad	80, 120, 142, 192/193, 194, 198, 206, 268
Karlsson, Jens/Hasselblad	16/17, 18/19, 37, 84, 112, 152/153, 154/ 155, 168, 176/177, 178/179, 180, 181, 184, 186, 188, 197, 200R, 212, 214, 218/ 219, 224/225, 256/257
Karlsson, Sture/Tiofoto	136/137
Linden, Mats	14/15, 57, 89, 90/91, 98/99, 110/111, 123, 146/147, 149, 156/157, 170/171, 172, 185L, 190L, 200L, 203, 204/205, 211, 217, 222/223, 226, 238R, 243, 244, 255, 258, 259, 262, 263, 264, 265, 274/ 275, 283, 291, 297, 306
Lloyd, John	292, 293
Löfgren, Claes/Tiofoto	61, 119, 151
Mikrut, Jack/Tiofoto	117
National Museum	40, 44, 49
Naylor, Kim	2, 102, 189, 266/267
Norenlind, Nils Johan/Tiofoto	65, 67, 81, 87, 88, 109, 114, 126, 239, 245, 247, 276
Per-Olle Stackman/Tiofoto	122, 124/125
Reitz, Jan/Tiofoto	134, 135
Röhsman, Björn/Hasselblad	284/285, 288/289, 300/301
Swedish Institute	34L, 36, 39, 41, 45, 53, 58, 59L&R, 66, 73, 78/79, 83, 85, 107, 127, 129, 131, 195, 233, 236
Swedish Tourist Board	cover, 9, 22, 23, 24, 25, 26, 27, 34R, 51, 63, 64, 72, 92/93, 94, 95, 96/97, 100/101, 103, 104L, 105, 108, 115, 121, 138, 139, 140/141, 148, 164, 166, 167, 174, 175, 185R, 190R, 191, 199, 201, 207, 210, 213, 215, 216, 221, 227, 231, 232, 234, 235, 237, 238L, 240, 241, 242, 246, 248, 249, 250, 251, 253, 254, 261, 269, 270, 272, 277, 278, 279, 280, 281, 286/287, 295, 296, 303, 305, 307, 308, 309
Tiofoto	77, 104R
Topham Picture Library	35, 43, 50, 69, 76, 118, 133, 169, 220, 294, 302

INDEX

K

L

M

T

U

V

W–Z

B
C
D
E
F
G
H
I
J
a
b
c
d
e
f
g
h
j
k
l

NOTES